ROMANTIC TO MODERN LITERATURE

ROMANTIC TO MODERN LITERATURE

Essays and Ideas of Culture
1750-1900

JOHN LUCAS

Professor of English, Loughborough University

THE HARVESTER PRESS · SUSSEX

BARNES & NOBLE BOOKS · NEW JERSEY

First published in Great Britain in 1982 by
THE HARVESTER PRESS LIMITED
Publisher: John Spiers
16 Ship Street, Brighton, Sussex

and in the USA by
BARNES & NOBLE BOOKS
81 Adams Drive, Totowa, New Jersey 07512

© John Lucas, 1982

British Library Cataloguing in Publication Data

Lucas, John, 1937-
  Romantic to modern literature: essays on literature
  and ideas, 1750-1914.
  1. English literature — History and criticism
  I. Title
  820.9   PR403

  ISBN 0-7108-0405-9

Library of Congress Cataloging in Publication Data

Lucas, John, 1937-
  Romantic to modern literature.

  1. English literature — 19th century — History and
criticism — Addresses, essays, lectures.   2. Romanticism
— England — Addresses, essays, lectures.   3. Dickens,
Charles, 1812-1870 — History and criticism — Addresses,
essays, lectures.   I. Title.
PR453.L8   1982   820'.9'007   82-6842
ISBN 0-389-20311-4   AACR2

Typeset in Times 11/12 point by Alacrity Phototypesetters,
Banwell Castle, Weston-super-Mare
and printed in Great Britain by
The Thetford Press Ltd, Thetford, Norfolk

For Ben and Emma

Contents

Chapter 1

Introduction

THE following essays were written at different times and they employ a variety of approaches. They also demonstrate some of the proper areas of concern that may be grouped together under the general title of 'English Studies'. At least, I hope that they do. We hear much nowadays about the crisis in English Studies. I think that there probably is one and that one of its most important causes is ignorance, although few people are prepared to admit as much. This is perhaps because those who speak most passionately about the crisis began their intellectual life in the 1960s, which was the decade that did a great deal to raise ignorance to the level of sanctity. And if that remark seems unwarrantably tendentious, I can only say that it seems to me that between 1960 and 1969, and particularly in the later years of that decade, a tradition which had taken for granted a respect for knowledge, a concern over facts, and a reverence for memory—that tradition was abandoned or attacked by those spray-gunners of the anti-culture and their allies, whose major visible achievement was to cover walls with the motto: 'The tigers of wrath are wiser than the horses of instruction'.

Of course, there are explanations for it all. If you were a student at university during the 1950s the chances were that you would be taught by old-style scholars who typically thought of themselves as wine-tasters of literature, and for whom the question of taste could be resolved by the litmus test of whether or not one was a gentleman. I can recall listening to a lecture by a senior and much-admired editor of Shakespeare who assured his audience that 'To like Scott is the test of a gentleman'. If you did not like Scott you at least knew where you were. It is hardly surprising that the young turks took against this, nor that they spent time and energy in attacking the old guard's taste and in insisting on the virtues of such non-gentlemen as Blake and Lawrence. The weapon to hand was

1

the New Criticism, and the fact that you could use it utterly to rout your opponents amounted to a double victory. In the first place it proved the deficiencies of 'gentlemanliness'; and in the second it demonstrated the superiority of 'rigorous critical thought' over the pallid assertions of 'taste'. It was heady stuff, and there is no doubt that the enemy was repeatedly put to flight. Yet the pursuit of rigour itself became something of a pose. The display of strenuous attention to the text went with an almost coenobitic devotion to a presumed Great Tradition which could be identified in terms of 'the quality of felt life', 'mature intelligence', 'a grasp on the actual', and so on. And going with that was a rather unpleasant kind of moral self-righteousness, often as nasty as the sterile snobbishness it largely replaced.

Or nearly so. For there was not much that could justify those gentlemen-scholars against whom the attacks were mounted; and even from this distance I can feel the old anger rising when I think of their assumption that they somehow naturally knew the best that had been thought and said. They created an orthodoxy which simply had to be knocked down. The trouble was that the New Criticism brought with it its own orthodoxy, its own set of conventions. Above all, that Criticism made it possible for what was called responsibleness to harden into a series of ritualistic gestures. (At the mere mention of the name Shelley, for example, there would be a switched-on sneer, or a murmur of 'nothing for the adult mind *there*'.) And with that went the cultivation of ignorance.

Now this may seem grossly unfair. After all, the New Criticism was surely a way of re-opening avenues to the past; it was about revaluation; it sought to dust off forgotten heroes and put them on view once again? I do not deny that this was the theory. In practice, however, the effect was quite different. For there was so much you need no longer bother to read. Moreover, since *in practice* English Studies were now narrowed to critical enquiry, and since *in practice* critical enquiry itself narrowed to reader and text, and since *in practice* the reader was to be congratulated in so far as he relied on what was called 'personal response', it followed that a kind of ignorance became not only defended but aggressively championed. Blake and Dickens were put to uses that would have horrified both of them. 'Holy Thursday', of the *Songs of Innocence*, and *Hard Times* were repeatedly invoked as texts which showed that the child's free, untrammelled imagination should not be violated by facts or by the imposition of any knowledge. And since the child was father of the man, men, too, were blessed in so far as they rejected what were presumed to be the emotionally and intellectually crippling demands of knowledge, of scholarship. Memory was distrusted as a form of tyranny; 'learning by heart' became 'learning by rote' and was to be avoided at all costs. The result is that the present crisis in English Studies ought to be seen not so much in terms of whether we should support this -ism against that -ology, but as partly resulting from the incontestible fact of an ignorance which has become so deep-rooted that very often people do not even know how to set about knowing.

I realise that all this may sound like the cry of the elitist. It is not. I write as a socialist, and I rejoice to concur with R. H. Tawney's great essay on 'An Experiment in Democratic Education', and in particular with the following words.

If persons whose work is different require, as they do, different kinds of professional instruction, that is no reason why one should be excluded from the common heritage of civilization of which the other is made free by a university education, and from which ... both, irrespective of their occupations, are equally capable, as human beings, of deriving spiritual sustenance. Those who have seen the inside both of lawyers' chambers and of coal mines will not suppose that of the inhabitants of these places of gloom the former are more constantly inspired by the humanities than are the latter, or that conveyancing is in itself a more liberal art than hewing.[1]

Now the ideal of personal response was justified on the grounds that it allowed for the humanity of anyone to be applied to a text, irrespective of whether he had those educational advantages that went with being a gentleman. So, at least, one was asked to believe. Yet in fact, the New Criticism was part of a restrictive and rigid cultural conservatism, and it is no accident that its most important champion in this country, F. R. Leavis, should have been so ready to repeat that 'It must be obvious that there are comparatively few who are capable of profiting from the study of literature'. And if one asks why Leavis should have thought that 'obvious', the answer must be that he took for granted a cultural context in which only 'gentlemen' would be engaged in pursuing the kind of study he had in mind. Such a context would guarantee a certain amount of knowledge, and that knowledge could be put to use when the matter of personal response became the issue.

Let me illustrate this by a simple example. In his wonderful elegy 'To the Memory of Mr Oldham', Dryden makes a comparison between Oldham and himself by noting that 'Thus *Nisus* fell upon the slippery place, / While his young friend perform'd and won the Race'. It is one thing to know who Nisus was, and quite another to see how finely the reference fits into what Dryden is saying. The 'gentleman-scholar' typically thinks he has done enough merely by pointing out that Dryden's mind was attuned to classical literature and that the analogy thus came easily to him. The New Critic, on the other hand, will want to concentrate on the appropriateness, or otherwise, of the reference, and appropriateness will include tone, the weight that should be given to 'perform'd', and the judicious rhyme of place / Race. Both assume that the reader will know who Nisus was. Yet the truth is that the average student, who for better or worse is the average reader, will not know. What is more, he may well think that there is no reason why he *should* know. And if that is how he thinks, part of the fault must lie with a critical orthodoxy which has filtered down into the schools and which has argued for an exclusive concentration on text, even while assuming knowledge of a kind that in practice it has done a great deal to outlaw as valueless.

In his recent book, *The Pursuit of Signs*, Jonathan Culler quotes E. D. Hirsch as suggesting that we 'should abandon the idea that has dominated scholarly writing for the past forty years: that interpretation is the only truly legitimate activity for a professor of literature. There are other things to do, to think about, to write about'.[2] Yes and no. If interpretation is limited to the methods that stem from the New Criticism and which have turned into the muscle-bound exercises that one so often comes across, or if it is a matter of the absurd psychoanalytic 'explanation' for a work's existence, then perhaps yes; and yet even those approaches may have individual justifications. Moreover, since interpretation means trying to answer the question 'What is this about', it seems arrogant and perverse in equal measure to claim that such a question is somehow unnatural. I count myself fortunate in that I was taught by a very great scholar, the late D. J. Gordon. Gordon was perhaps best known as an historian of ideas; but anyone who heard him lecture — on Jane Austen, Wordsworth, Shakespeare, Henry James, Lawrence, Yeats, Pope, Spenser, and many others — will agree that he was also a marvellous critic. Indeed, he would not have thought that you could separate out the two activites. He took for granted that to ask of a work of art 'What is it about' was a meaningful question. But he also assumed that if you were to answer the question you had to know as much as possible about the circumstances of the work's production, its effect on a contemporary audience, how its meaning and presence changed for successive audiences, and so on. In short, he was essentially pluralistic in his approach and he thought such an approach was essential for anyone who concerned himself with art. (And I mean anyone: for in spite of a certain trivial snobbishness Gordon was wonderfully contemptuous of those who went about saying that more will mean worse, or who insisted that only a few could profit from the study of literature.) He assumed that if you were in his company — and that could mean the enforced company of a seminar quite as much as the chosen company of a pub — you were as interested as he was in everything to do with the life of the mind.

Men meet and discuss. There is hesitation, curiosity, interest, eagerness for knowledge. We ought to have learned about that. Can't we learn about it? We *will* learn about it, and we will find a man to help us if a man is to be found. Fortunate teacher, who is sought and not avoided! Thus the medium is created; the spirit finds a body; the solitary student finds that he is one of a crowd. Education is not put on like varnish. It springs like a plant from the soil, and the fragrance of the earth is upon it.[3]

Reading those words of Tawney's, it is Gordon I immediately think of, not so much because he was the fortunate teacher as that we were the fortunate crowd: we became a body because in his presence it was impossible to ignore the fact that enquiry, interest in and concern for literary matters were thought to be entirely proper.

Gordon was by nature a pessimist. 'We shall never know', was one of his favourite remarks, uttered with a kind of gloomy relish. Or, as variation, 'I don't know, *nobody* knows'.

(Which struck the right note, of course, for if he didn't know, who could?) Yet the effect of such pessimism was entirely bracing. For although I have no wish to underplay Gordon's pessimism, which was intense, the truth is that to watch him at work was to be at least partly committed to and able to profit from the excitement he generated. I think that most of his students revered in him his extraordinary passion for knowledge. (And although the phrase is a cliché it is the only one I can think of that will do him any kind of justice.) I do not for a moment suppose that he would have approved of these essays. He was far too exact and exacting a scholar for that. But I hope that something of his example has gone into them and that they suggest ways of breaking free from the largely self-imposed crisis into which English Studies has drifted over the past twenty or so years.

Notes

1 R. H. Tawney, *The Radical Tradition: Twelve Essays on Politics, Education and Literature*, ed. Rita Hinden, Harmondsworth (1966) pp. 75-6.
2 Jonathan Culler, *The Pursuit of Signs* (1981) p. 17.
3 Tawney, *op. cit.*, p. 81.

Chapter 2

The Idea of the Provincial

We learned that a gentleman never misplaces his accents,
  That nobody knows how to speak, much less how to write
English who has not hob-nobbed with the great-grandparents
  of English....

Louis MacNeice, Autumn Journal

IN May 1860, Charles Kingsley received a letter from Lord
Palmerston, offering him the Regius Chair of Modern History
at Cambridge. The offer seems to have been made at the
insistence of Queen Victoria, whose favourite preacher
Kingsley was becoming, and whose son, Prince Albert, also
liked him. Bertie was shortly due to spend some time as an
undergraduate at Cambridge, and the Queen hoped that Kingsley would be able to exert 'a good manly influence over the
indolent Prince'.[1] Not surprisingly, perhaps, Kingsley accepted
the offer and later that year took himself off to Cambridge,
having first lectured his parishioners on their foolhardiness in
complaining about the appallingly rainy summer, and having
printed and circulated his sermon, 'Why Should We Pray for
Fine Weather?', in which he pointed out that incessant rain
cleansed the drains and therefore kept down cholera — tidings
which were unlikely to bring comfort and joy to a parish
composed almost entirely of farmers.

On 13 November 1860, Kingsley delivered his inaugural
lecture as Regius Professor. It was called 'The Limits of Exact
Science as Applied to History', and according to one of his
biographers, when printed it 'was reviewed, not too kindly, by
Justin McCarthy and many other critics.[2] That is something of
an understatement. The lecture was scornfully dismissed, both
before and after its publication, as was the man who gave it.
For McCarthy did not merely review the lecture, he also
recorded his personal impressions of Kingsley. The new
Professor was, he wrote:

Rather tall, very angular, surprisingly awkward, with thin staggering legs, a hatchet face adorned with scraggy whiskers, a faculty for falling into the most ungainly attitudes and making the most hideous contortions of visage and frame; with a rough provincial accent and an uncouth way of speaking that would be set down for caricature on the boards of a theatre.[3]

Five years later the then Professor of Poetry at Oxford, Matthew Arnold, published a volume of essays, called *Essays in Criticism*, including one essay, 'The Literary Influence of Academies', which has established itself as a classic. I shall return to this essay later but I want to note here the terms of Arnold's praise for the idea of an Academy, and above all for the fact that it encouraged the tone of the centre, and as such could usefully criticise and set standards against much in our literature that was, according to Arnold, 'full of hap-hazard, crudeness, provincialism, eccentricity, violence, blundering.'[4]

Between them, Oxford and Cambridge in the middle of the nineteenth century appear to define the idea of the provincial. Whether in speech or habit of thought the provincial is uncouth, crude, and therefore — you can hardly miss the implicit claim — essentially uncivilised. For it is surely the case that both McCarthy and Arnold think that they speak from a position of authority? They have, that is, an unquestioning trust in the rightness of their notion of the civilised, the central, the urbane. So that when they point to what they regard as 'provincial', they are not merely describing, they are making value judgements, and highly unfavourable ones. Now this may seem obvious enough; and after all we must accept the fact that in twentieth-century usage the word 'provincial' carries a highly pejorative set of meanings. What interests me is why this should have come to be so. For words have histories and belong to history; and that is true of the word 'provincial'. It comes into the language as a response to certain new experiences, and once it is in use it helps to shape and to define those experiences.

We can see how this is so if we consider that had McCarthy and Arnold been writing a century earlier they would have been very unlikely to have used the word at all. 'Uncouth', 'vulgar' or 'lacking in polish'; yes, those and other related terms were certainly available in the middle of the eighteenth century and, as we shall see, were much used. But 'provincial' was only just beginning to make its way. I want, therefore, to set myself to answer two questions: first, when did the word come into use; and second, and much more interestingly, why did it?

If we are to begin to answer these questions we need to go back to Dryden, because Dryden was the first of the modern law-makers for the English language. In the Preface to his play, *Troilus and Cressida*, published in 1679, Dryden writes:

In the age of [Aeschylus] the Greek tongue was arrived to its full perfection; they had then amongst them an exact standard of writing and speaking. The English language is not capable of such a certainty; and we are at present so far from it that we are wanting in the very foundation of it, a perfect grammar. Yet it must be allowed to the present age that the tongue in general is ... much more refined since Shakespeare's time ....'[5]

And in 1693 he returns to the subject in his 'Discourse Concerning the Original and Progress of Satire':

... we have ... not so much as a tolerable dictionary, or a grammar; so that our language is in a manner barbarous; and what government will encourage any one, or more, who are capable of refining it, I know not.'[6]

What Dryden has in mind is plain enough. The British government should follow the example that Cardinal Richelieu had set in France, in 1629: establish an Academy which would set standards for language. The Restoration court of Charles II was much influenced by the court of Louis XIV, which is hardly surprising since most Royalists had spent the Commonwealth years in exile at Louis's court. Dryden, one might say, is speaking as Restoration man when he pleads for both a grammar and a dictionary. But I think there is rather more to it than that, as his use of the word 'refine' suggests. Originally a term that identifies the process of purifying or separating metals from dross, alloy, or other extraneous matter, 'refine' as Dryden uses it hints at a cleansing process which has social and even political implications. For a 'refined' language is available only to those who know the rules of grammar and accept dictionary definitions, always supposing they can be provided. And it is small wonder that the poet who spoke out against the private spirit in religious matters should see that spirit as a threat to the stability of the nation. 'For points obscure are of small use to learn, / But common quiet is mankind's concern'

(*Religio Laici*). Substitute 'words obscure' for 'points obscure' and you are in the realm of the ranters, diggers, levellers, anabaptists, of all those sects which Christopher Hill has written about so brilliantly in *The World Turned Upside Down*, and whose private languages would undoubtedly seem part of a threat to the fragile order of post-1660 England. 'All I have writ concerning the matter of digging,' Winstanley wrote in December 1649, 'I never read it in any book, nor received it from any mouth ... before I saw the light of it rise up within myself.'[7] Indeed, the puritan is likely to distrust words simply because they belong to others, and do not proceed from his own experience. Thus John Hall could write, also in 1649, that it was 'better to grave things in the minds of children than words'.[8] Such a distrust of other people's words is, I think, deep in the English experience; and it partly explains why that bizarre figure, Krook, in *Bleak House*, insists on teaching himself to read and write rather than risk being 'learned' by others. But *Bleak House* belongs to the middle of the nineteenth century and by then the language had become systematised, whereas when Dryden died in 1700 there were still no dictionaries or grammars to speak of.

But in the eighteenth century they began to appear in abundance. I do not know that they have received a great deal of study, but the work has begun; and for most of what follows I am indebted to an as-yet unpublished PhD. thesis by Dr Olivia Smith, of the University of Birmingham. Among the more important studies of grammar are James Harris's *Hermes, or a Philosophical Inquiry concerning Universal Grammar*, which appeared in 1751; Joseph Priestley's *The Rudiments of English Grammar*, 1761; Robert Lowth's *A Short Introduction to English Grammar*, which was published the following year; and last, Lindley Murray's *English Grammar*, which appeared in 1795, and which soon established itself as the orthodox text. (It went through more than fifty major editions, and there were at least 120 abridgements, besides countless piracies and thinly disguised imitations.)[9] And the dictionaries? Only one counts, Samuel Johnson's great *Dictionary of the English Language*, published for the first time in 1755. With the appearance of these works is born the idea of what Dryden had called 'an exact standard of writing', or a proper language; and it becomes possible to think of fixing, stabilising such a language.

At the same time it becomes necessary to assert that this language is somehow the official language of the nation — why otherwise have it? — so that whoever speaks it speaks for England. In other words, a certain kind or class of person becomes thought of as the keeper of the language. The language is appropriated by this class because it is appropriate to it. And what is proper therefore becomes the property of — but of whom? Well, here is Joseph Priestley, arguing that it would be a good idea to incorporate the classical languages into English because then writers would avoid the dangers of

... debasing their style, by vulgar words and phrases, or such as have been long associated with, and in a manner appropriated to, vulgar and mean ideas; than which nothing can be more unworthy of the mind, much more the compositions, of a gentleman, or person of liberal education.[10]

That was written in 1761. The following year, when Lowth published his *Short Introduction to English Grammar*, he remarked that anyone wanting to learn the English language thoroughly must first frequent polite society; secondly, read the best authors; and thirdly, know the classical languages properly. Put Priestley and Lowth together, and it follows that for a gentleman to have a liberal education is a tautology; after all, the gentleman belongs to polite society, the authors he reads will be thought as the 'best', and the school he attends will have at the core of its curriculum the teaching of the classical languages. Just what this could mean in terms of controlling knowledge becomes clear if we consider the case of the governors of Leeds Grammar School who, as J. W. Adamson tells us in his monograph on *English Education, 1789-1902*, applied in 1805 to be allowed to widen the curriculum. The judgement went against them, and Lord Eldon ruled that 'a free school meant a free grammar school, and a grammar school as defined in Johnson's dictionary was a school for teaching the learned languages. The governors could not therefore lawfully use the endowment for teaching anything else.'[11]

The grammar school thus teaches a 'refined' language, purged of the vulgar and the mean. In short, by the middle of the eighteenth century the word 'refined' has attached itself very firmly to the idea of class, so that 'vulgar' is in class opposition to it. The only person who seems to have resisted this development of the word's meaning was, as one might perhaps expect, David Hume. In his essay, 'Of Simplicity and Refinement in Writing', the great Scottish philosopher wittily links refinement with conceit and what he calls 'the overloaded style'.[12] Hume obviously knew that in defining the excess of refinement he was describing a certain kind of English gentleman.

But Hume is exceptional. Priestley speaks for the developing orthodoxy when he says that 'vulgar words and phrases' are unsuitable for 'a gentleman'. And it is at this point — when the ideas of proper language and gentleman have come together — that the word 'provincial' makes its appearance. The crucial definition is Johnson's, but before I come to that I want to glance at Johnson's ideas for the *Dictionary*. He set these out in *The Plan of a Dictionary of the English Language*, which he drew up in 1747, and in the *Preface*. In the *Plan* Johnson said that he wished to include in his *Dictionary* 'words and phrases used in the general intercourse of life, or found in the works of those we commonly stile polite writers . . . '.[13] What does he mean by general intercourse? In the first place, Johnson claims that it is his duty to 'secure our language from being over-run with *cant*, from being crowded with low terms, the spawn of folly or affectation, which arise from no just principles of speech, and of which no legitimate derivation can be shewn.'[14] Never mind the question-begging phrase about 'just principles of speech'; what really matters is Johnson's determination to outlaw all argot, slang, dialect words. For if we turn to the *Dictionary* itself, we find that Johnson offers the following definitions of 'cant':

    (i)   a corrupt dialect used by beggars and vagabonds;
    (ii)   a particular form of speaking peculiar to some certain class or body of men;
    (iii)   barbarous jargon.[15]

It comes to this: that if the grammarians were busy outlawing certain *forms* of expression, Johnson was bent on outlawing certain *kinds* of expression. And between them, they threaten to expel from all consideration what we might call the idiom of the people. We can be sure that Johnson did intend this because he claimed in the *Plan* that it was his intention to brand with infamy, 'barbarous or impure words and expressions'; and as his authority for doing so he referred to Boileau's proposal to the French Academicians, that they should 'review all their polite writers, and correct such impurities as may be found in them, that their authority might not contribute, at any distant times, to the depravation of the language.'[16] And in the *Preface* Johnson said that he had refused to acknowledge

the diction of the laborious and mercantile part of the people [because it] is in great measure casual and mutable; many of their terms [being] formed for some temporary or local convenience, and though current at certain times and places, are in others utterly unknown. This fugitive cant, which is always in a state of increase or decay, cannot be regarded as any part of the durable materials of a language, and therefore must be suffered to perish with other things unworthy of preservation.[17]

General intercourse must then certainly leave out 'the laborious and mercantile part of the people'. Which is surely rather a lot of them? Moreover, Johnson doesn't merely disapprove of their 'casual and mutable' language. There is also the matter of pronunciation. For many words, Johnson says, have been 'altered by accident, or depraved by ignorance, as the pronunciation of the vulgar has been weakly followed....' Which is not to deny that language changes, but it is to say — at least if you are Samuel Johnson — that language can change for the better only when there is leisure for new thoughts, 'in a people polished by art, and classed by subordination'.[18] And although we might perhaps be tempted to think that Johnson is using the word 'vulgar' in its older sense, 'of the people', we have only to turn to his *Dictionary* to find that he more typically defines the word as 'mean, low'. So that 'vulgar' opposes 'a people polished by arts', whose liberal education is a means of securing a 'refined' language freed from impurities both of vocabulary and pronunciation that define the low and mean. And from this it follows that the 'gentleman' — the man of liberal education — is now the instrument through which the English language is to live.

There's an obvious consequence to all this. Eighteenth-century grammars and dictionaries conspire to make numbers of people invisible; their syntax is not English because it isn't derived from the classic languages; their very language is not English because it is 'cant'. They are exiles in their own land,

and they can become English only by denying their own language. Or they can stay as they are, in which case they are at best 'provincial'. And at this point we need Johnson's definition of the word. He gives four separate definitions, three of them of no great significance. One, however, is crucial:

(i)   relating to a province;
(ii)   appendant to the provincial country;
(iii)   belonging only to an archbishop's jurisdiction; not ecumenical;
(iv)   not of the mother country; rude, unpolished.

As example of this fourth use of the word, Johnson cites Swift: 'A country 'squire having only a provincial accent upon his tongue, which is neither a fault, nor in his power to remedy'. Johnson is in fact quoting from one of Swift's letters, published after his death in 1745. In other words, this use of 'provincial' is as near contemporary with Johnson's own *Dictionary* as one could wish for. Yet even so, Johnson has partly to adapt Swift's meaning, since Swift doesn't think of that provincial accent as being a fault. Johnson, on the other hand, does. For you cannot separate his definition of 'provincial' from his definition of 'cant'. In Johnson's terms, he who speaks with a provincial tongue is, at least metaphorically, 'not of the mother country'; he is banished to the provinces.

To sum up so far: we can say that the word 'provincial,' in that sense to which both McCarthy and Arnold appeal, makes its first appearance in Johnson's *Dictionary*, and that it does so because Johnson, along with Grammarians, wants to appropriate the English language. From now on, only a certain use of the language is to be regarded as the proper one, which is as much as to say that only certain people are allowed to speak for England. We can see that this is so if we glance at Hugh Blair's *Lectures on Rhetoric and Belles Lettres*, which were first published in 1783, and went through many editions, though God knows why, because they are quite incredibly tedious. Blair, who was Professor of Rhetoric and Belles Lettres at Edinburgh University, and who was quite incapable of original thought, always says what everyone else is thinking. As Leslie Stephen remarked, he had 'an infinite capacity for repeating the feeblest of platitudes'. Blair can therefore be taken as a reliable guide to the obvious when, in the course of Lecture 33, on 'Pronunciation, or Delivery', he tells his students that a public speaker must observe 'propriety of pronunciation; or the giving to every word which he utters that sound, which the most polite usage of the language appropriate to it; in opposition to broad, vulgar, or provincial pronunciation.'[19] I do not know what effect this statement would have had on Blair's largely Scottish audience; but it perhaps helps to explain Hume's witty attack on the language of refinement, and may also have contributed to that cultural schizophrenia which David Craig has so well analysed in his *Scottish Literature and the Scottish people*, and which no doubt appreciably deepened in the middle of the nineteenth century, when the philologist Alexander J. Ellis established, to his own satisfaction at least, the idea of 'received pronunciation'.

Now this grand act of appropriating the language inevitably created some pretty fierce opposition. And in case it's thought that I overstate the case in talking about such appropriation, I perhaps ought to point out that during the hundred years with which I'm concerned, one of Parliament's arguments for turning down various petitions for universal suffrage was that they were written in coarse or offensive language: which means that those who can't speak or write what has become 'official' English are plainly not fit to vote, or to exercise a share in democracy. Indeed, I can make the same point, and perhaps more tellingly, if I note that during the latter half of the eighteenth century the many acts of land enclosure were accompanied and in a sense confirmed by the enclosing of the language. And I will add — although in parenthesis, for I can't establish this as fact — that I strongly suspect that at exactly this same period, and unconsciously but revealingly, language becomes an expression of Capital: the custodians of the language are to be on their guard against a debasing of its currency. Priestley, we remember, had cautioned gentlemen against 'debasing' their style ('what we have we hoard'); they have to beware of the 'coining' of words and phrases, and have therefore to test words, to find whether they ring true or false.

It isn't surprising, therefore, that those who fought against what was being done to the language were radicals. One of the first into the attack was the politician John Horne Tooke.

Tooke is a shadowy figure, but a deeply attractive one, a sometime parliamentarian, an ally, though not I think a friend, of liberty and of Wilkes; and a marvellously witty, learned and intelligent man. In 1786 Tooke produced what Hazlitt, who wrote about him in *The Spirit of the Age*, called 'one of the few philosophical works on Grammar that were ever written',[20] and which he sharply contrasted with Harris's *Hermes* and Murray's *Grammar*. Tooke called his work *The Diversions of Purley*, and the title slyly disowns any other claim than that of being the trifling reflections of a gentleman in retirement; it hints at a kind of scaled-down Horatianism. But in fact, as Hazlitt recognised, the *Diversions* perform a wonderfully neat demolition job on those who believe that if you formally translate the Latin Grammar into English you have written an English grammar.[21] And yet Hazlitt had also to admit that 'prejudice and party spirit' allowed Horne Tooke's work to sink, while Murray's grammar continued to float on a sea of general approval; and this, although Murray 'confounds the genius of the English language, making it periphrastic and literal, instead of elliptical and idiomatic. According to Mr Murray, hardly any of the best writers ever wrote a word of English.[22] No wonder that Hazlitt should prefer Horne Tooke, and no wonder that Wordsworth and Coleridge should have been so indebted to him when they came to write the *Lyrical Ballads* (though the nature and extent of their debt seem to have had little recognition). The *Preface to the Lyrical Ballads*, with its famous statement of intent about using the language of men in low and rustic life because they 'hourly communicate with the best objects from which the best part of language is derived',[23] is very close to Horne Tooke's insistence that the English language is essentially idiomatic.

What may come as a surprise is the fact that Murray was an American; for one would expect Americans, and especially at this period, to challenge precisely those assumptions about language and grammar which Murray upholds. Thus the great American lexicographer, Noah Webster, remarked in his *Dissertations on the English Language*, published with emblematic rightness in 1789, that

when a particular set of men, in exalted stations, undertake to say, 'We are the standards of propriety and elegance, and if all men do not conform to our practice, they shall be accounted vulgar and ignorant', they take a very great liberty with the rules of the language and the rights of civility.[24]

And it was while William Cobbett was in America that he sent those wonderful letters to his son, James, which in 1817 were to be published as a *Grammar of the English Language*, and in which he gives a lucid, commonsense account of grammatical rules, and at the same time provides an unforgettable testament of the radical spirit. As an example of how to use the hyphen, Cobbett writes, 'The never-to-be-forgotten cruelty of the Borough Tyrants'; of a compound sentence, 'The people suffer great misery and daily perish for want'; and of the subjunctive mood, 'If he write, the guilty tyrants will be ready with their dungeons and axes'. To illustrate the verb 'to be' and some of its uses, he writes, 'The curse of the country is the corruption of the law-makers and the frauds of the makers of paper-money'; and again, 'It were a jest indeed, to consider a set of seat-sellers and seat-buyers as a lawful legislative body'. As an example of an active verb he offers, 'Pitt restrained the Bank', and of time, present, past and future, 'The Queen defies the tyrants, the Queen defied the tyrants, the Queen will defy the tyrants'. (I should point out that the *Grammar* is dedicated to Queen Caroline.) Figurative speech is instanced by 'The people would live amidst abundance if those cormorants did not devour the fruit of their labour'. And Cobbett gives the following examples of collective noun: 'Mob, parliament, rabble, House of Commons, regiment, Court of King's Bench, den of thieves'.[25]

It is perhaps not surprising, although much to be regretted, that Cobbett's *Grammar* did not supplant Murray's as the standard school text.

From Murray, one might say, the road runs clear to McCarthy's account of Kingsley as exhibiting 'a rough provincial accent and an uncouth way of speaking', and to Arnold's anathematising an English literature that is 'full of hap-hazard, crudeness, provincialism, eccentricity, violence, blundering'. And yet it is important to note that McCarthy and Arnold do not, in fact, mean quite the same thing. Their uses of the word are complementary rather than synonymous. For McCarthy the provincial is a matter of style; for Arnold it's a

habit of thought, and as such is an index to matters of wider
cultural significance. Indeed, when Arnold uses the word he
gives it an impetus which frees it from the casual cliché that it
has become for McCarthy. McCarthy's use of the word is very
close to Johnson's key definition, whereas Arnold is extending
its meaning beyond anything we can find in Johnson's *Dictionary*. For Johnson the provincial is 'rude, unpolished', and for
McCarthy it is 'uncouth'. But for Arnold the provincial is the
opposite of urbane; and although this definition in part derives
from the provincial as being 'not of the mother country' — that
is from the root, Latin, meaning of a province as a principal
division of a kingdom or empire — and although it implies a
metaphoric thrust similar to that found in Johnson's definition,
it goes much further. For the tone of the provincial can now be
more accurately measured against what is said to be the tone of
the centre. At least that is what Arnold undertakes to do. And
lying behind what he says is, of course, an awareness that
because of events belonging to the first half of the nineteenth
century, and which Johnson couldn't have anticipated, the
idea of the provincial now attaches to new towns and cities. As
it does so, quite new pejorative implications become clear.

We can see this if we look at the following definition of the
word, as supplied by the 1933 edition of the *Oxford English
Dictionary*: 'provincial: having the manners of speech of a
province or "the provinces"; exhibiting the character,
especially the narrowness of view or interest, associated with
or attributed to inhabitants of "the provinces"; wanting the
culture or polish of the capital'. And who is quoted in support
of this definition? Why, none other than Dr Johnson —
'provincial: rude, unpolished'. But as we have seen, that is *not*
what Johnson meant by the word. It couldn't be; for he was
not concerned with 'the narrowness of point of view or interest, associated with or attributed to inhabitants of "the provinces".' Which is not to deny that this meaning of the word
can emerge from the work that he and eighteenth-century
grammarians did on the language; but it is to say that such a
meaning can be fixed only when 'the provinces' themselves
have been thought to come into existence. And the plain fact of
the matter is that they didn't exist — weren't perceived to exist
— in the eighteenth century. Such a perception belongs to the

nineteenth century, and the definition of 'provincial' which the *Oxford English Dictionary* credits to Johnson it ought really to give to Arnold. For it is Arnold, not Johnson, who thinks of 'the provinces' as 'wanting the culture of the capital'. That, after all, is what 'urbanity' originally means: 'the state, condition, or character of a town or city'. And that effectively means London, the centre. Why otherwise use the word 'capital'?

We come here on a very interesting question. Why weren't eighteenth-century towns beyond London thought of, or called, 'provincial'? It wasn't that they did not exist. In fact there were plenty of them; but you have only to think of the ways in which they had come into existence, of how they had so slowly grown or declined, and of what happened to them during the eighteenth century, to realise that they didn't really require a word of their own. They weren't anything new. On the contrary, most of them were of a great age, and since many had been founded by the Romans, they could legitimately be regarded as *urbs*. Besides, as Kerry Downes has shown in his work on the architecture of Georgian cities,[26] during the eighteenth century there emerged something like a national style of architecture: what Buxton has in common with Bristol, shall we say, both have in common with London: examples of the work of such architects as Nash, Soane, Adam, Kent, Wyatt, can be found in all of them. Churches, spas, town villas, assembly rooms; look where you will, during the eighteenth century you find a conformity, if not uniformity, of architectural styles about England's towns and cities, aided by the fact that they were largely places for living in rather than for work. Moreover, Squire A.B., Sir B.C. and Lord E.F. would not only have houses in London, they would also own property in other English towns, and they would spend time in each, so that there is a network of social correspondence in which everything appears as familiar and accustomed. Leominster might be tiny compared to London, but it had always been there, you knew the kinds of people who lived in it, they were country cousins, and nobody would have thought you needed a special word either for them or for the place. The perceived opposition is not therefore between town and town but between town and country, and although such an opposition may seem grandly vague it makes sufficient sense. Quite simply, the country is whatever isn't London. Such an opposition survives at least until Jane Austen's *Pride and Prejudice*, published in 1813. In Chapter 9 of that novel, Mrs Bennet says to Mr Bingley,

> 'I cannot see that London has any great advantage over the country for my part, except the shops and public places. The country is a vast deal pleasanter, is it not, Mr Bingley?'
>
> 'When I am in the country,' he replied, 'I never wish to leave it; and when I am in town it is pretty much the same. They have each their advantages, and I can be equally happy in either.'[27]

Yet at about this time the country is beginning to be provincial, as we can see if we look at a poem of Robert Bloomfield's. Bloomfield, who had come to fame with *The Farmer's Boy*, produced in 1806 a volume of poems called *Wild Flowers*, and one of these poems is a ballad, written in the Suffolk dialect, and called 'The Horkey', which means 'Harvest-Home Feast'. Bloomfield sub-titled the poem 'A Provincial Ballad'.[28] It seems to me that he did so because it is about 'rude, unpolished' people, who are seen through a haze of genteel sentimentality, which is the more poignant when you remember that Bloomfield came from such people. In making them merely quaint, he has distanced himself from his own roots, has in a sense denied his own identity. Their language is not his. He aspires to the centre. (I will note in passing that Bloomfield is by no means the only poet at the end of the eighteenth century to write dialect poems out of what it seems proper to call a troubled conscience, wanting to preserve a language which at the same time must, so it feels, be renounced: hence the quaintness.)

With Bloomfield, therefore, 'provincial' ceases to be metaphoric of the region; it becomes identified with actual geographical place. And that identification is, of course, what comes to dominate in the nineteenth century, when the new towns and cities are created. They can be provincial as Buxton, Bristol and Bath, for example, couldn't be. They are brash and new, and they do not share assumptions with 'the town'; they are expressions of a spirit which in language and ways of thinking is beyond the pale. Manchester, Birmingham, Leeds,

Bradford, and the rest of them: these are the provincial cities, and, by implication, it is here that we are to find a narrowness of view and interest, the wanting of the culture of the capital, which Arnold deplored, and which largely because of him led to the commonplace assumption that provincial culture is a contradiction in terms.

Yet just how wanting are these towns? Let's take Manchester as our example, because in the nineteenth century everyone did. And by 'everyone' I mean those southern or foreign travellers — de Tocqueville, Faucher, Engels, Ruskin, Dickens — who came to be shocked and went away appalled.[29] In 1780 Manchester was a small market town with a population of 40,000. By 1850 that population had become over a quarter of a million. Manchester was *the* type of emergent industrial city, in which, according to Engels, the population was more or less divided into a middle class motivated entirely by self-interest and a vast working class condemned to a life of 'unexpungeable ... uniformity — uniformity of life, of style, even of colour'.[30] You can't get much narrower than that. Engels' account of Manchester may seem a form of special pleading, but he really speaks for all visitors to the city, even if he does so with an unusual eloquence and to greater purpose. And yet by 1838 Manchester had built not only the largest Exchange Room in Europe, but a very handsome one — as handsome as most of its warehouses which were going up all the time. It also had the first public parks of any city outside London. (In 1844 alone three such parks were opened.) In 1851 Owen's College came into existence, with five professors and two other teachers, and from this was to grow the University, which received its charter in 1880. In 1852 a splendid free library was established. Manchester officially became a city in 1853 and had its own Great Exhibition, held in an exhibition centre called Piccadilly. In 1856 the Free Trade Hall was opened, a fine building in the Venetian Lombard style. In 1857 the city staged the first art exhibition of its kind to be held anywhere in England — of work from private collections. And in 1858 the Hallé Orchestra was founded.[31] Not bad for a place condemned to be 'provincial'.

Now one might well protest that Arnold, at least, never makes such a condemnation. Nor does he. Arnold is a slippery customer, and when he opposes the provincial to the centre he names no names. Indeed, it is doubtful whether he would have thought of London as a centre of real culture. On the other hand, when you look at the terms in which he describes the provincial spirit you can hardly avoid seeing that he has real places in his sights. For example, Arnold says that

the provincial spirit ... does not persuade, it makes war; it has not urbanity, the tone of the city, of the centre ... the provincial tone is more violent, and seems to aim rather at an effect upon the blood and senses than upon the spirit ... [32]

That comes from his essay on 'The Literary Influence of Academies' and if you want to know where Arnold thinks such violence is to be found, you need look no further than *Culture and Anarchy*, which he published in 1869. For there we are told that a dominant spirit of the times is 'fire and strength', which seeks to justify 'vulgarity, hideousness, ignorance, violence'[33] — a list, it will be noted, very similar to that which is offered against all that's wrong with English literature: 'hap-hazard, crudeness, provincialism, eccentricity, violence, blundering'. And where is that spirit of fire and strength above all to be found? Where else but in the new cities. Arnold doesn't say so — of course not — but he would hardly need to draw his readers' attention to what others had repeatedly pointed out: that the skyline of these cities was dominated by tall chimneys which belched out fire and smoke; so that his apparently metaphoric language claims a basis in fact.

It is the same when Arnold talks in *Culture and Anarchy* of 'Hebraism' and 'Hellenism'. By the former he means 'strictness of conscience', 'conduct and obedience', and 'energy and honesty'. (In his essay on 'The Literary Influence of Academies' Arnold characterises energy and honesty as 'the chief spiritual characteristics' of the nation.) I do not see how anyone reading Arnold's words could fail to understand that what he is really talking about is the spirit of non-conformity. And where is that spirit most to be found? In the provincial cities. The word 'energy', however, needs closer attention: for it defines a particular class of person, as Arnold perfectly well knew, because he had certainly read John Stuart Mill's essay on 'Civilization', first published in 1836, in which Mill had remarked that 'the energies of the middle classes are almost confined to money-getting, and those of the higher classes are nearly extinct'.[34]

This is a most important point. Mill's remark closely anticipates the notorious anecdote in which Engels records his meeting with a middle-class manufacturer in Manchester:

... these English bourgeois are good husbands and family men, and have all sorts of other virtues ... but how does this help matters? Ultimately it is self-interest, and especially money-gain, which alone determines them. I once went into Manchester with such a bourgeois and spoke to him of the bad, unwholesome method of building, the frightful condition of the working-people's quarters, and asserted that I had never seen so ill-built a city. The man listened quietly to the end, and said at the corner where we parted: 'And yet there is a great deal of money made here; good morning, sir'.[35]

Again, you can't get a much narrower view than that. And yet remember how much Manchester had achieved even by the time that conversation took place — presumably some time in 1843. Why is *that* not to count? Why is the provincial city wanting the culture of the capital? Why in his essay should Arnold say that 'to get rid of provinciality is a certain stage in culture'?

For it plainly won't do to assert that the middle classes were motivated solely by an energy to make money. What did they do with it when they got it? One answer is that they made Manchester — and other cities for that matter — places of such enviable cultural riches that even a combination of Hitler's bombs and the town planners of the 1960s couldn't entirely destroy what they had created. (And I am not thinking merely of the architecture.) Another answer, a much more ambiguous one, is to be found in *North and South*, the novel which Elizabeth Gaskell published in 1855, and which is for the most part set in Manchester — or 'Miltern Northern' as she there calls it. There is a finely pointed scene where Mr Thornton, a middle-class manufacturer of Milton, finds himself in conversation with Mr Bell, an Oxford don, a custodian of culture whom chance has brought to Milton. Bell asks Thornton:

'I wonder when you Milton men intend to live. All your lives seem to be spent in gathering together the materials for life.'
'By living, I suppose you mean enjoyment?'

'Yes, enjoyment — I don't specify of what, because I trust we should both consider mere pleasure as very poor enjoyment.'

'I would rather have the nature of enjoyment defined.'

'Well! enjoyment of leisure — enjoyment of the power and influence which money gives. You are all striving for money. What do you want it for?'

Mr Thornton was silent. Then he said, 'I don't really know. But money is not what I strive for.'

'What then?'

But Thornton cannot answer. Why he can't is best explained, I think, by understanding the power of that word 'leisure'. For after all, if the middle class is to be identified with energy, it can't also want leisure without being untrue to itself. Yet leisure is becoming thought of as essential to culture or the acquiring of culture. That is why Thornton stays silent. Because from Bell's — orthodoxy's — point of view he can't be cultured. I have already quoted Johnson's remark that those who change language for the better are those with 'leisure for new thoughts', who are 'a people polished by arts, and classed by subordination'. Much more important though is a passage in Mill's essay on Coleridge, published in 1840, in which Mill notes how Coleridge saw that 'cultivation, to be carried beyond a certain point, requires leisure; that leisure is the natural attribute of a hereditary aristocracy....'[36] It certainly isn't the natural attribute of the Hebraic. For the Hebraic spirit is characterised by energy, and the energetic are the money-makers of provincial cities, so that it follows that they are defined in opposition to leisure: therefore they must want for culture.

As I have said, Arnold opposes the Hebraic by the Hellenic. And he characterises the Hellenic in terms of 'sweetness and light'. Again the language is metaphoric, but again nobody reading Arnold's words in 1869 could avoid knowing that provincial cities were literally the opposite of sweetness and light. They stank — as Engels had memorably recorded; and to the southern imagination, in particular, they were places of such darkness that it is not surprising that they seemed hell on earth.[37] Indeed, if you look at illustrations of the new towns made by southern artists during the latter half of the nineteenth century, you will see that those cities are turned into regions that resemble, above all, the kind of illustrations of hell that were at the same period accompanying texts of Milton's *Paradise Lost* and Dante's *Inferno*.

Of course, this is an exaggerated reaction. You have only to compare any of the well known mid-century illustrations of the *London Illustrated News* of the Black Country (although the soubriquet is itself significant) with contemporary photographs of Wolverhampton to see how far southern imagination exceeds Midland reality. But the point to make is that those who came to call the new cities 'provincial' did so partly because they couldn't in any sense conceive of them as being places of 'sweetness and light'. The very phrase hints at Mediterranean sunlight: it conjures up the classical world of Greece and Rome which Arnold had particularly in mind when he came to use it. At the very least sweetness and light will be linked with the south, fire and energy with the north. And since the new industrial cities were in what came to be thought of as the north, once you have fixed the terms of culture as Arnold did you have automatically placed the provincial as beyond the pale of serious cultural consideration.

And this makes for a further, all-important, point. For as soon as you have put people beyond the pale, have turned them into quasi-colonials, you have demonologised them. And you therefore fear them. So you justify your fear in terms of their presumed violence. (Colonials don't know what is good for them: the natives are always growing restless.) Given this, it is hardly surprising that Arnold should make such ritualistic use of the word 'violence'. We will recall that he links provincial literature to violence; he thinks the provincial tone is violent; and the provincial spirit seeks to justify violence. What can Arold mean by so repeatedly invoking the word? More Sheffield outrages? More Chartist demonstrations? More rick burnings? Well, yes and no. For behind that slippery language lurks the genuine fear that attaches itself to the appropriator. It is a fear that is interestingly betrayed in Henry James's very Arnoldian novel, *The Princess Casamassima*, in which at one point James has his hero reflect, of a working-class girl, that

...she had given rein to a fine faculty of free invention of which he had had frequent glimpses, under pressure of her half-childish, half-plebeian impulse of destruction, the instinct of pulling down what was above her, the reckless energy that would, precisely, make her so effective in revolutionary scenes.

What comes out there, though in an involuntary manner, is guilt: the guilt of the appropriator who has decided what shall be thought of as 'above'; and who sees it not only in class, nor in geographical, but in absolute terms.

Yet the crucial matter is that such guilt is usually and successfully transferred to those who are presumed to be 'below'. They are required to apologise for their exclusion from, their inferiority to, what has been appropriated. The ultimate absurdity of the colonial is that he has to apologise for being colonial. The ultimate absurdity of the provincial is that he has to apologise for being provincial. And he does it.

I can pinpoint this simply by noting that when Arnold Bennett came to write his first novel he called it *A Man from the North*. The man in question is Richard Larch, a would-be writer, who wants to escape from what he regards as the stultifying small world of Stoke to London. Now Stoke isn't really the north at all, and I don't know any citizen of the town who would think it was. But for the young Bennett it was the essence of 'provincial' — the later fiction makes handsome amends for this judgment — and can therefore be called 'the north'. And it is also worth noting that in his autobiography *An Only Child*, published in 1961, Frank O'Connor speaks of Daniel Corkery, a friend of his early manhood, as having 'a good deal of the harshness and puritanism of the provincial intellectual which I share.'[38]

One can't, it hardly needs saying, reverse history, and it is plainly impossible to undo the meanings that over the past 200 years have attached themselves to the word 'provincial'. But it is at least possible to see why the word developed those meanings, and to demystify the kinds of presumed authority which those who did most to develop such meanings take for granted. By what right do those people claim to appropriate the English language and its culture? By right of 'leisure' and 'cultivation' perhaps? But leisure and cultivation are themselves complicated words, ones that Dickens wonderfully dissects in *Dombey and Son*; and there is the jolt 'cultivation' gets from George Orwell, lying in bed in his last illness, listening to what he called the 'cultivated' voices of hospital visitors:

And what voices! A sort of over-fedness, a fatuous self-confidence, a
constant bah-baing of laughter at nothing, above all a sort of heaviness and
richness combined with a fundamental ill-will — people who, one instinct-
ively feels, without being able to see them, are the enemies of anything
intelligent or sensitive or beautiful.

I will end this essay, as I began it, with a lecture. It is by the
poet Seamus Heaney, and it is called 'The Sense of Place'.
Heaney remarks that 'we are dwellers, we are namers, we are
lovers, we make homes and we search for our histories'.[39] That
is both true and important. It also refers us to matters that the
language of the Academy, the culture of the centre, will not
help us to define. On the contrary, *that* language, *that* culture,
are likely to thwart or impoverish any attempt at a fit utterance
of such matters. This is what Hardy recognised, when he jotted
down in a Notebook of 1880 his conviction that 'Arnold is
wrong about provincialism.... A certain provincialism of
feeling is invaluable. It is of the essence of individuality....'[40]
And, I will add, of community. For as Hazlitt saw, all that is
greatest in our literature is dependent on such feeling. Talk of
the centre, of regulated language, becomes a trivial irrelevance,
for example, when we are faced with John Clare's 'The Flit-
ting', which is one of the greatest of all poems of the nineteenth
century, and which is about the agony of being dispossessed
precisely of that sense of place which Johnson and Arnold
would think of no account, and which, moreover, celebrates
the possession of a language, a dialect, that they regard as
utterly provincial and therefore of small value.
    Or is this to be unfair? For interestingly enough, though
both Johnson and Arnold begin by championing the idea of
the French Academy, when it comes to the pinch neither of
them actually wants anything like it to take root in England. In
the *Preface to the English Dictionary*, Johnson allows himself
to imagine the establishing of an academy 'for the cultivation
of our stile', but then confesses that 'I, who can never wish to
see dependence multiplied, hope the spirit of *English* liberty
will hinder or destroy [it].'[41] And at the end of his essay on 'The
Literary Influence of Academies', Arnold admits that 'an
Academy quite like the French Academy, a sovereign organ of

the highest literary opinion, a recognised authority in matters of intellectual tone and taste, we shall hardly have, and perhaps we ought not to wish to have it.'[42]

Notes

1 Una Pope Hennessy, *Canon Charles Kingsley* (1948) p.195.
2 *Ibid.*, p.201
3 *Ibid.*, p.121.
4 Matthew Arnold, *Essays in Criticism, First Series*, Macmillan (1925) p.55
5 *John Dryden: Selected Criticism*, ed. J.Kingsley and G.Parfitt (1970) p.159.
6 *Ibid.*, p.276.
7 Christopher Hill, *The World Turned Upside Down: Radical Ideas during the English Revolution*, Harmondsworth (1975) p.368.
8 *Ibid.*, p.369.
9 H.A. Gleason, *Linguistics and English Grammar*, New York (1966) p.71.
10 Joseph Priestley, *The Rudiments of English Grammar* (1761). The quotation is from Olivia Smith.
11 J.W. Adamson, *English Education, 1789-1902* (1902) p.43. *Ibid.*
12 David Hume, *Essays*, (London and New York u.d.) p.142.
13 *The Plan of a Dictionary of the English Language*, in *Samuel Johnson: Prose and Poetry*, ed. Mona Wilson (1957) p.123.
14 *Ibid.*, p.129.
15 *Samuel Johnson: A Dictionary of the English Language*, facsimile edition, Times Newspapers (1979).
16 *The Plan, op. cit.*, p.136.
17 *Preface to the Dictionary, op. cit.*, unpaginated.
18 *Ibid.*
19 Hugh Blair, *Lectures on Rhetoric and Belles Lettres* (1825) p.445.
20 William Hazlitt, *The Spirit of the Age* in *Hazlitt's Works*, ed. W.Carew Hazlitt (1886) p.89.
21 *Ibid.*, p.95.
22 *Ibid.*, p.94.
23 *Wordsworth and Coleridge: Lyrical Ballads*, ed. R.L.Brett and A.R. Jones (1963) p.239.
24 Noah Webster, *Dissertations on the English Language* (1789). The quotation comes from Olivia Smith.
25 Quoted in W.Baring Pemberton, *William Cobbett*, Harmondsworth (1949) pp.121-2.
26 Kerry Downes, *The Georgian Cities of Britain* (1979).
27 Jane Austen, *Pride and Prejudice*, Oxford Edition (1971) p.19.
28 Robert Bloomfield, *Poetical Works* (1867) pp.165-71.
29 See Asa Briggs, *Victorian Cities* (1963), chapter on Manchester.

30 Freidrich Engels, *The Condition of the Working Class in England in 1844*,
    text of Institute of Marxist-Leninism, introduction by Eric Hobsbawn,
    p. 168.
31 See Briggs, *op. cit.*
32 *Essays in Criticism, op. cit.*, p.67.
33 Matthew Arnold, *Culture and Anarchy* (1869).
34 J.S. Mill, *Essays on Politics and Culture*, ed. Gertrude Himmelfarb, New
    York (1963) p.57.
35 Engels, *op. cit.*, p.301.
36 J.S. Mill, *op. cit.*, p.126.
37 For more on this, see my essay on 'Engels, Mrs Gaskell and Manchester',
    in *The Literature of Change* (1977/80).
38 Frank O'Connor, *An Only Child* (1961) p.151.
39 Seamus Heaney, *Preoccupations* (1980) p.149.
40 Florence Emily Hardy, *The Life of Thomas Hardy* (1965) pp.146-7.
41 Preface to a *Dictionary of the English Language, op. cit.*
42 *Essays in Criticism, op. cit.*, p.78.

Chapter 3

The Poet in His Joy: How and Why a Word Changed Its Meaning during the Eighteenth Century

IN 1841 John Clare was entered into Northampton General Lunatic Asylum, victim of insanity which, according to Dr Fenwick Skrimshire, who had attended the poet since 1824, had been brought on 'after years addicted to poetical prosings'. Those 'prosings' did not cease when Clare entered the asylum and one of them is of immediate relevance to my theme. It is called 'The Peasant Poet', it is about Clare himself, and it ends with the following lines: 'A silent man in life's affairs, / A thinker from a boy, / A peasant in his daily cares, / The poet in his joy.'[1] We may find it odd, indeed deeply upsetting that Clare of all people should insist on joy as the defining characteristic for the poet. But there it is. *The* poet, not *a* poet. The phrase is peremptory and absolute. And it is echoed by Matthew Arnold in the very long 'Empedocles on Aetna'. For late in that poem Empedocles remarks to himself that 'something has impair'd thy spirit's strength / And dried its self-sufficing fount of joy.'[2] Different as they may be, both Clare and Arnold accept the equation of poet *as* poet with 'joy' and in doing this they are, of course, following a convention that had been established by the great Romantic poets, especially Wordsworth and Coleridge. Time and again in their work 'joy' is invoked in such a way that it seems to have an almost talismanic power. And so it is for their successors. Which may help to explain why Arnold could call the Augustan age one of prose. For no matter how finely you comb the works of Dryden and Pope you will find no evidence to suggest that they thought of the poet or the act of creating poetry in terms of joy. Wit, yes; judgement, fancy, reason, art and nature, yes, yes, yes and yes again. But joy? No, never.

30

Where then did this equation come from? Or to put the matter another way, how did Wordsworth and Coleridge find it possible to make such constant and emphatic use of the word and to link it so intimately with the nature and function of poetry?

By way of beginning to answer this question I want to note that at least some eighteenth-century poets were capable of linking joy, if not with poetry itself, then with fancy. For example, in Book 1 of the first version of his *The Pleasures of Imagination* (1744), Mark Akenside offers a purely conventional account of fancy as the pleasing lie. It properly functions by kind permission of Reason, and when it does 'the intellectual power / Bends from his awful throne a wondering ear, / And smiles; the passions, gently smoothed away, / Sink to divine repose, and love and joy / Alone are waking....'[3] It is obvious that Akenside is here accepting the Lockeian claim that the pleasure of imagination must not be confused with the truth. (A claim which had been erected into a principle of sorts in Addison's famous papers 411-421 of the Spectator).[4] So it should come as no surprise that on this occasion at least Akenside chooses to think of joy as a placid and serene emotion. And it is worth noticing that this is how joy is regarded in Langhorne's four elegies, *The Visions of Fancy*, written about 1750. True, the last stanza of the first elegy may at first glance seem to say more than that, but Langhorne hedges too many bets for us to regard him as in any way Romantic in his use of the word. 'Ecstatic hours! so every distant day / Like this serene on downy wings shall move: / Rise crown'd with joys that triumph o'er decay, / The faithful joys of Fancy and of Love.'[5] 'Ecstatic' there hardly survives the 'serene and downy wings'. And in the other elegies joy is simply equated with the pleasant but unimportant reign of Fancy. Moreover, since it is so equated you are bound to get a rude awakening if you hope for any more. In this context it is worth mentioning Sir William Hamilton's 'Ode to Fancy'. The date of this is uncertain, but it was published in his *Poems on Several occasions* (1749) and is unlikely to have been written before he had read Joseph Warton's 'Ode to Fancy', which had been first published in 1746 as one of Warton's *Odes on Various Subjects*. Hamilton enquires of Fancy 'why didst thou decoy / My thoughts into this dream of joy, / Then to forsake me all alone, / To mourn the fond delusion gone?'[6]

Even so, Hamilton's dream of joy has very little suggestion of power about it, and the fact is that none of the eighteenth-century writers I have so far mentioned think of joy as an exultant emotion.[7] Why this should be need not surprise us if we remember that Locke had remarked that joy is 'a delight of the mind, from the consideration of the present, or assured possession of a good.'[8] This fairly enough suggests that the Augustans thought of joy in terms of rational and controlled emotion. They did not expect to be surprised by joy. 'If the thing we think of is great,' John Dennis wrote in *The Advancement of Reformation of Modern Poetry*, 'why, then, admiration attends the idea of it; and if it is very great, amazement. If the thing is pleasing and delightful, why then joy and gaiety flow from the idea of it.'[9]

What Dennis had said in 1701, Langhorne, Hamilton and Akenside repeat in the middle of the century; and the Lockeian influence is still there at the century's end. In 1798 Thomas Campbell published *The Pleasures of Hope*, and there we can read of a woman whose husband is drowned at sea, but to whom 'Mercy gave, to charm the sense of woe, / Ideal peace, that truth could ne'er bestow; / Warm on her heart the joys of Fancy beam, / And aimless Hope delights her darkest dream.'[10]

And yet in the year in which the *Pleasures of Hope* made its appearance, Wordsworth and Coleridge published the *Lyrical Ballads*, and in one of the great poems of that volume we find Wordsworth writing: 'While with an eye made quiet by the power / Of harmony and the deep power of joy / We see into the life of things.'[11] There is an enormous gap between the ways in which Campbell and Wordsworth use the same word.

For the moment I want merely to register the fact of that gap and to suggest that it is of great importance to Coleridge. There can be no doubt that Coleridge's crucial uses of the word are indebted to Wordsworth. In a very real sense Wordsworth invented the modern meaning of 'joy'. Certainly there is nothing in early Coleridge to suggest the strength that the word will come to have in his poetry. Where 'joy' occurs it is in contexts and with definitions that Augustan poets would have unhesitatingly approved. So 'An Invocation' (1790) begins

'Sweet Muse! companion of my hour! / Voice of my joy! Sure soother of the sigh!' and in 'Domestic Peace', a poem written four years later, Coleridge speaks of 'Memory, bosom-spring of joy'.[12] Since Locke regarded memory as the source of nearly all ideas of the imagination, Coleridge is being no more than orthodox in making a double equation between joy, memory and fancy. (The equation of joy and fancy was by now a cliché).

The 'Eolian Harp' (1795) contains Coleridge's first important use of 'joy', but this in fact proves my point about his indebtedness to Wordsworth. For the lines in which the word occurs (26-33) were not included in the poem until the three-volume edition of 1828, though they were printed in the errata to *Sibylline Leaves* (1817). Thus they must have been written after the 1803 edition of the poems. The key lines run 'O! the one Life within us and abroad, / Which meets all motion and becomes all soul, / A light in sound, a sound-like power in light, / Rhythm in all thought, and joyance every where.'[13] Coleridge speaks here of an innate power in the human mind which *recognises* the essential vitality of the universe by means of a matching vitality. In short, he is prepared to journey beyond Hartley's associationist theory which had earlier contented him. And beside Hartley we may place Alexander Gerard, whose *Essay on Genius* (1774) is important to any consideration of eighteenth-century accounts of the functioning of the imagination. Speaking of the imagination's power in Part i, Section iii of his essay, Gerard remarks that it can 'transpose, vary and compound our perceptions into an endless variety of forms, so as to produce numberless combinations that are wholly new.'[14] The statement may seem to look forward to Coleridge's famous definition of the secondary imagination as that which 'dissolves, diffuses, dissipates, in order to re-create',[15] but there is a crucial difference. For Gerard is forced to regard all perceptions as retained wholes since he has no satisfactory explanation of how the imagination can activate — and so recreate — them. Gerard's problem becomes especially obvious as soon as he says that the imagination 'darts with the quickness of lightning, through all possible views of the ideas which are presented' — for although he sees genius as the possession of true poets he can only and lamely

say that its workings require 'a peculiar vigour of association'. No effort of genius can make for the creative bringing
together of ideas; instead, ideas themselves have qualities
which lead to their being regularly associated with each other
and 'it is impossible to give a reason why these qualities unite
ideas.'[16]

One would be correct in calling this mechanical association-
ism, and yet in admitting to the peculiar vigour of genius
Gerard half anticipates Coleridge's leap by means of which
qualities are transferred from the ideas themselves to the mind
which entertains them. The imagination of genius does not
work mechanically but organically; and its power is signalled
by joy. We here approach the crux of the matter. As Humphry
House remarked, 'the "joy" of "Dejection" must be understood as involving the "deep delight" which "Kubla Khan"
shows as the centre of creative happiness'.

> Joy, lady! is the spirit and the power,
>   Which wedding Nature to us gives in dower
>   A new Earth and new Heaven,
> Undreamt of by the sensual and the proud —
> Joy is the sweet voice, Joy the luminous cloud —
>   We in ourselves rejoice!
> And thence flows all that charms or ear or sight,
>   All melodies the echoes of that voice,
> All colours a suffusion from that light.[17]

Those lines from the 'Dejection Ode' may be compared with
some lines from Book 3 of the *Prelude*: 'I had a world about
me; 'twas my own, / I made it; for it only liv'd to me, / And to
the God who look'd into my mind.'[18] In the 1850 version the
last of those lines was changed to 'And to the God who sees
into the heart', and Wordsworth's retreat from his earlier
position is not unlike a retreat from joy. For joy not only
signals the power of imagination working in genius, it also
confirms the truthfulness of the imagination's transforming
power.

But Coleridge had his doubts. And at this point I need to
make brief mention of the *Biographia Literaria* and especially
of the persuasive account of it offered by J. A. Appleyard in his
Coleridge's Philosophy of Literature. Appleyard follows
I. A. Richards in feeling that the argument of the *Biographia*

doesn't really hold water, and in the course of his important discussion of it, he says that

Since... 1801 [Coleridge's] speculations had been directed to the recon-ciliation of the Cartesian dualism by a knowledge theory which would provide both for a formative, creative activity of the mind and for the objective reality of what was known.... The theory of imagination grew out of certain experiences — the lessons of Boyer, the reading of Bowles and especially of Wordsworth, and, obviously, Coleridge's own once-total in-volvement with the creation of poems — which testified to this unity of the knowing mind and the known object, and was an attempt, even prior to the *Biographia*, to provide a rationale for the apparent connaturality of the two.

I think that both Richards and Appleyard are right in arguing that Coleridge fails to provide the rationale, even if he testifies to the 'one life within us and abroad'. Moreover, Appleyard convincingly explains why Coleridge withdrew from the opportunity of providing the rationale that Schelling seemed to offer. Schelling, whose work Coleridge certainly knew by the turn of the century, proposed the identity of mind and nature at the point at which they meet in an Absolute where all prior antitheses disappear, and he further argued that imagin-ation provided the verification of this identity because it could objectify the inward intuition of the subject-object identity. At first glance such a line of argument seems to be exactly one to appeal to Coleridge. It provides a medium between knower and known and it give imagination its contact with the real.

Yet Coleridge rejected this argument and he did so because, in Appleyard's words, 'it offered too much... it collapsed all distinctions between the world and the self insofar as it did not distinguish between the world and God — everything became only a moment in the dialectical act of knowing that constituted the existence of the Absolute. [19] In other words, Coleridge was too serious a Christian to risk advancing the theory. This means, of course, that he is left with the problem that imagin-ation may be the sweet lie of Locke's account. And it then follows that the power of joy which he wants to regard as integral to the poetic process may itself delude the poet into identifying it with inspiration, that is, truth.

Of course, to suggest that inspiration equals truth is to make another leap, but it had in fact been made before Coleridge began to worry about the truth or otherwise of imagination.

Indeed, by the end of the eighteenth century it had become a commonplace to accept that inspiration was the source of all true poetry. We are by now a long way from Johnson's gruff 'Sir, a man may write at any time if he will set himself *doggedly* to do it'. And also a long way from the demand that poets should be scholar poets. So, as Robert Anderson pointed out, Burns could — justifiably — make money from his poems by gulling polite society into the belief that 'he was an illiterate ploughman who wrote from pure inspiration...in company he would not suffer his pretensions to pure inspiration to be challenged, and it was seldom done where it might be supposed to affect the success of the subscription for his Poems.'[20] I do not think that it is necessary to trace in any detail the rise in the fortunes of 'inspiration' during the century, but a few points are important. First, and perhaps most significant, Milton becomes *the* inspired poet. 'Milton, thou shouldst be living at this hour.' Well, to all intents and purposes he was. Blake after all saw himself as Milton's reincarnation, and was proud to quote his remark that a true poem is 'Not to be Obtain'd by the Invocation of memory and her syren Daughter, but by Devout Prayer to that Eternal Spirit, who can enrich with all utterance and knowledge and sends out his Seraphim with the hallowed fire of his Altar to touch and purify the lips of whom he pleases.' And he knew, as did Wordsworth and Coleridge, Milton's claim that poetic abilities 'wheresoever they be found, are the inspired gift of God.'[21]

It is also important to note that, probably because of the gigantic influence of Milton, Augustan poets came to accept that poetry was the gift of God. Even the most sceptical admitted that true poetry might snatch a grace beyond the reach of art, and the less sceptical were forthright in their acceptance of the notion. Thus Thomas Parnell, in his 'The Gift of Poetry', could write

> My God! from whom proceed the gifts divine
> My God! I think I feel the gift is thine.
> Be this no vain illusion which I find,
> Not Nature's impulse on the passive mind,
> But Reason's act, produc'd by good desire,
> By grace enliven'd with celestial fire.

And for Parnell the true poet tells God's truths. The vision with which the poem ends has him casting a retrospective eye over human history and coming to understand why poets were created. 'Where first the morning stars together sung, / Where first their harps the sons of glory strung / With shouts of joy.'[22] Parnell died in 1718, but his verse continued to enjoy some popularity, as is evident from any anonymous essay which appeared in the *London Magazine* in 1735, in the course of which the author argued that 'there is nothing more proper to furnish us with *sublime Sentiments* and *poetical Images* than a view of the magnificent Structure of Things, than that vast *Idea* which made *Morning Stars sing together, and the sons of God shout for joy.*'[23] Parnell's sons of glory have now become sons of God. The invocation to rejoice in the Lord is now seen as being specifically the poet's duty (and pleasure).

Again, it is important to recognise that the belief that God's laws in nature are a discoverable certainty has much to do with the identification of the poet with inspiration. To see this spelt out we must turn to Akenside's *The Pleasures of Imagination*, not because it is a successful poem (it has some good passages but they are few and far between) but because it is a virtual anthology of contemporary thinking about poets and poetry, and because it was attentively read by Wordsworth. Near the beginning of the poem, Akenside writes 'From Heaven my strains begin; from Heaven descends / The flame of genius to the human breast, / And love, and beauty, and poetic joy, / And inspiration.'[24] These lines are later altered (Akenside spent the remainder of his life tinkering with the poem, which was left incomplete at his death in 1770), so that 'poetic joy' becomes 'poetic wonder', and 'the human breast' becomes 'the chosen breast'. The first change is unimportant (there is plenty about joy elsewhere in the poem). The other change is a different matter. It insists that the poet is chosen by God, and thus makes emphatic what had been implicit in the first version. Later on in the first book, Akenside reveals what it is that the chosen poets receive from God.

> To these the Sire Omnipotent unfolds
> The world's harmonious volume, there to read
> The transcript of Himself. On every part
> They trace the bright impressions of his hand:
> In earth or air, the meadow's purple stores,

> The moon's mild radiance, or the virgin's form
> Blooming with rosy smiles, they see portrayed
> that uncreated beauty, which delights
> The mind supreme. They also feel her charms;
> Enamoured, they partake the eternal joy.[25]

The inspired poet is placed in the way of receiving God's truths and of communicating them. Partaking in the eternal joy is expressive as well as receptive.

Later, however, in one of his more complicated passages, Akenside seems to contradict this position in the interest of what might be called a pre-Romantic commitment to imagination's transforming powers. 'Mind, mind alone, (bear witness earth and heaven!) / The living fountains in itself contains / Of beauteous and sublime: here, hand in hand, / Sit paramount the Graces: here, enthroned, / Celestial Venus, with divinest airs, /Invites the soul to never-fading joy.'[26] Such joy as this appears to go clean counter to the principle of eternal joy and I suspect that Akenside himself must have felt unhappy with what almost certainly appeared to him to be an impious assertion. In the later version 'Mind, mind alone' is therefore altered to 'He, God most high' — which neatly enough demonstrates the problem about the mind's imaginative powers that was to plague far greater poets than Akenside.

Akenside never resolved the problem to his own satisfaction. It is perhaps no accident that his poem remained unfinished at his death. Generally speaking, the earlier version is the more confident and the more coherent, perhaps because it relies more on Milton's 'Celestial Light' which will 'shine inward, and the mind through all her powers / irradiate': perhaps also because it more powerfully asserts the fact of joyance everywhere. In Book II, for example, Akenside writes of the Sovereign Spirit of the world.

> Within his own deep essence he beheld
> The circling bounds of happiness unite;
> Yet, by immense benignity, inclined
> To spread around him that primeval joy
> Which filled himself, he raised his plastic arm,
> And sounded through the hollow depth of space
> The strong, creative mandate.[27]

Universal joy proceeds from God, it is communicated to poets who 'trace everywhere the bright impressions of his hand', and they communicate it to others in 'shouts of joy'.

Joy. The word keeps coming up and it seems right to ask why. Well, partly because it is the Psalmist's word, and partly because a radically new (or renewed) emotionalism in religion is discoverable during the years with which I am concerned. In her invaluable study, *The Happy Man*, Maren-Sofie Rostvig offers conclusive evidence of the fact that eighteenth-century man went in search of God in nature by means of that 'charming enthusiasm' which Shaftsbury had felt to be the source of all true knowledge. In this context 'joy' indicates the triumphant conclusion of the search. In the words of Mrs Elizabeth Rowe, 'In nature's lovely and unblemish'd face / With joy his sacred lineaments I trace.'[28] The lines may stand for the many examples Rostvig cites of what was familiar in the literature of the period. I do not mean to suggest that this is a remarkable use of the word 'joy'. Given the nature of the search it is an inevitable one. The Happy Man has every reason to obey the Psalmist's injunction to rejoice in the Lord. But that the search for God should be conducted 'enthusiastically' does need noting, because it goes beyond anything that Akenside proposes. (Even if he hints at it when he says of God's nature that the poet 'feels her charms').

It is James Thomson who provides the perfect example of the 'enthusiastic' search for and discovery of God. I think particularly of these lines in *Spring*, where Thomson writes that 'By small degrees the love of nature works, / And warms the bosom; till at last arriv'd / To rapture, and enthusiastic Heat, / We feel the present Deity, and taste /The joy of God, to see a happy world.'[29] We have now moved some distance from Parnell. God's gift of joy is not communicated by Reason's act but by 'Rapture and enthusiastic Heat'.

In her study of *Enthusiasm* Susie Tucker says that those eighteenth-century devotees of enthusiasm who believed that you could find its true meaning by tracing its etymology were simply being naive. 'The Greek', she says, 'implies real possession by a God, or at least "an intercourse with him" in Dr Johnson's words. But the seventeenth and eighteenth century critics... believed that such a state never existed — it was always a false, vain confidence.'[30] Maybe, but such critics had to take very seriously indeed the claims made by Thomson and others, if only because the claims were so many, so intense and so persistent. And they had the inevitable attraction of being able to get round a difficult problem. For although Pope had announced that 'God said Let Newton be and All was Light', the fact remained that nature and nature's laws still lay hid in night. Bother light, therefore, and bother laws. Or rather bother such lights and laws as weren't those of inspiration, of Celestial Venus, of God himself.

How to answer this? The opponents of inspiration were quick to insist that it proceeded from the heat-oppresséd brain. And this leads us to the next point, which is that during the earlier part of the eighteenth century inspiration is commonly associated with the 'psychopathology of enthusiasm', which phrase I take from F.E. Manuel's *The Eighteenth Century Confronts the Gods*, where it provides the title for one of that great book's sub-chapters. There we find a fascinating discussion of the deist, John Trenchard, who in 1709 published an essay called *The Natural History of Superstition*, in which he rehearsed most of the arguments that were to become standard in eighteenth-century deistic arguments against the belief in 'inspiration' as emotional cognition of God. Trenchard argued that in times of so-called inspiration what actually happened was that inner stimuli of the body aroused visions that were not contradicted by the senses because there was a blockage of communication with the real world. These internally generated images, he claimed, are continually 'striking upon, and affecting the Brain, Spirits, or Organ where the imaginative faculty resides'. And he took this explanation to be sufficient to account for the 'inward light' of visionaries. Trenchard, moreover, identified the visionary with the enthusiast, whom he characterised as a type of the melancholy man, afflicted by 'Inquietude and Alienation of Thoughts, Anxious and Panick Fears, and a desire for Solitude'.[31]

We come now to a further point, which is the connection of the poet with melancholia and solitude. The attack on solitude as a means of feeding the visions of enthusiasm is familiar enough to require no comment here. What is perhaps less familiar is the way in which inspiration came to be defended just because it could be linked with enthusiasm and solitude;

and how all could be seen as defining characteristics of the true poet. A. S. P. Woodhouse argued that William Collins was greatly concerned with the poet's prophetic role, which he thought couldn't be defensible 'unless the creatures of the poet's imagination were in some sort true'. Where could Collins have found evidence for the imagination's essential truthfulness, Woodhouse wondered, and suggested a possible source in Puttenham's statement that 'A poet is as much as to say a maker . . . Such as (by way of resemblance and reverently) we may say of God; who without travell to his divine imagination made all the world of nought.'[32] But you don't have to go to a source as remote as Puttenham (which anyway we have no evidence that Collins had read). The fact is that by the middle of the eighteenth century the notion that the poet was a prophet, because inspired with God's truths, had become too wide-spread for Collins to have missed it. (After all, it was he who called Thomson a druid.)

The most convenient text to refer to here is Young's *Conjectures on Original Composition* (1759), for in the course of that essay Young makes a famous distinction between two kinds of poets. On the one hand there are the 'scholar poets', and on the other those 'divinely-inspired enthusiasts' who are the true geniuses — and who are remarkable for their determination to cross 'all public roads into fresh untrodden ground'.[33] Young puts metaphorically what was coming to be accepted as a literal fact; that the true poet is a solitary. Or, as James Grainger was to write in his 'Solitude: An Ode' (1758), 'Inspiration, Nature's child / Seek[s] the solitary wild'.[34]

Not surprisingly the old order drew back from this insistence that the poet's divine inspiration is to be nurtured in solitude. Even Gerard, who toys with the idea of the poet as divinely inspired, won't finally commit himself to the proposition. 'The fire of genius', he says, 'like a divine impulse, raises the mind above itself, and by the natural influence of imagination actuates it as if it were divinely inspired.'[35] The caution is typical.

Yet at the same time those who insisted on the fact of the divinely-inspired enthusiast, nurturing his truthful visions in isolation, could find support in a new element which had entered eighteenth-century religious language (or, perhaps more likely, the two were mutually supportive). 'Inspiration', Isaac Watts wrote, 'is when an overpowering impression of any proposition is made upon the mind by God himself, that gives a convincing and indubitable evidence of the truth and divinity of it; so were the prophets and apostles inspired.'[36] And so, we may add, were eighteenth-century poets. Or so the belief ran. As Ernest Tuveson has pointed out, the imagination can become a means of grace;[37] and by extension (though we lack a sophisticated study of the subject) druids, bards, and minstrels can become interchangeable titles. Thus Beattie, in the preface to his *Minstrel* notes that

The design was, to trace the progress of a Poetical Genius, born in a rude age, from the first dawning of fancy and reason, till that period at which he may be supposed capable of appearing in the world as a MINSTREL, that is, as an itinerent poet and musician: — a character which, according to the notions of our forefathers, was not only respectable, but sacred.[38]

It is now becoming clear that for the Romantic poets 'joy' can call up the notion of sacred truth, and therefore become a metaphysical cum theological assertion which can manage to do what their epistemology and psychology cannot: that is, 'prove' the truth of imagination as at once projective and realistic. Yet though Wordsworth and Coleridge do use the word in this way they are still haunted by doubts. For on the one hand, if God grants joy he may also deny it — may suddenly cease to regard a poet as one of the chosen; and on the other, joy may itself be a psychological state with no explanation beyond the strains and stresses that the human mind can become victim of. The Deists could be right after all. The poet as solitary may — and indeed can often be — the poet as melancholy man, characterised (to recall Trenchard's words) by 'Inquietude and alienation of thoughts, Anxious and Panick fears'.

> But as it sometimes chanceth, from the might
> Of joy in minds that can no further go,
> As high as we have mounted in delight
> In our dejection do we sink as low;
> To me that morning did it happen so;
> And fears and fancies thick upon me came;
> Dim sadness — and blind thoughts, I knew not nor could name.

As Wordsworth makes clear in his great poem, 'Resolution

and Independence', he considers himself to be a solitary; 'Far from the world I walk and from all care'. And the immoderate joy that results from solitary communication with nature may therefore well be proof of a psychological imbalance. In his *Anatomy of Melancholy*, Burton had spoken of some who had fallen into the malady as a result of the fact that they 'for joy ran mad'. And he cites the case of 'Epaminondas ... [who] the next day after his Leuctrian victory " came abroad all squalid and submiss", and gave no other reason to his friends of so doing, than that he perceived himself the day before ... to be too insolent, overmuch joyed.'[39] Wordsworth had read his Burton (as had Trenchard) but he could have found the same kind of case much nearer to hand.

In 1791 appeared the first English version of a work which had originally been written in German, and which was to go into at least ten editions by 1800. *Solitude, or the Pernicious Influence of a Total Exclusion from Society upon the Mind and Heart*, was the work of J. G. Zimmerman, a Swiss doctor who had spent much time in England and who was extremely well read in English literature, especially literature of the eighteenth century. His attitude to solitude was typically Augustan. On the whole it was a bad thing. Solitude, he remarked, 'excites and strengthens the powers of the imagination to an uncommon degree, and thereby enfeebles the effect of the controlling powers of reason.'[40] And he makes an interesting distinction between the 'happy enthusiast', who is concerned to record the benevolence of God in the Universe, and the 'fanatical visionary' who

feels, like the happy enthusiast, the same agitation of passions, and the same inflammation of mind; but as the feelings of the one are founded upon knowledge, truth and nature, so the feelings of the other are the result of ignorance and error, and all the glittering meteors of his brain the effects of imposture and deception.[41]

In other words, the fanatic visionary does not, as he supposes, receive his visions from God; and as he awakens to this fact he becomes a type of the melancholy man, passing from glittering delight into the opposite state of mind. His soul 'sinks day after day into deeper dejection, and threatens Nature with madness and Death'.[42] 'We poets in our youth begin in gladness, / But thereof come in the end despondency and madness.' The lines are at least a possible gloss on Zimmermann's account of the melancholy man, and suggest that Wordsworth was well aware of the area of opinion which Zimmermann's book covers.

As Zimmermann recognises, his treatise and its arguments form a rearguard action against the growing indentification of emotion with truth about which W. J. Bate writes so well in *From Classic to Romantic*.[43] In this context it is worth noting Abraham Tucker's *The Light of Nature Pursued*, which appeared between 1768-78, which Hazlitt abridged, and which had some effect on Keats. Tucker stresses the use that imagination may make of the totally unconscious mind; and he argues that there is an unusual intensity and instinctive facility that accompanies such a use. For Tucker as for Blake, genius has no error.

Wordsworth was unwilling to accept that much without question, as the speculative nature of 'Resolution and Independence' shows. Yet he does not abandon the idea, and his use of the word joy shows how he could cling on to it. For when he speaks of joy he accepts, I think, that the word has religious implications which silence doubts as to its authenticity. At the beginning of the eighteenth century joy was equated with fancy, and was commonly reckoned to be a mild emotion. But by the end of the century it had become equated with religious inspiration, religious inspiration itself had become identified with fancy, and joy could therefore now be seen as a violently — and validly — powerful emotion, a guarantee of truth, of God's presence, of the fact that the poet was a chosen man, a prophet, a seer blest.

But where is there evidence of the link between joy and religious inspiration? For an answer to that one has only to turn to Wesley's *Journal*, open it at random, and read passages such as the folllowing:

While I was speaking, several dropped down as dead; and among the rest, such a cry was heard, of sinners groaning for the righteousness of faith, as almost drowned my voice. But many of these soon lifted up their heads with joy.

And

At that hour one who was bitterly mourning after Christ . . . was filled with joy unspeakable.

And

[She still remained] in settled despair: but afterwards God turned her heaviness into joy.

And

One young man was in a violent agony, and could not refrain from crying aloud. Several continued with him in prayer till ten o'clock. He was then filled with joy unspeakable.[44]

It is obvious that Wesley uses the word in a semi-technical sense. Joy signifies the moment of sudden intrusion of God's grace, his overwhelming 'inspiration', a word which Johnson defined as 'a breathing into; or, infusion of ideas into the mind by a superior power'.[45] In Wesley's formulation, God gives you life by an infusion of the felt idea of Him. Rebuking Stinstra's *An Essay on Fanaticism*, Wesley says that 'the very thing that Mr Stinstra calls fanaticism, is no other than heart religion; in other words, righteousness and peace and joy in the Holy Ghost. These must be felt, or they have no being.'

Behind certain experiences that Wordsworth records in the *Prelude* we may detect the tradition represented in the writings of Akenside and Wesley: the knowledge of joy eternal felt, if not as heart religion, then at least 'felt in the blood and felt along the heart'. I think for instance of the passage which begins 'I felt the sentiment of being spread / O'er all that moves . . .' and which concludes 'I saw one life, and felt that it was joy.'[46] And I also think that the tradition is behind Coleridge's 'Dejection Ode'. 'Joy, virtuous Lady! Joy that ne'er was given, / Save to the pure, and in their purest hour, / Life, and Life's effluence, cloud at once and shower . . . .' So far as I am aware none of Coleridge's commentators has stressed how specifically religious his use of the word is in the context of this poem. It is not surprising that his guilt feelings in addressing it to Sarah Hutchinson should be so evident; but it seems to me certain that he considers that joy has been withdrawn from him because of his own impurity. Literally, he has been denied inspiration (in the sense in which Wesley used the word). Only if you think of the word in purely secular terms will you think it a paradox that Coleridge should be able to write a great poem about his failed powers.

By way of identifying the religious meaning of the word in Coleridge's poem I want to note his significant, and I suspect largely unconscious, echo of *Samson Agonistes* (an echo which seems to have gone unremarked). Appleyard says that Coleridge feels in the poem that he cannot summon joy. But the point is that it isn't his to summon.

> My genial spirits fail;
> And what can these avail
> To lift the smothering weight from off my breast?
> It were a vain endeavour,
> Though I should gaze for ever
> On that green light that lingers in the west:
> I may not hope from outward forms to win
> The passion and the life, whose fountains are within.[47]

These lines are surely an echo of Samson's despairing speech?

> All otherwise to me my thoughts portend,
> That these dark orbs no more shall treat with light,
> Nor th'other light of life continue long,
> But yield to double darkness nigh at hand:
> So much I feel my genial spirits droop,
> My hopes all flat, nature within me seems
> In all her functions weary of herself;
> My race of glory run, and race of shame,
> And I shall shortly be with them that rest.[48]

Coleridge's awareness of the loss of joy is very close indeed to Samson's awareness of his loss of grace; for both, the principle of life summed up in the phrase 'genial spirits' fails at their abandonment by God.

A last point: Coleridge's lines have some connection with *Resolution and Independence*, as is well known. But it is important to note how Wordsworth accepts that no matter what the source of inspiration it will in time fade. For joy is to be primarily associated with youth, because youth is the time of imagination's power. In the words of the Psalmist, 'Weeping may tarry for the night, but joy cometh in the morning.' And Hartley had put the matter in these terms:

As the Pleasures of Imagination are very prevalent, and much cultivated during Youth; so, if we consider Mankind as one great individual, advancing in Age perpetually, it seems natural to expect, that in the Infancy of knowledge, in the early Ages of the World, the Taste of Mankind would turn much upon the Pleasures of this Class.[49]

Believe that and you are more likely to believe in the authenticity of the *Ossian* poems. Thus Gray, writing in 1763, told the Rev. James Brown that he was sorry their friend, Mr Howe, had not heard of the poems, and wished he could send them to him, for 'He would there see, that Imagination dwelt many hundred years ago in all her pomp on the cold and barren mountains of Scotland. The truth (I believe) is that without any respect of climates she reigns in all nascent societies of men...'[50] Imagination and its signal, joy, are to be found in youthful societies and in the youth of men. Among eighteenth-century texts which make the connections between youth and imagination and youth and joy, I note Langhorne's *Fables of Fancy*, the later version of *The Pleasures of the Imagination* (especially Books 2 and 4), Beattie's 'The Triumph of Melancholy' (especially stanzas 47-8) and Campbell's 'The Pleasures of Hope' (part 2). And I would suggest that both Wordsworth and Coleridge see Chatterton and Burns as joyful possessors of imagination because they were poets; because they came from 'nascent societies of men'; because they were or could be seen as solitaries; and because they died young.[51]

I do not pretend that I have done more than outline the various ways in which joy changed its meaning — mostly through altered associations — through the eighteenth century, and I am certain that a great deal more work can and should be done to show how and why it becomes so important, so *defining* a word for the poet during the Romantic period.[52] But at least it may now be possible for us to recognise that when Clare referred to himself as 'The poet in his joy' he was assuming a connection between words which would have been unimaginable a hundred years earlier, and yet which he could take for granted.

Notes

1 *John Clare: Selected Poems*, ed. J. W. and Ann Tibble (1965) p. 326. Oddly enough, Geoffrey Grigson, in his selection of the poems, prints 'A poet in his joy', thus ruining the force of the line.
2 *The Poetical Works of M. Arnold*, ed. Tinker and Lowry (1950) p. 429.
3 *The Poetical Works of Mark Akenside*, Aldine edition, Book 1, 11, 127-31.

4 Addison published the papers as a separate essay which was widely known and much referred to during the eighteenth century.

5 *Langhorne's Works*, Cooke's edition, p. 142.

6 My text is *Bell's Classical Arrangement of Fugitive Poetry*, Vol. XII (1790) p. 70. Bell prints four other Odes to Fancy, including Warton's.

7 Johnson relegated joy as violent emotion to the tail end of his account of the word's meaning.

8 In his *Essay Concerning the Human Understanding*.

9 See *English Critical Essays, XVI-XVIIII Centuries*, World's Classics, p. 206. For other Augustun texts which link joy with tranquility or serenity, see e.g. Lyttleton's 'To Mr West at Wickham', where joy is equated with 'tranquility and love', and Henry Baker's 'The Universe: A Philosophic Poem', in which joy is linked with 'calm' and 'repose'.

10 *The Poetical Works of Thomas Campbell*, n.d., p. 12. It is only fair to say that in the same poem Campbell also links joy with melancholy and with grief. There is a good deal of gothickry about his use of the word: it defines a pleasing shudder.

11 'Tintern Abbey', 11. 47-9.

12 *Coleridge's Poems*, ed. E. H. Coleridge (1912) Vol. 1, pp. 16 and 72.

13 See E. H. Coleridge, *ibid.*, Vol. 1, p. 101.

14 *An Essay on Genius*, Alexander Gerard (1774) p. 30.

15 *Biographia Literaria*, Ch. 13.

16 Gerard, *op. cit.*, p. 57.

17 *Coleridge's Poems, op. cit.*, Vol. 1, p. 336. This is the version of the poem which Coleridge chose to publish in his life-time and not the 'Letter' which Humphry House prefers. See his *Coleridge* (1953).

18 *The Prelude*, ed. E. De Selincourt (1926). I quote the 1805-6 version, 111, 142-5.

19 *Coleridge's Philosophy of Literature*, J. A. Appleyard (1965) pp. 204-206.

20 See *Burns*, T. Crawford (1965) pp. 198-9.

21 Milton, *The Reason of Church Government*, opening of Bk. II.

22 My text is the edition of the Poetical Works (1786) pp. 147-50.

23 Quoted by Maren Sophie-Rostvig, *The Happy Man*, 2nd edn revised (1962) p. 161.

24 Akenside, *op. cit.*, Book 1, 11. 56-9.

25 *Ibid.*, 11. 99-108.

26 *Ibid.*, 11. 481-6.

27 *Ibid*, Book 2, 11. 311-15.

28 See *Elizabeth Singer Rowe*, Henry F. Stecher (1973) p. 211. A large number of poems in which this equation between joy and enthusiasm makes itself felt is referred to by Maren Sophie-Rostvig, *op. cit.*

29 *The Seasons*, 1730 (Scholar Press facsimile), 'Spring', 11. 861-5.

30 Susie Tucker, *Enthusiasm* (1972) p. 21.

31 *The Eighteenth Century Confronts the Gods* (1959) especially pp. 72-80.

32 See his essay on Collins in *From Sensibility to Romanticism*, ed. Hilles and Bloom (1965) p. 108.

33 *English Critical Essays, op. cit.*, p. 289.

34 *Bell's Classical Arrangement, op. cit.*, Vol. XIII, p. 30.

35 Gerard, *op. cit.*, p. 68.
36 See Johnson's *Dictionary*, where he quotes Watts as the source for this definition of inspiration.
37 See his *Imagination as A Means of Grace* (1960).
38 *The Poetical Works of Beattie, Blair and Falconer*, ed. Gilfillan (1854).
39 *The Anatomy of Melancholy* (1849 edn), p. 198.
40 I use the edition of 1808. See Vol. II, Ch. IV, especially pp. 150-72.
41 *Ibid.*, Vol. II, p. 152.
42 *Ibid.*, p. 153. cf. Dr Cotton, who attended Cowper during his first period of insanity, noting signs of hypermania, and becoming fearful 'lest the sudden transition from despair to joy should terminate in a fatal frenzy'. Quinlan, *Life of Cowper (1953) p. 78.*
43 See Chapters IV and V.
44 *Wesley's Journals*, 8 vols., 1909-16. It is worth noting that Mill Flanders remarks that her husband, when she finally makes good, thanks God 'with an ecstasy of joy'. There is a very funny, obscene incident in Anstey's *New Bath Guide* in which a young lady is filled with joy — by Roger.
45 Johnson's *Dictionary, op. cit.*
46 *The Prelude, op. cit.,* 11. 420-30.
47 *Coleridge's Poems, op. cit.*, Vol. 1, p. 365.
48 I use F. T. Prince's edition (1957) p. 45. The speech is at 11. 590-8.
49 *Observations on Man* (1749) Vol. 1, p. 431.
50 *Letters of Thomas Gray* (1951) p. 250.
51 I think here not only of 'Resolution and Independence' but of the extraordinary myth-making that goes on in Coleridge's 'Monody on the Death of Chatterton', *Coleridge's Poems, op. cit.*, Vol. 1, pp. 13-16. And also of Wordsworth's two poems to Burns, part of the *Memorials of a Tour of Scotland.*
52 The next stage would be to show various of the ways in which 'joy' made it possible for non-'school' poets to claim a right to attention. 'Joy' democratises the poet, and takes inspiration out of the control of a cultural/class minority. This period sees the rise of the 'natural' poet, and his rise is connected with 'joy' and 'inspiration'.

Chapter 4

Wordsworth and the Anti-Picturesque

BOOK XI of *The Prelude* — I speak of the 1805-6 version — is called 'Imagination, how Impaired and Restored'. In it, Wordsworth looks back to moments of his early manhood when his 'growing mind' had been most pleased by 'Reason, not the grand / And simple Reason, but that humbler power / Which carries on its no inglorious work / By logic and minute analysis . . . ' (11. 123-6). Such power has obvious benefits, the poet claims, but it carries with it great dangers:

> to speak
> Of all the narrow estimates of things
> Which hence originate were a worthy theme
> For philosophic Verse; suffice it here
> to hint that danger cannot but attend
> Upon a Function rather proud to be
> The enemy of falsehood, than the friend
> Of truth, to sit in judgement than to feel. (11. 130-7)

And that appears to be that. It isn't, however. For in spite of the apparent finality of those lines, Wordsworth has more to say. What comes next is an attack on the tyranny of the eye. 'The most despotic of our senses', he calls it, and he emphasises the fact that sight conditions the perceiver to accept or reject what is seen according to 'rules of mimic art transferr'd / To things above all art'.

Why should Wordsworth be so severe on this point? To answer the question, we have to look at the lines immediately following, where the poet claims that

> this,
> Although a strong infection of the age,
> Was never much my habit, giving way
> To a comparison of scene with scene,

Bent overmuch on superficial things,
Pampering myself with meagre novelties
Of colour and proportion, to the moods
Of time and season, to the moral power
The affections, and the spirit of the place,
Less sensible. (11. 155-64)

What we have here, of course, is an attack on the picturesque, that 'strong infection of the age'. The age in question is
the late 1780s and early 1790s, which was the time of Wordsworth's late adolescence and early manhood, of his Cambridge
years, and of his earliest attempts to write poetry. As he
admits, he had for a while himself caught the general infection;
the virus of 'humbler' reason had worked in him temporarily
to deaden his sensibility to the *living* qualities of place. (Indeed,
Wordsworth had originally written that the infection had
made him 'insensible', which word he softened to the 'less
sensible' of the 1805-6 text, although he later reinstated it, and
'insensible' is in the 1850 text of the *Prelude.*)

The syntax of the lines quoted above seems to me evasive. It
isn't easy to tell whether Wordsworth is saying that he did or
didn't share the strong infection of the age: was it the age or
himself who gave way to 'a comparison of scene with scene'
and so on? The answer of course is: both. But the leap from
'never much my habit' (itself an evasive phrase, does he mean
not long indulged or never completely given into, or are we
to understand that he only pretended to the habit?) — that leap
to 'giving way', without the intervention of a pronoun, suggests a kind of covering up, the reason for which becomes
clearer once we take note of the fact that as a young man
Wordsworth had written some decidedly picturesque poems,
and was to return to the picturesque mode in his *Guide to the
Lakes*. In other words, the picturesque was an infection which
Wordsworth never entirely shook off, even though he
recognised that it *was* an infection, and had indeed shown it to
be so in some of his greatest poetry. The syntax of the passage I
have been considering is evasive, I think, because Wordsworth
himself is in some difficulties at this point. On the one hand, he
presents himself as the radical critic of the deadening aesthetic
/social concept that is embodied in the picturesque; on the
other, he has against him the awkward evidence of his own past

poetry, which is manifestly poetry of the picturesque, and which he doesn't want to disown.

Still, I don't want to make too much of this. It is enough for my present purpose to note that Wordsworth was in a very good position to recognise the signs and consequences of the infection because he himself had been infected; and that this gives an especial authority to his anti-picturesque poetry. But I will start with those 'meagre novelties' with which he admits to have pampered himself at some time in the past. He must surely be referring here to his Cambridge period, for it was then that he began seriously to write poetry, and three long poems which belong to those years, 'The Vale of Esthwaite', 'An Evening Walk', and 'Descriptive Sketches', are all very obviously picturesque, in inspiration and expression.

I am not going to offer detailed accounts of the poems, but it is important to make a few points about them. And first, it is worth remarking that 'The Vale of Esthwaite', some of whose matter was to be incorporated into 'An Evening Walk', is the kind of prentice work which tries out all sorts of poses, and includes varieties of fashionable material, from druids, lonely castles, ghosts and dungeons — all very Gothicky, of course — through to romantic chasms and moonlit landscapes. 'An Evening Walk' is also prentice work, but of a rather more substantial nature. It was written during one of Wordsworth's vacations from Cambridge, and Mary Moorman tells us that an anonymous reviewer speaks of 'having used Wordsworth's poem as a companion during a tour of the lakes'. Which is apt, since as she later points out, 'An Evening Walk' is not only 'almost an anthology of borrowing and adaptations from the landscape poets, from Milton to Beattie'; it is also a poem that fittingly belongs to the century 'in which guide-books began to be written for the service of tourists, with a marked emphasis on the "picturesque". The point is that Wordsworth was familiar with many of those Guides, and when he wrote *An Evening Walk* he placed himself deliberately among the writers of the "landscape" school.'[1]

As for 'Descriptive Sketches', I think it enough to quote Moorman's remark that 'it affects to represent [Wordsworth] in a melancholy frame of mind'; and that it contains 'even more literary borrowings and fewer patches of intimate observation and truth of detail than *An Evening Walk*'.[2] Moorman's implied judgement on 'An Evening Walk' is too severe. It is in its derivative way a perfectly well-written poem, packed with truth to detail. But I am content to take that for granted. What concerns me are the kinds of truth that the details record; and they concern me because they obviously concerned Wordsworth when he came to write Book XI of the *Prelude*.

In his invaluable essay on 'The Picturesque Moment', Martin Price points out that a crucial element of picturesque theory was its 'dissociation of visual, pictorial, or generally aesthetic elements from other values in contemplating a scene'.[3] In other words, the picturesque does not concern itself with moral, metaphysical, social or political matters, a point which Ruskin seized on when he argued that even in so apparently 'neutral' a matter as presentation of landscape, aesthetic and moral may well conflict. Pathos, however, is allowable. The picturesque, Price remarks, 'turns to the sketch, which precedes formal perfection, and the ruin, which succeeds it. Where it concentrates upon a particular object, the aesthetic interest lies in the emergence of formal interest from an unlikely source (the hovel, the gypsy, the ass), or in the internal conflict between the centrifugal forces of dissolution and the centripetal pull of form (ruined temples, aged men).'[4]

It is well said, but it leaves out a matter of great importance. For one of the presiding moods of the picturesque is genteel melancholia: one is brought face to face with natural forces which emphasise or at least imply man's helplessness before fate, his inevitable transience, decay and downfall. At least, that is the intention. Yet a question must surely be asked about such an intention. Is a hovel quite the same as a ruined temple? For after all, the ruins made by time are not the same as the ruins made by man, and to pretend that they are is to mystify. In his sometimes-picturesque poem, 'The Task', Cowper wrote with melancholic resignation that 'All has its date below: the fatal hour / Was register'd in Heaven ere Time began'. Such a view of history rules out any intervention by man. Simply, this is how things have to be. Hovels, gypsies, ruined temples, aged men: they are all brought together in a seamless fabric which denies the possibility of the social process as in any sense determined by men. Price seems to accept this. He remarks that

The typical picturesque object or scene — the aged man, the old house, the road with cart-wheel tracks, the irregular village — carries within it the principle of change. All of them imply the passage of time and the slow working of its change upon them.[5]

But can one really call this the principle of change? I would have thought that the point about scenes such as those Price describes is that in registering them one shouldn't be able to, or be asked to, or be expected to, account for anything so grand as 'the principle of change'. Rather, one is meant to accept change as an undeniable and unremarkable fact. If that amounts to a principle it does so only at the level of unexamined tautology: change is change, 'and there's an end on't.' The picturesque aims not at tragedy, but at pathos, and the pathetic is inseparable from a certain complacency precisely because it invites you to consider that nothing can be, other than what is. Acceptance, not enquiry, is of the essence of the picturesque.

Yet consider that 'slow working' of the passage of time that we are to read into irregular villages, and so on. For those who were experiencing the effects of enclosure during the eighteenth century time didn't so much move slowly as with catastrophic suddenness. To imply that there is a *principle* of change behind all that was happening in the century is therefore to mystify, to pretend that there aren't very different practices of change. And of course you are bound to realise that mystification is necessary as soon as you consider that the audience for the picturesque was likely to be largely composed of those who enforced changes of the kind that enclosure brought about, or who profited by it in a manner that might well seem to be the opposite of principled. And you also realise that a consequence of the implicit collusion between artist and audience in this world of the picturesque is that both accept that it shall typically be drained of human activity. As Christopher Salveson has pointed out, 'the most noticeable quality of Gilpin's little scenes is their emptiness'. True, Salveson is specifically concerned with the formlessness of Gilpin's work, but it is proper to remark that in Gilpin's many sketches not only is there 'no sense of control', as Salveson rightly indicates

('What is left is vague emotion, expressed in shadowy mass and luminous haze'), but there is no sense of the human, either.[6]

The point needs to be stressed, because it explains something about Gilpin to which Price draws attention but which he doesn't account for.

> Gilpin is not much interested in the treatment of commonplace humans. His wild landscapes require banditti; neither people of elegance nor 'peasants *engaged in their several professions.*' ... more than this, however, Gilpin dislikes 'all *vulgarity* of form — modern dresses — modern utensils — anything, that occurs commonly to the eye. I consider painting as a kind of poetry, which excludes all vulgarisms'.[7]

Vulgarity ... vulgarisms. They are betraying words. Early in the eighteenth century 'vulgarity' meant simply 'being usual, ordinary, or commonplace'. But by 1774 the word more typically became identified with 'unrefined, or coarse'. 'Refined' has its own very interesting history,[8] but without going into it here we may note that during the eighteenth century 'vulgarity' moves from being a word that one wouldn't mind having applied to oneself to being a word reserved for others, who are considered to be social inferiors. (And of course the quickening sense of class-consciousness inevitably goes hand in hand with the shifting meanings of the word.)

The history of 'vulgarism' is also instructive. At the beginning of the eighteenth century it means 'a common or ordinary expression'; but by the second half of the century it has come to stand for 'a colloquialism of a low or unrefined character'. I draw attention to this because we need to realise that when Gilpin speaks of excluding 'vulgarity of form' and 'vulgarisms' from the picturesque, what he is really doing is to set up an aesthetic which can be insulated from pressures that threaten to blow apart the notion of 'the principle of change'. The picturesque is a debilitating aesthetic, not only because of its characteristic concern with the pathetic (to register a sense of pathos marks you out as a person of feeling, and is meant to endorse a comforting notion of your humanness and humaneness), but also because it is so sterile in its self-reflectiveness. That is to say it nurtures, feeds and protects an attitude to history and to change that circles round from observer/contemplator of object to object itself and back again. Nothing is allowed to upset this closed circuit, which is set up by the discoverer of apparently fortuitous but in fact carefully calculated landscape 'compositions', de-humanised and thus de-humanising. And indeed how could it be otherwise? For all vulgarities have been excluded.

There is an instructive episode in the history of the picturesque which deserves to be better known than it is, because it is such a perfect give-away. Tours of England in search of the picturesque had, of course, become a commonplace by the 1780s, when a certain Mr Byng set out on his tour, which he decided to record for posterity. He also decided to take himself into Derbyshire, being reasonably certain that he would find there any number of picturesque landscapes, and very little human activity. Indeed, he looked for no more than some simple peasants 'sequestered' in the vales. (That is, not being peasants at all.) But to his vast dismay he discovered that instead of peasants in the vales there were the new cotton mills, built by Arkwright and others, and that potentially picturesque scenes were entirely spoiled, rendered totally unpicturesque, by the presence of what he calls 'impudent mechanics'.[9]

This brings us back to Wordsworth. 'The Evening Walk' is, I have said, a picturesque poem, and indeed the title itself hints at the fact; for it is not being over-ingenious to suggest that evening signifies the ruin of the day, and inspires a pleasing-pathetic melancholia; it calls up thoughts of the fading of light and of the coming darkness. The world of 'An Evening Walk' is a sticky-sweet world of 'Sweet rills', 'sweetly ferocious' cockerels, 'sweet sounds', 'sweet...streamlet murmurs', and so on, and on. But there are, or may seem to be, discordant notes. One such note is struck by the description of quarry men at work, another of a beggar woman and her two starving children. Beggars, of course, *can* belong in the picturesque, (though they are preferable when disguised as gypsies — more like banditti, that is, and less resonant of social/political concerns). But what of workers? Surely they can have no place in a picturesque landscape? To include them goes clean counter to all that Gilpin had insisted on. Well, here is Wordsworth's description.

> I love to mark the quarry's moving trains,
> Dwarf pannier'd steeds, and men, and numerous wains:

How busy the enormous hive within,
While Echo dallies with the various din!
Some, hardly heard their chisel's clinking sound,
Toil, small as pigmies, in the gulph profound;
Some, dim between th' aerial cliffs descry'd,
O'er walk the viewless plank from side to side;
These by the pale-blue rocks that ceaseless ring
Glad from their airy baskets hang and sing. (11.141-50, 1793 text)

It's all right, you see, they aren't really working at all. The men
are viewed from so far off that their labour can only be guessed
at, and anyway what matters is the fact that they can easily be
absorbed into the picturesque landscape, made objects of
purely aesthetic contemplation. ('I love to mark'.) They blend
into the aerial cliffs, gulph profound and pale-blue rocks, and
their toil is made as unreal as possible. Even their 'various din'
wittily reduces them to the picturesque, since the orderly
variety of a scene is an essential requirement of the picturesque.
('Various' is one of its key words.) Moreover, the scene is
carefully 'composed'; the observer's vantage-point is deliberately chosen in order to make the quarry's moving trains
most aesthetically effective — effective according to the dic-
tates of the picturesque, that is.

The case of the beggar woman is, however, rather different.
Her story occupies some sixty lines of the 1793 text, and these
were cut to fewer than thirty in the later version of the poem,
published in 1820. Mary Moorman comments:

Into the peaceful landscape of *An Evening Walk* Wordsworth introduced one
significant human group — a Beggar-woman and her two children, who after
suffering privations of heat and cold are overtaken by a storm in which the
two children perish. In 1794, when he was revising *An Evening Walk* at
Keswick, he turned this passage into a description of an actual tragedy which
had occurred two years previously on Stainmore... when 'a poor woman
was found dead with two children whom she had in vain attempted to protect
from the storm in the manner described.'[10]

These last words come from Wordsworth's own note to the
revised passage which, however, 'he did not make use of when
he republished *An Evening Walk* in 1820'. And Moorman adds
that 'The introduction of the Beggar-woman was bad for the
poem from a critical point of view, for the sixty lines he gives to
her are the weakest in it....'[11] It seems fairly clear that

Moorman says this by way of offering an explanation for Wordsworth's decision to cut the passage by over a half in 1820. It doesn't, however, explain why he decided not to publish his note, which would be perfectly relevant to the passage as that eventually saw the light of day. What will explain the omission, and the cutting, is the fact that the 1820 version of 'An Evening Walk' is a very picturesque performance, and that 'an actual tragedy' can have no place in such a poem. Wordsworth, that is, has once more gone down with 'the strong infection of the age', but he possesses sufficient literary skill to know that he can't mix modes and expect to produce a poem acceptable to an audience which by the second decade of the nineteenth century he had begun to pander to, even though in the great Preface to the *Lyrical Ballads* he had spoken of it with a proper scorn, refusing to 'furnish food for fickle tastes and fickle appetites', and condemning those 'who talk of Poetry as a matter of amusement and idle pleasure; who will converse with us as gravely about a *taste* for Poetry, as they express it, as if it were a thing as indifferent as a taste for Rope-dancing, or Frontiniac, or Sherry'.[12] Or the picturesque?

The picturesque, let us remind ourselves, prefers pathos to tragedy, and certainly Wordsworth's revisions to 'An Evening Walk' — ones clearly made later than 1794 — are intended to turn the beggar woman and her children into objects of pathos. This is how the episode ends in the 1820 version:

> Press the sad kiss, fond mother! vainly fears
> Thy flooded cheek to wet them with its tears;
> No tears can wet them, and no bosom warms,
> Thy breast their death-bed, coffined in thine arms!
>
> Sweet are the sounds that mingle from afar,
> Heard by calm lakes, as peeps the folding star....

As the transition from one verse to another reveals, the mother and her dead children are 'tastefully' contained by the picturesque conventions which the poem manipulates. And the pathos is pointed up by the exclamation mark after 'coffined in thine arms', a trick which Wordsworth hadn't thought of in 1793, but which increases the pathos of the episode. Indeed, the 1793 version is far less 'tasteful' than that of 1820, a fact which seems to me altogether to Wordsworth's credit, but which no doubt explains why he decided to cut the episode so drastically. In the first version it is so nakedly *tasteless*, by which I mean that the actuality of the episode quite wrecks the picturesqueness of what comes after. Moorman is quite wrong to say that lines in the 1793 version are poetically weak. And anyway, it's precisely the strongest lines which Wordsworth cut out:

> —no more her breath can thaw their fingers cold,
> Their frozen arms her neck no more can fold;
> Scarce heard, their chattering lips her shoulders chill,
> And her cold back their colder bosoms thrill....

Even allowing for the weak syntax of the second line, the over-all effect is surely to haul us out of the tastefully composed world of the picturesque into one of real, appalling suffering. The lines provide for a radical de-mystifying of beggardom. Moorman remarks that Wordsworth's 'natural attraction to the ragged vagrant world no doubt moved him to describe her, and his admiration for Crabbe's *Village* and Langhorne's *Country Justice* encouraged him to introduce a figure of forlorn destitution into his poem'.[13] But that is a hopelessly muddled sentence. Natural attraction to the ragged vagrant world — a very obvious requirement of the picturesque — can hardly explain the decidedly un-picturesque beggar woman of 'An Evening Walk'. And the appeal to Crabbe and Langhorne, as though the beggar woman can somehow be thought of as belonging merely to a literary tradition with which those two poets equally identify, makes no sense once we remember that the *Village* is a caustic attack on the sentimentalities of that pastoral convention into which Langhorne's poem neatly slots. 'I paint the cot / As truth will paint it, and as bards will not', Crabbe wrote in the *Village*. This is not to deny that much eighteenth-century poetry of a kind which the *Village* comes out of, at an odd angle, made use of aged solitary women as parts of the landscape; there are, for example, the cress-gatherer of Goldsmith's *Deserted Village*, that 'sad historian of the pensive plain', and Crazy Kate of Cowper's *Task*. And to be fair I think that in both these cases we have to recognise a need on the part of the poets to acknowledge and try to register the horror of dispossession and enforced deprivation, imaged in terms of loneliness, of an individual who has been denied community. But equally one has to say that both Goldsmith and Cowper control the presentation of their aged solitaries in such a way that we don't feel shocked by their appearance. (The words 'sad' and 'pensive', for example, establish a tone of melancholy resignation that comes to more or less the same thing as accepting 'the principle of change'.) Whereas we do feel shocked by the beggar woman of 'An Evening Walk'. For there is no way in which her 'actual tragedy' can be accommodated to a world of sweetness; and so the episode has to be cut.

At which point I think it worth drawing an analogy between 'An Evening Walk' and the early work of another great, revolutionary writer. The presiding tone of *The Pickwick Papers* is one of genial comedy. Though there are numerous incidents and people who threaten to dull the comic glow, they are always subdued to it — largely through the unruffled suavity of Sam Weller. But there is at least one occasion on which the tone itself is subdued, and is indeed temporarily lost to the novel. When Mr Pickwick is put into the Fleet he, and we, become aware of individuals who are well beyond the saving grace of Sam's comic spirit, so much so that to try to apply the spirit to them would be shocking. As a result, the chapters which deal with Pickwick in prison seriously threaten the tone of *The Pickwick Papers* and Dickens, no doubt recognising the fact, hurriedly organises Pickwick's release. It is his forced solution to a problem which, in an admittedly lesser way, Wordsworth had to face in 'An Evening Walk'. For what do you do when you discover that a fictional world your art is intending to celebrate and recommend as some sort of ideal (and the world of Dingley Dell is as carefully 'composed' as any picturesque landscape) is willy-nilly invaded by matter that destroys the compositional 'effect', the tone, the wished-for unity of appearance? In the cases of Dickens and Wordsworth the answer is more or less the same. Both great men recognise that they 'cannot live in art'.[14] Dickens writes *Oliver Twist*, Wordsworth the *Lyrical Ballads*.

To put it that way is, of course, drastically to foreshorten a complicated sequence of events. But this much at least is true, that many of Wordsworth's poems in the *Lyrical Ballads* use

picturesque material, indeed entice the reader in search of the
picturesque into their world, only for that reader to discover
painful actualities that insult his expectations. And in this
sense the ballads are profoundly revolutionary poems. Octavio
Paz has argued that 'poetry is a food which the bourgeoisie —
as a class — has proved incapable of digesting'. For poetry
tries to abolish the distance between the word and the thing,
both by dissolving the self-consciousness that separates us
from nature, and by offering 'a conquest of the historical world
and of nature'. Both are ways of bridging the gap and reconcil-
ing alienated consciousness to the world outside. The picturesque is art for the bourgeoisie precisely because it accepts an
alienated consciousness — the observer/contemplator is not
implicated in the scene he views from a chosen vantage point,
which emphasises distance; and because it de-historicises
actuality, gestures towards 'the principle of change'.[15] Wordsworth's lyrical ballads are typically anti-picturesque, and in
Octavio Paz's sense they are therefore anti-bourgeois.

To take an example: 'Simon Lee, the Old Huntsman, with
an incident in which he was concerned'. The title suggests that
we are in for a narrative poem, of the kind to which readers at
the end of the eighteenth century were fairly used. And the
poem opens in a way that would hardly be likely to disturb.

> In the sweet shire of Cardigan,
> Not far from pleasant Ivor-Hall,
> An old man dwells, a little man,
> I've heard he once was tall.
> Of years he has upon his back,
> No doubt, a burthen weighty;
> He says he is three score and ten,
> But others say he's eighty.[16]

The first half of the stanza introduces us to a world which we
are surely made to feel is a remote one. We are off on a guided
tour of a picturesque spot, the 'sweet shire of Cardigan', and of
a picturesque 'little man'. Except that the whole feeling of the
opening lines, and it's one sustained throughout the stanza, is
of a scarcely-suppressed chortle: the little man is the kind of
'character' whom we, the polite audience, will spot as someone
very like John Gilpin. And granted the poem's full title, we
expect a diverting history, something to laugh over. (The

laughter is already there, of course, in the feminine rhymes, 'weighty', and 'eighty', and in the slightly antiquated 'burthen'.) But what follows, although it offers itself as a kind of narrative, utterly upsets our expectations. And here it is worth making the obvious but important point that when it comes to upsetting audience expectations a poem enjoys one clear-cut advantage over a painting. For a poem exists in time, whereas a painting exists in space. A painting's incongruities can therefore be taken in at a glance, but a poem's can be held back and only gradually discovered and registered. In short, an anti-picturesque painting cannot use the delayed shock tactics of the anti-picturesque poem, simply because it cannot employ a narrative method. 'Simon Lee', as I have said, is something of a narrative; but as we read forward we are shaken out of our complacent, condescending view of the old man and are brought to recognise him as uncomfortably, because irreducibly, human. Our 'old huntsman' escapes from type into individuality. The incident in which he is involved turns out to be of significance, but not because it is blessedly comic, even though it looks as if it will turn out to be just that. ('The mattock totter'd in his mind' — how avoid the comedy of 'totter'd'?) No, the point is rather that we are set up for a comic denouement of a trivial tale only to discover that we have to choke back our guffaws, and accept, chilled and chastened, the uncompromisingly human, plain and awkwardly truthful lines with which the poem ends:

> — I've heard of hearts unkind, kind deeds
> With coldness still returning.
> Alas! the gratitude of men
> Has oftener left me mourning.

Those lines are a straightforward rebuke to the picturesque.

Or consider 'Old Man Travelling; Animal Tranquility and Decay, A Sketch'. The title is fully within the picturesque tradition. The picture-poem is offered as that quintessential picturesque type, 'the sketch'; and we are to contemplate the typical picturesque object, an old man, with all those implications of 'the passage of time and the slow working of its change' upon him. There is also a hint that this old man is a 'genteel' beggar: after all, he is 'travelling', and he is part of the natural order of things. 'Animal tranquility and decay' is not a phrase calculated to disturb any sensibility attuned to the picturesque. On the contrary, it is accommodatingly pathetic, hinting at 'the principle of change'.

The poem itself opens in deliberate sketch-like manner, with a mere half-line. We recall Price's remark that the picturesque favoured the sketch, 'which precedes formal perfection'. It is as though the subject can be 'delicately', aesthetically handled by avoidance of a fully-committed formal concern. (As who should say, 'We are persons of taste, and we agree, don't we, that it would be wrong to make too much of this?') 'The little hedge-row birds, / That peck along the road, regard him not.' I don't deny that the rapt, grave tone of the poem goes beyond anything that would be recognisably appropriate for the picturesque, but it is nevertheless a fact that the poet appears as an observer/contemplator of a scene whose compositional unity of tone is broken only when the old man begins to speak, and thus disturbs the point of view which, no matter how sympathetic to him, is finally a kind of aesthetic tyranny over the actual.

> —I asked him whither he was bound, and what
> The object of his journey; he replied
> 'Sir! I am going many miles to take
> A last leave of my son, a mariner,
> Who from a sea-fight has been brought to Falmouth,
> And there is dying in an hospital.'

End of poem. In the *Lyrical Ballads* version, at least. But of course in later life, when the strong infection of the age was once more doing its deadly work, Wordsworth cut the old man's words, just as he tidied up the sea captain's words in 'The Thorn', and no doubt for the same reason: that he wanted his poems to become exercises in the picturesque. For 'The Thorn' is a much safer, more pathetic poem, once we cease to wonder about the nature of the garrulous old bore who tells the tale. The great Wordsworth, however, is not the conformist who bowed down to models of correct taste, but the poet who challenged such models, seeing in them mere evasions of that necessary confrontation with the irreducible fact of the human to which all true poetry must address itself. And we may note that in this context his true successor is William Carlos

Williams, at least where Williams willingly allows for the intrusion of reality into the otherwise self-enclosed 'beautiful' work of art. As here in Book One of *Paterson*.

> Two half-grown girls hailing hallowed Easter,
> (an inversion of all out-of-doors) weaving
> about themselves, from under
> the heavy air, whorls of thick translucencies
> poured down, cleaving them away,
> shut from the light: bare-
> headed, their clear hair dangling —
> Two —
>   disparate among the pouring
> waters of their hair in which nothing is
> molten —
> two, bound by an instinct to be the same:
> ribbons, cut from a piece,
> cerise pink, binding their hair: one —
> a willow twig pulled from a low
> leafless bush in full bud in her hand,
> (or eels or a moon!)
> holds it, the gathered spray,
> upright in the air, the pouring air,
> strokes the soft fur —
>   Ain't they beautiful   (Book One, Section II)

But by far the most important of all Wordsworth's assaults on the picturesque is 'Michael'. To put it that way is, I suppose, unfair. After all, the poem is one of the very greatest in our language, and in no sense is it to be accounted for simply in terms of the anti-picturesque. Yet it does, deliberately, assault the picturesque sensibility, and is among many other things a radical critique of that sensibility's incuriosity (for all its gawping habit), and de-humanised, emotional sterility (for all its concern with the pathetic). 'Michael' begins with some lines that seem to offer themselves as an obvious kind of 'Guide'.

> If from the public way you turn your steps
> Up the tumultuous brook of Green-head Gill,
> You will suppose that with an upright path
> Your feet must struggle; in such bold ascent
> The pastoral Mountains front you, face to face.
> But, courage! for beside that boisterous Brook
> The mountains have all open'd out themselves,
> And made a hidden valley of their own.

The tone is not one that mocks an interest in the picturesque; on the contrary, it is deeply considerate of 'you', where 'you' may be presumed to stand for the genteel reader. Yet the considerateness in no way rules out the fact that 'you' will understand precious little of what is truly significant about this picturesque spot. It isn't, in short, to be prized in accordance with its scenic value but because there is: 'one object which you might pass by, / Might see and notice not. Beside the brook / There is a straggling heap of unhewn stones!' What matters about these stones is that they have led the poet to think 'On man; the heart of man and human life'. There is no room now for reflections in accordance with the picturesque. What we have here is something altogether more important, or so Wordsworth insists. And so: 'I will relate the same / For the delight of a few natural hearts, / And with yet fonder feeling, for the sake / Of youthful Poets, who among these Hills / Shall be my second self when I am gone.'

The point to make about this odd, and apparently directionless introduction to the poem, is that Wordsworth is plainly concerned with the landscape which he describes because it has a specific human significance, one that we discover is inseparable from work. For Michael is known through his work, as is his wife. However, we do not need to trace that through the poem. It is enough that we should recognise the ways in which 'Michael' is, among so much else, a rebuke to the picturesque idea that somehow landscape is knowable and lovable through and because of 'scenic' values. On the contrary, what makes this landscape cherishable is its connection with human endeavour: Michael and his wife are not merely 'as a proverb in the vale / For endless industry'. They are also important because they mark the landscape with human aspiration, love, concern for perpetuity. Of course the marks can be erased, of course the concern is frail; but that does not alter the fact that it is of real significance, nor does it hide the passion, the human worthwhileness of what Michael and his wife attempt. Even more important, for Wordsworth at least, is the fact that what they stand for is destroyed, not by some abstract 'principle of change', but by a registered actuality; the fact and consequence of Michael's becoming a bondsman, the vulnerability of his property (in given circumstances); and the tragedy that springs from the severance of relationship between land and labour. For it is such a severance which is wished on Michael, and his relationship with the land which is shown most grievously to be affected.

Once we put it that way we can see why Wordsworth should spend so much time emphasising Michael's relationship with his land, and why this relationship should be seen in terms of 'honourable gain'. For Michael in himself represents a moment of the relationship; of the small, independent farmer with his 'chosen' tract of land, the possession and loss of which define the outer and inner bounds of human possibilities for him.

> these fields, these hills
> Which were his living Being, even more
> Than his own Blood — what could they less? had laid
> Strong hold on his affections, were to him
> A pleasurable feeling of blind love,
> The pleasure which there is in life itself.

In his great *Preface* Wordsworth proclaimed that

in spite of difference of soil and climate, of language and manners, of laws and customs, in spite of things silently gone out of mind and things violently destroyed, the Poet binds together by passion and knowledge the vast empire of human society, as it is spread over the whole earth, and over all time.

'Michael' is undoubtedly a poem which embodies that proclamation, and in doing so it offers a definitive rebuke to the picturesque moment.

Notes

1 Mary Moorman, *Wordsworth: Early Years* (1968) pp. 115-16. Among the guide books which Wordsworth himself possessed, Moorman notes that 'Gilpin's *Observations* appeared in 1786 and was among Wordsworth's valued possessions. West's *Guide* came out in 1778 and James Clarke's Survey in 1787. Wordsworth must have studied this very soon after publication, for lines 175-190 of *An Evening Walk* (1793) are taken straight from it with a footnote of acknowledgement.'

2 Moorman, *ibid.*, p. 129.

3 Martin Price, 'The Picturesque Moment', in *From Sensibility to Romanticism*, ed. Hilles and Bloom (1965) pp. 260-4.

4 *Ibid.*, p. 277.

5 *Ibid.*, p. 285.

6 Christopher Salveson, *The Landscape of Memory* (1965) p.66.
7 Price, *op. cit.*, p.281.
8 I have tried to follow something of the word's history in my essay on 'Mrs Gaskell and Brotherhood', in *Tradition and Tolerance in Nineteenth Century Fiction* (1966).
9 See Benedict Nicolson, *Joseph Wright of Derby* (1968) p.167.
10 Moorman, *op. cit.*, pp.117-18.
11 *Ibid.*, p.118.
12 *Wordsworth and Coleridge: Lyrical Ballads*, ed. Brett and Jones (1963) pp.240 and 251.
13 Moorman, *op. cit.*, p.118.
14 'Cannot live in art'. The remark was made to Tennyson by his friend, Trench.
15 See Michael Hamburger, *The Truth of Poetry*, Harmondsworth (1972) p.44.
16 All the quotations of lyrical ballads are taken from the edition of Brett and Jones, *op. cit.*

Chapter 5

Dickens and America

'NOW to astonish you', Dickens wrote to his friend and biographer, John Forster, on 19 September 1841. 'After balancing, considering, and weighing the matter in every point of view, I HAVE MADE UP MY MIND (WITH GOD'S LEAVE) TO GO TO AMERICA — AND TO START AS SOON AFTER CHRISTMAS AS IT WILL BE SAFE TO GO.' Some three-and-a-half months later, on Tuesday, 4 January 1842, Dickens sailed out of Liverpool on the Cunard Steamer, *Britannia*, accompanied by his wife although not by the children he had at one time hoped to take with him. The voyage turned out to be a terrifying ordeal. In mid-Atlantic the ship was hit by gales of such violence that most of the lifeboats were smashed, the planking of the paddle-boxes was torn away, and the smoke-stack had to be secured with chains and ropes to prevent its being blown over and setting fire to the ship. But on Saturday, 22 January, the *Britannia* entered Boston harbour, and Dickens's tour of America had begun.

He was by no means the first English writer to undertake such a tour. Ten years previously Frances Trollope had published *Domestic Manners of the Americans*, the fruits of a lengthy visit to the United States, and her book has been accurately described as 'an acid portrait of the vulgarity and crudity of young America at a moment when the national pride of the United States was especially tender.'[1] The pride had shown itself in bitter protests that followed the book's publication in America.

Dickens had no intention of following Frances Trollope's example. When he had proposed to his publishers, Chapman and Hall, a project that was to grow into *Master Humphrey's Clock*, he had told them, 'I should be ready to contract to go at any specified time ... either to Ireland or to America, and to write from thence a series of papers descriptive of the places

68

and people I see, introducing local tales, traditions and legends, something after the plan of Washington Irving's *Alhambra*.'[2] *The Alhambra*, which was published in 1832, is a kind of sketch-book derived from Irving's stay of several months, in 1829, in the Alhambra, at Granada, a fortress-palace of the Moorish Kings. Dickens knew and liked the work, just as he knew and liked the author. He was in friendly, regular correspondence with Irving, and had been much moved by the American writer's praise of *The Old Curiosity Shop*.[3] It is unlikely that in planning his tour he had any thoughts of writing harshly about Irving's homeland.

Indeed, it is virtually certain he would have known Irving's essay, 'English Writers on America', which appeared in *The Sketch Book* (1820), and in that case he would have noted Irving's feeling of deep regret for

the literary animosity daily growing up between England and America ... English travellers are the best and worst in the world. Where no motives of pride or interest intervene, none can equal them for profound and philosophical views of society, or faithful and graphical descriptions of external objects; but when either the interest or reputation of their own country comes in collision with that of another, they go to the opposite extreme, and forget their usual probity and candour, in the indulgence of splenetic remark, and illiberal spirit of ridicule.

Those words might be applied to *Domestic Manners of the Americans*, but Dickens would not want them to become applicable to his projected sketch-book. Irving adds that another problem is that America seems to attract the worst travellers from England: 'the broken-down tradesman, the scheming adventurer, the wandering mechanic, the Manchester and Birmingham agent'. It isn't perhaps surprising, he reflects, that such men are incapable of understanding 'a country in a singular state of moral and physical development; a country in which one of the greatest political experiments in the history of the world is now performing; and which presents the most profound and momentous studies to the statesman and philosopher'. On the other hand,

Possessing ... as England does, the fountainhead whence the literature of the language flows, how completely is it in her power, and how truly is it her duty, to make it the medium of amiable and magnanimous feeling—a stream where the two nations might meet together, and drink in peace and kindness.[4]

The significance of those words would hardly be lost on Dickens. 'The medium of amiable and magnanimous feeling': why, it might almost be Boz's epitaph!

And there is a further reason why Dickens would not want to be classed with Irving's worst travellers. 'A country in which one of the greatest political experiments in the world is now performing.' Awkwardly put, but the meaning is clear enough, and certain to gain the novelist's approval. for Dickens had come to his enormous fame not simply as a novelist of comedy and pathos, of 'amiable and magnanimous feeling', but as a radical, the scourge of bumbledom, officialdom, and 'all the rest of it with blast of trumpet'. Forster reports that in August 1841, Dickens wrote him a letter in the course of which he remarked, 'By Jove, how radical I am getting! I wax stronger and stronger in the true principles every day.' And Forster adds that, 'He would at times even talk, in moments of sudden indignation at the political outlook, of carrying off himself and his household goods, like Coriolanus, to a world elsewhere.'[5] I do not deny that there is sometimes an element of play-acting in all this, yet we have to remember that when the Houses of Parliament burnt down in 1833, Dickens was among the cheering onlookers; and his ballad, 'The Fine Old English Gentleman, New Version, to be said or sung at all conservative dinners', has the note of genuine radical feeling about it — a feeling which surges through *Oliver Twist, Nicholas Nickleby, The Old Curiosity Shop* and *Barnaby Rudge.*

> The good old laws were garnished well with gibbets,
>   whips, and chains,
> With fine old English penalties, and fine old English
>   pains,
> With rebel heads, and seas of blood once hot in
>   rebel veins;
> For all these things were requisite to guard the
>   rich old gains
>   Of the fine old English Tory times;
>   Soon may they come again![6]

Moreover, Dickens was bound to have been well aware of the fact that the great English Romantic poets had seen America as a promised land, a country to which the future belonged, a utopia of the (projected) Pantisocracy, where, as Coleridge put it, 'O'er the ocean swell / Sublime of Hope, I see the cottage'd dell / Where Virtue calm with careless step may stray', or where, in Shelley's words, one could find 'A People mighty in its youth / A land beyond the Oceans to the West, / Where, though with rudest rites, Freedom and Truth / Are worshipped'. (*The Revolt of Islam*, Canto 11, stanza xxii).

In short, when Dickens made his decision to visit America, and told Chapman and Hall that he meant to 'keep a notebook, and publish it for half-a-guinea or thereabouts, on my return,'[7] he must have seen himself in the role of traveller as philosopher, determined to exhibit amiable and magnanimous feeling, and to bring to the attention of perfidious Albion the triumph of that new land which, to quote Shelley again, 'draws the milk of Power in Wisdom's fullest flow.'

If we accept this, we can account for something that otherwise will strike us rather odd about the *American Notes*, which is that they fail to begin with a series of sketches such as Boz's audience would naturally expect. (The journey over is a different matter, but then as a ship's passenger Dickens was not on official duty, so to speak. He was Boz rather than Charles Dickens, novelist, radical, and friend of America.) Instead, we get some rather ponderous generalisations about Boston and a determined tour of its institutions. Boston is a city of 'intellectual refinement and superiority', Dickens assures us, and he thinks the virtues owe a good deal to the influence of the nearby University.

Whatever the defects of American universities may be, they disseminate no prejudices; rear no bigots; dig up the buried ashes of no old superstitions; never interpose between the people and their improvement; exclude no man because of his religious opinions; above all in their whole course of study and instruction, recognise a world, and a broad one too, lying beyond the college walls.

After this enthusiastic opening, with its implied rebuke to Oxford and Cambridge, Dickens spends some time describing and commending the Perkins Institution and Massachusetts Asylum for the Blind, where he not surprisingly applauds the absence of uniform. ('Nothing but senseless custom and want of thought would reconcile us to the liveries and badges we are so fond of at home' — a statement that may well contain the seeds of Rob Toodles' experiences at the Charitable Grinders.) He then goes on to the State Hospital for the insane and is deeply impressed by the humane and enlightened treatment of the inmates, speaks with delighted approval of the House of Industry, for old or otherwise helpless paupers ('It is not assumed that being there they must be evil-disposed and wicked people, before whose vicious eyes it is necessary to flourish threats and harsh restraints'), visits a House of Reformation for Juvenile Offenders ('the importance of such an establishment in every point of view, and with reference to every consideration of humanity and social policy, requires no comment'), and finally examines the State prison, about which he has some doubts — isn't it a bit *too* unlike a jail for its inmates' ultimate good — but about which he nevertheless brings himself to say that 'the subject of Prison discipline is one of the highest importance to any community; and... in her sweeping reform and bright example to other countries in this head, America has shown great wisdom, great benevolence, and exalted policy.'

If we add to all this Dickens's statement that 'the tone of society in Boston is one of perfect politeness, courtesy, and good breeding', we have an account of the city which is at once a decisive rebuttal of Frances Trollope's findings about America, is all that Irving could have desired of the best English traveller, and which fits snugly into the radical/ Romantic view of the land which 'draws the milk of Power in Wisdom's fullest flow'.

Why, then, did it all go wrong? For the fact is that although Dickens went to America determined to love the country, he returned in a very different frame of mind. This is not to say that *American Notes* is as bitter or prejudiced a report as *Domestic Manners of the Americans*. It is however to observe that in both the *Notes* and in letters Dickens sent to Forster while he was on tour, letters which were to be used for the *Notes*, the tone changes from rapt (and perhaps dutiful) admiration, to scorn and indignation. And this is much more apparent in *Martin Chuzzlewit*, the novel he wrote after his return. Because the America that young Martin and Mark

Tapley discover is even more repellent than Frances Trollope's. And it won't do to say that Martin's and Mark's views can be discounted or explained away as those of the 'scheming adventurers' whom Irving had anathematised. Martin and Mark are adventurers, right enough: but there can be no doubt that Dickens shares their point of view. The Eden they eventually discover is an anti-utopian horror which is surely meant to give the lie to Southey's and Coleridge's dream of what life might be like beside the banks of the Susquehanna?

As they proceeded further on their track, and came more and more towards their journey's end, the monotonous desolation of the scene increased to that degree, that for any redeeming feature it presented to their eyes, they might have entered, in the body, on the grim domain of Giant Despair. A flat morass, bestrewn with fallen timber: a marsh on which the good growth of the earth seemed to have been wrecked and cast away, that from its decomposing ashes vile and ugly things might rise: where the very trees took on the aspect of huge weeds, begotten of the slime from which they sprung, by the hot sun that burnt them up; where fateful maladies, seeking whom they might infect, came forth at night in misty shapes, and creeping out upon the water, hunted them like spectres until day; where even the blessed sun, shining down on festering elements of corruption and disease, became a horror; this was the realm of Hope through which they moved. (Chapter 23)

Is this the promised end, or image of such horror?

I think we are bound to ask why Dickens makes this dystopia the journey's end for Martin and Mark. Why should the dream of America come to this? Well, one can of course itemise those features of American life which Dickens came increasingly to dislike as his tour went on. He was, for example, upset by the lack of privacy. Dickens, it hardly needs saying, was an intensely sociable, gregarious man, but he took for granted the fact that one *chose* to be sociable. In America, however, he found sociability thrust on him, whether he wanted it or not. In addition he found himself upset by American table-manners, by the habit, common among American men, of putting food into their mouths with their knives and then using those knives to supply themselves with butter from the general dish. He loathed the universal habit of spitting. He was inevitably outraged by slavery and the attitudes to negroes even in the 'free' states; and Chapter 17 of the *American Notes*, called 'Slavery', includes horrifying lists of advertisements which he had taken from newspapers, all of them pleading for information about runaway slaves, and all revealing the terrible brutality of which the slaves were victims. The chapter ends with a collection of newspaper reports, which tell of the frighteningly casual violence of American life and of the deaths by shooting of parties involved in argument. Yet Dickens doesn't make much of these last matters in *Martin Chuzzlewit.* About all we have on slavery is a reference to the theory of the genteel and 'enlightened' Morrises, who assume slavery is not a good thing, but that negroes are nonetheless 'funny', and an easy satire on the Watertoast Sympathisers, who style themselves Sons of Freedom and vigorously oppose 'Nigger emancipation'. And as far as violence is concerned we have to make do with the awkwardly introduced episode of Hannibal Chollop, who shows Mark his revolving-pistol, and tells him that '"It ain't long since I shot a man down with that, sire, in the State of Illi*noy*... for asserting in the Spartan Portico, a tri-weekly journal, that the ancient Athenians went ahead of the present Locofoco Ticket"' (Chapter 33).

On the other hand, Dickens makes a great deal of a matter that on the face of it seems trivial but which without doubt deeply upset him — the indifference of Americans to meals as social occasions. Dickens undoubtedly loved meals just *because* they were social occasions. He always took the keenest delight in arranging and presiding at dinner parties for his various friends; and even ordinary meals were likely to turn into celebratory events, in his life just as much as in his novels. The year after his return from America, he wrote to his friend, Felton, from Broadstairs, where he was at work on *Martin Chuzzlewit*, describing himself as

brown as a berry, and they *do* say he is a small fortune to the inn-keeper, who sells beer and cold punch. But this is mere rumour. Sometimes he goes up to London (eighty miles, or so, away), and then I'm told there is a sound in Lincoln's Inn Fields at night, of men laughing together with a clinking of knives and forks and wine glasses.[8]

American meals, however, failed utterly to provide the occasion for people to laugh together. In the *Notes*, Dickens reports life aboard a steamboat bound for Cincinnati:

There is no conversation, no laughter, no cheerfulness, no sociability, except in spitting; and that is done in silent fellowship round the stove, when the meal is over. Every man sits down, dull and languid; swallows his fare as if breakfasts, dinners, and suppers, were necessities of nature never to be coupled with recreation or enjoyment; and having bolted his food in gloomy silence, bolts himself, in the same state. But for these animal observances, you might suppose the whole male portion of the company to be the melancholy ghosts of departed door-keepers, who had fallen dead at the desk; such is their weary air of business and calculation. Undertakers would be sprightly beside them; and a collation of funeral-baked meats, in comparison with these meals, would be a sparkling festivity. (Chapter 11)

This observation finds its counterpart in *Martin Chuzzlewit*, both at the Pawkins', where 'all the knives and forks were working away at a rate that was quite alarming; very few words were spoken, and everybody seemed to eat his utmost in self-defence.... Dyspeptic individuals bolted their food in wedges; feeding, not themselves, but broods of nightmares who were continually at livery within them' (Chapter 16); and at the National Hotel, where 'tea, coffee, dried meats, tongue, ham, pickles, cake, toast, preserves, and bread and butter, were swallowed with the usual ravaging speed' (Chapter 21).

There are other features of America which Dickens came to dislike. he was incensed by the lies of the gutter press, and he didn't at all approve of the hard worhsip of the 'Almighty Dollar', nor of the 'smart' people who got rich by exploiting and cheating those many others who were innocent enough to trust them. But what I want to draw attention to is the fact that in the *Notes*, and even more in *Martin Chuzzlewit*, a rage of and contemptuous hatred for much of American life becomes the norm. Hence Eden, that symbolic anti-utopia, Martin and Mark's journey's end. And if we ask the question, why does Dickens develop this obsessional hatred, this 'splenetic remark, and illiberal spirit of ridicule' which Irving had so much regretted, I think the answer is not simply to be found in what he thought of America, but what he thought of England.

Let me at this point offer a suggestion. I think that Dickens went to America as a committed radical. I think he came home one. But I also think that his Englishness found him out in ways he could not have anticipated; and that when he was exposed to the American way of life he found he cared more deeply than he had suspected for tradition, custom, ceremony: matters which the radical is likely to treat with professional scorn. Look, for example, at this moment in *American Notes*, describing the journey by steamboat from Pittsburg to Cincinnati.

The night is dark, and we proceed within the shadow of the wooded bank, which makes it darker. After gliding past the sombre maze of boughs for a long time, we come upon an open space where the tall trees are burning. The shape of every branch and twig is expressed in a deep red glow, and as the light wind stirs and ruffles it, they seem to vegetate in fire. It is such a sight as we read of in legends of enchanted forests; saving that it is sad to see these noble works wasting away so awfully, alone; and to think how many years must come and go before the magic that created them will rear their like upon this ground again. (Chapter 11)

The fact that the trees are burning at the very least makes possible a clearing of the way for settlement, for human occupation. But what Dickens sees and feels is a sharp sense of loss; and in doing so he exhibits that very English feeling for the 'perishing pleasures' which Cowper had earlier mourned in 'The Poplar Field', and the 'beauty been' which Hopkins would later lament in 'Binsey Poplars'. So that when the radical Dickens comes to write *Martin Chuzzlewit*, he finds himself wanting to preserve England as a place of tradition and custom; he chooses to see it as a land rooted in past observances which have present strength. As a result, the England of that novel becomes a kind of golden pastoral.

In the *Melancholy Man* I remarked on what still seems to me to be a matter of some significance, which is that Dickens's description of the countryside round Salisbury is sharply at odds with Cobbett's description of it. And that this should be so makes clear how mythic the rural England of *Martin Chuzzlewit* actually is.

Here is Dickens:

It was a lovely evening in the spring-time of the year; and in the soft stillness of the twilight, all nature was very calm and beautiful. The day had been fine and warm; but at the coming on of night, the air grew cool, and in the mellowing distance smoke was rising gently from the cottage windows. There were a thousand pleasant scents diffused around, from young leaves and fresh buds; the cuckoo had been singing all day long, and was but just hushed; the smell of earth newly-upturned, first breath of hope to the first labourer after his garden withered, was fragrant in the evening breeze. (Chapter 20)

And here is Cobbett:

I have now been in nearly three score villages, and in twenty or thirty or forty hamlets of Wiltshire; and I do not know that I have been in one, in which I did not see a house or two, and sometimes more, either tumbled down, or beginning to tumble down. It is impossible for the eyes of man to be fixed on a finer country than that between the village of CODFORD and the town of WARMINSTER; and it is not very easy for the eyes of man to discover labouring people more miserable.[9]

The point I made, and which I still think valid, is that Dickens's countryside is strangely de-humanised, and therefore de-historicised. It thus amounts to an exercise in the genteel picturesque. What I now realise is that his American experience was crucial in making him turn away from precisely those matters that we might expect him, as radical, to be concerned with, and matters to which the radical Cobbett had drawn sharp attention. Instead, Dickens typically invokes in his novel a land of 'timeless' pastoralism, in which, for example, there is an ideal inn, called *The Blue Dragon*, though before the novel is done it changes its name to the *Jolly Tapler*, presided over by a 'rosy hostess, Mrs Lupin' — a very English flower[10] — who has a 'face of clear red and white, which, by its jovial aspect at once bore testimony to her hearty participation in the good things of the larder and the cellar' (Chapter 3). Mrs Lupin, that is, treats food and drink as elements of social ceremony; one can hardly avoid the implication of those qualifying words: *jovial* aspect, *hearty* participation, *good* things. And Dickens spells the matter out beyond any fear of misunderstanding, when he has Mark tell Tom Pinch, '"Lord, there's no dullness at the Dragon! Skittles, cricket, quoits, nine-pins, comic songs, choruses, company round the chimney corner every winter's evening. Any man would be jolly at the Dragon"' (Chapter 5). In short, *Martin Chuzzlewit* is perhaps the least radical of any Dickens novel. Indeed, I do not think it absurd to suggest that in many ways it is reminiscent of the Edmund Burke who wrote *Reflections on the Revolution in France*. And this is not merely because that passage about the burning trees is subtly akin to many passages in the *Reflections* that liken England and its history to a natural growth, a plant which draws its sustenance from its age. 'Rage and phrensy will pull down more in half an hour, than prudence, deliberation, and foresight can build up in a hundred years.' Thus Burke, and there is that in Dickens which, for all his delight at the burning down of Westminster, would be ready to agree. Yet the true, or nearer, kinship between *Reflections* and *Martin Chuzzlewit* can be located most persuasively in the sceptical tone that both men adopt towards the 'new', the 'free' and the 'independent'.

I think, for example, of that passage in which Burke writes of the men of the Revolution who are intent on destroying the past:

They despise experience as the wisdom of unlettered men; and for the rest, they have wrought underground a mine that will blow up, at one grand explosion, all examples of antiquity, all precedents, charters, and acts of parliament. They have the 'rights of men'. Against these there can be no prescription; against these no agreement is binding: these admit no temperament, and no compromise: anything withheld from their full demand is so much of fraud and injustice. Against these their rights of men let no government look for security in the length of its continuance, or in the justice and lenity of its administration.

And I think, by way of comparison, of Mr Chollop's claim that 'We are the intellect and virtue of the airth, the cream of human natur', and the flower of moral force. Our backs is easy ris. We must be cracked-up, or they rises and we snarls. We shows our teeth, I tell you, fierce. You'd better crack us up, you had' (Chapter 33).

Or I think of Burke remarking that

instead of casting away our old prejudices, we cherish them to a very considerable degree, and to take more shame to ourselves, we cherish them because they are prejudices; and the longer they have lasted, and the more they have prevailed, the more we cherish them.

And I think, again by way of comparison, of that moment when Martin and Congressman Elijah Pogram find themselves in argument, and Pogram tells Martin:

'We have no time to ac-quire forms, sir.' ...
'Acquire!' cried Martin, 'but it's not a question of acquiring anything. It's a question of losing the natural politeness of a savage, and that instinctive good breeding which admonishes one man not to offend and disgust another .... Now, observe what this comes to ... the mass of your countrymen begin by stubbornly neglecting little social observances, which have nothing to do with gentility, custom, usage, government, or country, but are acts of

common, decent, natural, human politeness. You abet them in this, by
resenting all attacks upon their social offences as if they were a beautiful
national feature. From disregarding small obligations they come in regular
course to disregard great ones....' (Chapter 34)

Dickens may seem to be having Martin argue the opposite case
from Burke, who would hardly be likely to accept that politeness has nothing to do with 'gentility, custom, usage, government, or country'. In denying this equation Dickens is, of
course, clinging to his radical status. ('Acts of common,
decent, natural human politeness'.) Yet what clearly concerns
him are *precisely* social observances, those things that Burke
calls prejudices. And the two men are at one in anathematising
any society which attempts to destroy them. They would
concur with Bacon who, in his *Essayes*, remarks that 'Not to
use Ceremonies at all, is to teach others not to vie them againe,
and so diminishe his respect; especially, they be not to bee
omitted to strangers and strange natures.' So that when Burke
declares that 'History consists, for the greater part, of the
miseries brought upon the world by pride, ambition, avarice,
revenge, lust, sedition, hypocrisy, ungoverned zeal, and all the
train of disorderly appetites', he would have an ally in the
Dickens who came to find in the act of writing *Martin Chuzzlewit* an unexpected regard for social observances which helped
to keep that train of disorderly appetites at bay (and for whom
appetite at meals is an apt metaphor of other appetites); and
who has Mark say that he would paint the American Eagle as
'like a Bat, for its short-sightedness; like a Bantam, for its
bragging; like a Magpie, for its dishonesty; like a Ostrich, for
its putting its head in the mud, and thinking nobody sees it...'
(Chapter 34). To repeat, *Martin Chuzzlewit* is perhaps the least
radical of Dickens' novels. It is, after all, an important feature
of the novel that everyone travels about England by stage-
coach, a matter which readers of 1843/4 probably found a little
odd, and to which I shall return.

Forster, it is true, thinks the novel not only an artistic
advance on Dickens's earlier fiction, but a concentrated attack
on the vices of the age, above all, Self. Dickens, Forster claims,
'now sent his humour and his art into the core of the vices of
the time' and he adds that

Debtors' prisons, parish Bumbledoms, Yorkshire schools, were vile enough, but something much more pestiferous was now the aim of his satire; and he had not before so decisively shown vigour, daring, or discernment of what lay within reach of his art, as in taking such a person as Pecksniff for the central figure in a tale of existing life.[11]

But is that *really* how the novel strikes us? I do not think so. On the contrary, it seems to me that we are much more likely to be struck by a feeling that the novel is somehow unfocussed, as though Dickens isn't quite sure what he wants to be writing about. And those phrases that Forster uses: 'of the time', 'existing life' — they surely apply more accurately to the great fable of 1843, *A Christmas Carol*, than they do to *Martin Chuzzlewit*, which is on the face of it hardly about the 1840s at all? And that isn't simply a matter of its mythic pastoralism. London, for example, is a good deal less alarming in this novel than it had been in either *Oliver Twist* or *Nicholas Nickleby*, because, as Chapter 9, 'Town and Todgers', makes clear, Dickens's writing about the city is often characterised by the same nostalgia as accompanies his writing about the country-side. For example:

To tell of half the queer old taverns that had a drowsy and secret existence near Todgers', would fill a goodly book; while a second volume no less capacious might be devoted to an account of the quaint old guests who frequented their dimly lighted parlours. These were, in general, ancient inhabitants of that region; born, and bred there from boyhood, and short of breath, except in the article of story-telling; in which respect they were still marvellously long-winded. These gentry were much opposed to steam and new-fangled ways, and held ballooning to be sinful, and deplored the degeneracy of the times; which that particular member of each little club who kept the keys of the church professionally, always attributed to the prevalence of dissent and irreligion: though the major part of the company inclined to the belief that virtue went out with hair-powder, and that Old England's greatness had decayed amain with barbers.

Dickens's relish for those men, the chuckly way he describes them, may look near to condescension. And I suppose it is. Yet it also seems to me that elsewhere in the novel he comes very close to endorsing their point of view. 'These gentry were much opposed to steam'. But then, as we shall see, so is Dickens. And if he sees these 'gentry' through an affectionate, nostalgic glow, that may be one way in which he tries to adjust to fears that urge themselves sharply on his consciousness, although he hopes to blunt them or turn them aside. The fears have to do with what he feels may be happening to England, and in *Martin Chuzzlewit* they are projected onto and realised in America; whereas in his next novel they are fully dramatised through the contrasting but connecting worlds of the Wooden Midshipman and the firm of Dombey. But to say this is to make it plain that there is more that divides *Martin Chuzzlewit* from *Dombey and Son* than the four years that intervene between the completion of the one and the commencement of the other. The point is not so much that 'the time' had changed, but that Dickens had. In *Dombey and Son* the characteristic mode of travel is the railway, whereas, as I have already remarked, in *Martin Chuzzlewit* it is the stage-coach.

Or rather, in the England of *Martin Chuzzlewit* people travel by stage-coach. And this is where we come on something of considerable interest. For when Martin and Mark are in America they travel by railway (as Dickens himself had done on his tour).

How the wheels clank and rattle, and the tramroad shakes, as the train rushes on! And now the engine yells, as it were lashed and tortured like a living labourer, and writhing in agony. A poor fancy; for steel and iron are of infinitely greater account, in this commonwealth, than flesh and blood. If the cunning work of man be urged beyond its power of endurance, it has within it the elements of its own revenge; whereas the wretched mechanism of the Divine Hand is dangerous with no such property, but it may be tampered with, and broken, at the driver's pleasure. Look at that engine! It shall cost a man more dollars in the way of penalty and fine, and satisfaction of the outraged law, to deface in wantonness that senseless mass of metal, than to take the lives of twenty human creaters. (Chapter 21)

There is not much point in trying to defend that passage. It is probably one of the most ill-considered pieces of writing that Dickens ever dashed off. Yet we can agree, I think, that what he is trying to identify is a dangerous worshipping of the machine and the machine-age, and he comes to see such worship as a part of the England of *Dombey and Son*. Hence the famous passage about the train journey that Dombey and Bagstock take to Birmingham, after Paul Dombey's death: 'away, with a shriek, and a roar, and a rattle, and no trace behind but dust and vapour; like as in the track of the remorseless monster, Death!'

The machine as Death. Yet actually a close study of the whole passage, from which I have quoted a mere fragment, reveals the fact that however Dickens may fear the spirit of machine worship, he can nevertheless respond positively to it. After all, the railway gives Toodle employment, and it sweeps away some of the worst slums.[12] Which is to say that in *Dombey and Son*, steel and iron and flesh and blood become complementary as well as oppositional forces. In *Martin Chuzzlewit*, on the other hand, it is surely the case that steel and iron, the spirit of the machine age, are to be identified with America, flesh and blood with England?

Now this is strange, to say the least. And it surely adds to the strength of my argument that Dickens is deliberately inventing or at least de-historicising the England of *Martin Chuzzlewit*. He is investing it with qualities whose typicality had been called in question by his friend, Carlyle, in that famous essay of 1829, 'Signs of the Times'.

Were we required to characterise this age of ours by any single epithet, we should be tempted to call it, not an Heroical, Devotional, Philosophical, or Moral Age, but, above all others, the Mechanical Age. It is the Age of Machinery, in every outward and inward sense of that word; the age which, with its whole undivided might, forwards, teaches and practises the great art of adapting means to ends. Nothing is now done directly, or by hand; all is by rule and calculated contrivance .... Our old modes of exertion are discredited, and thrown aside. On every hand, the living artisan is driven from his workshop, to make room for a speedier, inanimate one. The shuttle drops from the fingers of the weaver, and falls into iron fingers that ply it faster. The sailor furls his sail, and lays down his oar, and bids a strong, unwearied servant, on vaporous wings, bear him through the waters. Men have crossed oceans by steam; the Birmingham Fireking has visited the fabulous East: and the genius of the Cape, were there any Camoens now to sing it, has again been alarmed, and with far stranger thunders than Gama's. There is no end to machinery. Even the horse is stripped of his harness, and finds a fleet fire-horse yoked in his stead. Nay, we have an artist that hatches chickens by steam — the very brood-hen is superseded! For all earthly, and for some unearthly purposes, we have machines and mechanic furtherances; for mincing our cabbages; for casting us into magnetic sleep. We remove mountains, and make seas our smooth highway; nothing can resist us. We war with rude nature; and by our resistless engines, come off always victorious, and loaded with spoils.

'Men have crossed oceans by steam'. What Carlyle wrote in

1829 Dickens was to echo in 1842, when he crossed from Liverpool to Boston on the steamship *Britannia*.

But he came home by sail. That decision neatly emblematises his move from present to past, one that is dramatised in the novel by the fact that we switch from Mark and Martin on an American train to Tom Pinch on an English stagecoach.

Chapter 36 of *Martin Chuzzlewit* is largely taken up with a lengthy, exuberant account of Tom's journey from Salisbury to London, and it follows directly on Martin and Mark's re-arrival in England.

Yoho, behind there, stop that bugle for a moment! come creeping over to the front, along the coach-roof, guard, and make one at this basket! Not that we slacken our pace the while, not we: we rather put the bits of blood upon their mettle, for the greater glory of the snack. Ah! it is long since the bottle of old wine was brought into contact with the mellow breath of night, you may depend, and rare good stuff it is to wet a bugler's whistle with. Only try it. Don't be afraid of turning up your finger, Bill, another pull! Now, take your breath, and try the bugle, Bill. There's music! There's tone! 'Over the hills and far away', indeed. Yoho!

On the one hand, a solitary driver, and 'the engine yells'. On the other, conviviality, food and drink as social occasion, and 'There's music'. I have no doubt that the coaching bugle made excellent music, but the fact of the matter is that by the time Dickens was writing his novel it had largely faded from the roads of England. Instead, the yell of the engine was heard in the land. As Harold Perkin points out in his fine study, *The Age of the Railway*, most of the major rail lines had been established before the end of 1837. Senseless masses of metal, which in *Martin Chuzzlewit* are made to seem so peculiarly an American contrivance, were clanking and rattling across most of England by the time Dickens sat down to write his novel.

Now one might try to argue that this doesn't matter, because the novel is not set in the 1840s, so that it is unfair to suggest that Dickens's use of the stage-coach is somehow anachronistic. But the trouble with such an argument is that the American scenes of the novel are very *obviously* set in the present, that is, the 1840s. (America didn't have a railway system before England.) In other words, when Martin and Mark go to America they suddenly take a ten years' leap forward, or so it must seem. That is why I have drawn attention

to the novel's unfocussed feeling, and why Forster's claim that
the novel is 'of the time' will hardly do. We can underscore the
point by noting that when Dickens and Kate returned to
England from America, they journeyed down to London by
train, as Dickens himself records.

The country, by the railroad, seemed, as we rattled through it, like a
luxuriant garden. The beauty of the fields (so small they looked!), the
hedgerows, and the trees: the pretty cottages, the beds of flowers, the old
churchyards, the antique houses, and every well-known object: the exquisite
delights of that one journey, crowding in the short compass of a summer's
day, the joys of many years, with the winding up with Home and all that
makes it dear; no tongue can tell, or pen of mine describe. (*American Notes,*
Chapter 16)

There, you see, the railway isn't treated as a hostile spirit. It
simply puts Dickens in touch again with England. But 'no
tongue can tell, or pen of mine describe'. On the contrary, I
think that in passage after passage of *Martin Chuzzlewit*
Dickens tries very hard to describe those 'exquisite delights'
which create a myth of England as a pastoral golden world, a
myth which is already operating in the passage just quoted,
and which, *pace* Forster, makes it impossible for us to regard
the novel as a sustained satire on Self.

And with this in mind we may now be in a position to answer
the question of why Dickens sent Martin and Mark to America.
Edgar Johnson takes it for granted that the decision was
reached because Dickens thought it the most likely way to
boost the novel's disappointing sales — little over 20,000 copies
of the monthly instalments, compared with 100,000 of the
weekly instalments of *The Old Curiosity Shop.* 'A conference
was held at Chapman and Hall's', Johnson tells us. 'Something
clearly had to be done, and at the end of the fifth number
Dickens and Martin announce that he'd "go to America".'[13]
Forster, however, is a good deal more circumspect. He says of
Dickens's resolve to have Martin seek his fortune in America,
that although it was believed that this

might increase the number of his readers, that reason influenced him less
than the challenge to make good his *Notes* which every mail had been
bringing him from unsparing assailants across the Atlantic. The substantial
effect of the American episode upon the sale was yet by no means great. A

couple of thousand additional purchases were added, but the highest number at any time reached before the story closed was twenty-three thousand.[14]

Forster is in the right of it. Martin and Mark go to America, not so much to help sales of the novel, as to vindicate *American Notes*. What Forster does not say, however, though I think it clear beyond doubt, is that the American scenes allow Dickens the chance to spell out his fears of what might be happening to England, or be about to happen. When Forster tells us that *Martin Chuzzlewit* is 'of the time', and is a satire on Self, I have no doubt at all that he speaks with Dickens's authority. They were close friends and Dickens always discussed the progress of his fictions with Forster. But Forster is taking the intention for the deed. It is only the America of the novel which is truly 'of the time', and that same America embodies Self to a far greater degree than England. (Nothing Pecksniff does can rival the villainy of General Choke and Mr Scadder, for example.) If it is true to say that Dickens partly invents an America for *Martin Chuzzlewit,* one into which is drained all the infections of England as well as its own, the consequence is that he invents an England: an ahistoric, idyllic land which he wanted to believe in, and which embodied values he now realised that he cared for very deeply, but which he feared — though he could not bring himself to admit the fact — were under threat.

Notes

1 Anthony Trollope, *North America,* ed. Robert Mason with an introduction by J. W. Ward, Harmondsworth (1968) p.7.
2 John Forster, *Life of Charles Dickens* (1893) p.86.
3 *Ibid.*, p.129.
4 Washington Irving, the *Sketch Book* (1820) p. 34 *et seq.*
5 Forster, *op. cit.,* p.123.
6 *The Poems and Verses of Charles Dickens* (1903) pp. 59-60.
7 Forster, *op. cit.,* p.130.
8 Edgar Johnson, *Charles Dickens*, 2 vols. (1952) Vol. 1, p.458.
9 William Cobbett, *Rural Rides*, Harmondsworth (1967) p.334.
10 When I wrote that I was remembering the back garden of the house I lived in for some years as a child, which featured a large, flourishing bed of lupins: blue, white and purple. The lupin became then and has remained one of my favourite flowers. But I now discover — irony of

ironies — that it isn't native to England but was imported from north-western America. I doubt, however, if Dickens would have known that.

11   Forster, *op. cit.,* pp.221 and 224.
12   For an extended analysis of Dickens's ambivalent feelings towards the railway, and what it symbolises, see my essay on *Dombey and Son* in *Tradition and Tolerance in Nineteenth Century Fiction* (1966).
13   Johnson, *op. cit.,* Vol. 1, p.4531
14   Forster, *op. cit.,* p.216.

Chapter 6

Dickens and Arnold

I

ON the face of it the coupling is an unlikely one. Indeed, it may seem downright perverse to want to bring them together. Dickens clearly knew very little about Arnold and Arnold affected to know very little about Dickens. They are both writers living in Victorian England and there the similarities end. Dickens was a professional man of letters who had literally made his own way to absolute pre-eminence as a popular novelist. Arnold came from a cultured background, and although his educational experiences were, properly speaking, more extraordinary than Dickens's they are nonetheless the kind we expect our writers and intellectuals to enjoy. The fact that nearly all the greatest writers of the past 200 years — Blake, Dickens, Hardy, Lawrence, Yeats — *haven't* had such an experience has done little to remove the impression that Arnold's formative years were exemplary in opening the way for him to become an intellectual, a poet, and a social, cultural and literary critic. As Arnold saw himself so, one might say, his critics have seen him. Above all, they have taken him to be a central commentator on his age, operating from a position of enlightened liberal disinterestedness: cool, aloof, impartial, urbanely poised and able to speak with a measured finality on most if not all matters of significance. The contrast with Dickens — heated, avowedly partial, not at all withdrawn from battle, hugely and implacably involved — could hardly be more striking. Yet the odd fact is that Dickens is also seen as a central commentator of his age, even by those who wish to emphasise Arnold's centrality. Perhaps Dickens and Arnold have more in common than is usually allowed?

But, of course, they haven't. Nor can one simply say that the Victorian Age was complex enough to allow both of them to function properly as central commentators. No, the truth is that if Arnold is to be seen as occupying a central position, then Dickens's position must become marginal. And more than that, if Arnold is right in his prescriptions for and diagnoses of great literature, then Dickens is a minor writer. Certainly, it is impossible to argue for Dickens's greatness from an Arnoldian standpoint, and those critics who have tried to do it have succeeded only in making Dickens look pretty small beer. I have two reasons for bringing them together. First, I want to expose the customarily evaded contradictoriness of seeing both Dickens and Arnold as great creative critics of their age. Secondly, I want to suggest that Dickens's radical greatness makes Arnold look minor in comparison.

It is impossible to say how much Arnold actually knew of Dickens's writing. We know that in 1880, ten years after Dickens's death, he read *David Copperfield* for the first time, and to his surprise found that the satire on Creakle's academy was both accurate and intelligent.[1] The following year he went so far as to praise this part of the novel in one of his essays, pointing out how commendable the achievement was, considering that 'intimately indeed did Dickens know the middle class: he was bone of its bone and flesh of its flesh'.[2] The implication behind the remark is that one might have expected Dickens *not* to have attacked his own class, which suggests how little Arnold knew of Dickens's writing and also makes apparent the kind of expectations he had of it. For it is clear that previous to the reading of *David Copperfield* Arnold had thought of Dickens as the unambiguous champion of the philistines. In a cancelled passage of the Preface to the *Essays in Criticism* Arnold remarks that the Palatine Library of the future will be a philistine establishment, 'like the British College of Health enlarged', and the bookshelves will be free

from all the lumber of antiquity . . . Everything they contain will be modern, intelligible, improving: *Joyce's Scientific Dialogues, Old Humphrey, Bentham's Deontology, Little Dorrit, Mangall's Questions, The Wide Wide World, D'Iffinger's Speeches, Beecher's Sermons:* a library, in short, the fruit of a happy marriage between the profound philosophic reflection of Mr Clay and the healthy natural taste of Inspector Tanner.[3]

Most of the books Arnold lists were intended for children, so that the inclusion of *Little Dorrit* may indicate that he saw it as kid's stuff — a view which Arnoldian critics have tended to support even while finding themselves mysteriously drawn to Dickens, and which has been most firmly voiced by F. R. Leavis in his announcement that 'the adult mind doesn't as a rule find in Dickens a challenge to an unusual and sustained seriousness'.[4] And for Arnold to put *Little Dorrit* beside Bentham's *Deontology* is convincing evidence of his contemptuous belief in Dickens's philistinic, Utilitarian-like and middle-class mind. Of course, this only goes to show that Arnold hadn't read *Little Dorrit*, since not even he would have been able to explain away Pancks's bitter statements about 'the whole duty of man in a commercial society'.[5] And by the same token it is clear that he either hadn't read or hadn't understood *A Christmas Carol* or *Dombey and Son*. He might, however, have read *Bleak House*. In that novel Esther Summerson queries the value of Rick Carstone's learning the classics in what might well seem to be the manner of James Clay's attack on the middle-class education which gave, so Clay thought, far too much attention to Latin and Greek.[6] Looking at the irresolute and aimless Rick, Esther wonders whether the Latin verses he had made for eight years at public school 'often ended in this, or whether Richard was a solitary case' (Chapter 13). Now actually this isn't at all philistinic: Rick's education is, after all, one of the conditioning factors in his moral apathy. All the same, one can imagine Arnold raising an opprobrious eyebrow if he read Esther's words; and he might well have permitted himself to echo the phrase which J. S. Mill used after he had read *Bleak House:* 'that creature Dickens'.[7]

Yet it hardly matters what Arnold had or had not read of Dickens's work. For we can be sure that he thought of him as a popular writer in the worst sense — his fiction no better than vulgar books for children — and as one of the philistines, bone of its bone and flesh of its flesh. The judgement is hardly unique. George Eliot, Henry James, G. H. Lewes — they all thought of Dickens much as Arnold did. How representative their view was may be judged from Frederick Faber's remark to Newman, after Newman had published *Loss and Gain*. Faber informed Newman that his former Puseyite Friends considered him now to have 'sunk below Dickens'.[8] In our own century the view has been shared by such commentators as A. O. J. Cockshutt, Humphry House, F. R. Leavis (until his late conversion), K. J. Fielding, and many more, although the twentieth-century critics have differed from their predecessors in their discernibly embarrassed feeling that Dickens is somehow a great writer. Yet it must be clear that a writer with such crippling disadvantages as Arnold obviously thought Dickens possessed *isn't* great. So that what separates Arnold from, shall we say, Mr Cockshutt is not the assessment each makes of Dickens's qualities but Arnold's greater intellectual courage and consistency in claiming that such qualities put Dickens with Susan Bogart Warner's sentimental novel for juveniles, the *Wide Wide World*, rather than with Flaubert and Tolstoy, let alone Aeschylus and Shakespeare.

The last two names are not chosen at random. Arnold invoked them in *The Function of Criticism at the Present Time*,[9] that famous essay of his which is crucial to my present argument because it contains Arnold's fullest explanation of why he though the production of great literature impossible in Victorian England. 'At some epochs', he says towards the close of the essay, 'no other creation [than criticism] is possible'. Victorian England may produce fine criticism but it will certainly produce only "poor, starved, fragmentary, inadequate' art. In contrast:

The epochs of Aeschylus and Shakespeare make us feel their pre-eminence. In an epoch like those is, no doubt, the true life of literature; there is the promised land, towards which criticism can only beckon. That promised land it will not be ours to enter, and we shall die in the wilderness ... [10]

It is worth recalling that Arnold was writing these words late in 1864. The wilderness had therefore already produced *Dombey and Son, David Copperfield, Bleak House, Little Dorrit* and *Great Expectations;* and *Our Mutual Friend* was appearing in serial form.[11] It seems at least worth asking why Arnold could not see that the full flowering of Dickens's art entirely transformed the wilderness (not that it was ever *that* barren). The answer is not simply that Arnold was looking in the wrong direction — towards poetry and drama. True, he was accustomed to think of literary and poetic greatness as being one and the same. But as I have already remarked, the point is not that Arnold didn't see Dickens, but that he didn't like what he saw. Besides, Arnold could not have believe Dickens to be a great writer since Dickens plainly contradicted every prescription for the creation and nourishing of greatness laid down in *The Function of Criticism at the Present Time.* Nor is it quite fair to say so much the worse for the prescriptions. After all, they are given tacit approval by a great many critics. And the fact is that if Arnold is right then Dickens is not a great writer. In other words, it is not merely that Arnold's ideas about the pre-conditions of great art blurred his appreciation of Dickens's worth. More profoundly, when Arnold looked at Dickens's work he could not see any reason to doubt the worth of his own arguments.

Two essential factors must come together for the creation of great art, or so Arnold claimed: genius and the apt historical moment:

The grand work of literary genius is a work of synthesis and exposition . . . its gift lies in the faculty of being happily inspired by a certain intellectual and spiritual atmosphere, by a certain order of ideas, when it finds itself in them; of dealing divinely with these ideas, presenting them in the most effective and attractive combinations, — making beautiful works with them, in short. But it must have the atmosphere, it must find itself amid the order of ideas, in order to work freely; and these it is not so easy to command. This is why great creative epochs in literature are so rare, this is why there is so much that is unsatisfactory in the productions of many men of real genius; because for the creation of a master-work of literature two powers must concur, the power of the man and the power of the moment, and the man is not enough without the moment; the creative power has, for its happy exercise, appointed elements, and those elements are not in its own control.[12]

The major question this passage raises is, of course, how are we to recognise the apt historical moment? Arnold's answer is not very helpful. The ideal moment, he says, allows for one or both of what he calls 'complete culture and unfettered thinking', such as existed in the Germany that produced Goethe; and the 'national glow of life and thought', such as existed in the England that produced Shakespeare.[13]. All of which is decidedly vague. Indeed, one has the strong impression that Arnold's analysis of the apt historical moment is a piece of *arrière pensée.* Yet it has to be admitted that he is fully prepared to follow the implications of his own statements through to their

logical end. That is why he is so cautious about the achievement of Romantic art. For the Romantics did *not* live at an apt
historical moment:

At first sight it seems strange that out of the immense stir of the French
Revolution and its age should not have come a crop of works of genius equal
to that which came out of the stir of the great productive time of Greece, or
that of the Renascence, with its powerful episode of the Reformation. But
the truth is that the stir of the French Revolution took a character which
essentially distinguished it from such movements as these. These were, in the
main, disinterestedly intellectual and spiritual movements; movements in
which the human spirit looked for its satisfaction in itself and in the increased
play of its own activity. The French Revolution took a political, practical
character.[14]

The more one considers this passage the more evasive and
dishonest it becomes. There is, for example, the pure invention
of a Periclean Athens and Renaissance Europe that never were
on land or sea. Arnold's epochs are every bit as mythical as
Ruskin's Gothic or Morris's medieval world and quite without
the generosity of social and political thought that led to their
recreations of the past. We have also to note the unfocussed
and, surely, indefensible use of such abstractions as 'disinterestedly intellectual and spiritual movements', and 'the
human spirit'. Most disturbing of all, there runs beneath the
quasi-historical argument an appeal for an art that shall be
uncommitted to its own ideas. Just after the sentences already
quoted, Arnold adds that the French Revolution 'found undoubtedly its motive power in the intelligence of men and not
in their practical sense'.[15] It is of course true that if we take this
sentence on its own it may not seem to be driving a wedge
between ideas and commitment to ideas. Yet Arnold goes on to
say that 'the mania for giving an immediate political and
practical application to all these fine ideas of the reason was
fatal',[16] and at once we are forced to notice his real detestation
of commitment, his wish that the free play *of* ideas should be
taken to imply no more than a playing *with* ideas.

I realise that what I am saying may appear a brutal way of
treating Arnold's efforts at discrimination, but I think it
necessary. Arnold has been protected for too long. He is not
the disinterested, enlightened man that he took himself to be
and we need to be clear about the fact. We need also to expose

the assumptions on which his position rests (as opposed to the assumptions on which he thought or claimed it rested, and which far too many of his commentators have been content to take at face value). When Arnold praises Goethe's Weimar for supplying that great writer with 'complete culture and unfettered thinking', and when he speaks of great artists as dealing divinely with ideas, 'presenting them in the most effective and attractive combinations', it ought to be perfectly obvious that he is wanting to free literature from a commitment to history or politics as shaping forces. Instead, the artist must — but must what? Well, shape a *possible* history, a *possible* politics, built a Platonic world, in short. For how else can we explain a remarkable passage where Arnold claims that even if an artist does not live in an environment of 'free thought, intelligent and alive', he can go some way to creating it: 'books and reading may enable a man to construct a kind of semblance of it in his own mind, a world of knowledge and intelligence in which he may live and work'.[17] This is very close to Newman's idea of a university education, of course: close, too, to nineteenth-century arguments about the integrity of the University which have proved so persistent in the twentieth. But Arnold is thinking exclusively of the artist. It is *he* who needs to construct a free, untrammelled world of ideas in which to nurture his art.

That Arnold nonetheless thought such an effort of construction difficult — indeed impossible — in his own century we know from his repeated references to the contemporary wilderness[18] and also from the famous Preface to the volume of his poems published in 1853. For it is here that he speaks of the artist's predominant desire to construct images of noble and significant action, and of his need for great actions, 'calculated powerfully and delightfully to affect what is permanent in the human soul'.[19] Unfortunately, neither the actions nor the opportunity for them exist in the nineteenth century. Hence the need for criticism — including criticism of the age — to supply the sort of ambience in which a great creative epoch can establish itself. It might of course be argued that what Arnold thinks of as criticism others would think of as art. But Arnold would himself reject any such equation. In common with most Victorians he did not believe in the value of satire. That is why he disliked Voltaire, and why he could not see that Swift and

Pope were great writers.[20] Artists, he said, 'wish neither to applaud nor to revile their age: they wish to know what it is, what it can give them and whether this is what they want'.[21] Moreover, artists

do not talk of their mission, nor of interpreting their age, nor of the coming Poet; all this, they know, is the mere delirium of vanity; their business is not to praise the age, but to afford to the men who live in it the highest pleasure which they are capable of feeling.[22]

Arnold's admirers may dislike having to admit it, but that passage is surely very close to the famous last sentences of Pater's *Renaissance:*

What we have to do is to be for ever curiously testing new opinions and courting new impressions ... For art comes to you, proposing frankly to give nothing but the highest quality to your moments as they pass, and simply for those moments' sake.[23]

And for Arnold, every bit as much as for Pater, the artist's effort to promote pleasure automatically rules out the possibility that he can operate as a critic. For in a very real sense Arnold wants the artist to be outside history:

He will not, however, maintain a hostile attitude towards the false pretensions of his age; he will content himself with not being overwhelmed by them. He will esteem himself fortunate if he can succeed in banishing from his mind all feelings of contradiction, and irritation, and impatience; in order to delight himself with the contemplation of a heroic time, and to enable others, through his representation of it, to delight in it also.[24]

It seems extraordinary that Arnold should claim that the artist will not maintain a hostile attitude towards the false pretensions of his age. Why on earth shouldn't he? Yet to ask the question is immediately to recognise what anathema Dickens would be for Arnold. And not because Arnold thought Dickens praised the age, but because, whether Arnold knew it or not, Dickens exactly contains within his art 'feelings of contradiction, and irritation and impatience', because he maintains a hostile attitude towards the pretensions of his age, and because there is nothing in his work which Arnold would be able to recognise as a worthy prescription for modes of being that offer a way out of the wilderness. For Arnold, Dickens would typify the artist who steadfastly refused to beckon to the

promised land. Dickens's art, in other words, is diametrically
opposed to all that Arnold thought art should be.

And there is a further point. Arnold suggests that the artist,
in seeking not to be overwhelmed by the false pretensions of his
age, must do all that he possibly can to keep apart, to keep his
language pure, uninfected by the general corruptions. The
task, however, is difficult, and there is no guarantee that the
most self-conscious of artists can escape contamination:

Where shall we find language innocent enough, how shall we make the
spotless purity of our intentions evident enough, to enable us to say to the
political Englishmen that the British Constitution itself, which, seen from the
practical side, looks such a magnificent organ of progress and virtue, seen
from the speculative side . . . our august Constitution sometimes looks — for-
give me, shade of Lord Somers! — a colossal machine for the manufacture of
Philistines? How is Cobbett to say this and not be misunderstood, blackened
as he is with the smoke of a lifelong conflict in the field of political practice?
How is Mr Carlyle to say it and not be misunderstood, after his furious raid
into this field with his *Latter-Day Pamphlets?* How is Mr Ruskin, after his
pugnacious political economy? I say, the critic must keep out of the region of
immediate practice in the political, social, humanitarian sphere, if he wants
to make a beginnning for that more free speculative treatment of things,
which may one day make its benefits felt even in this sphere, but in a natural
and thence irresistible manner.[25]

For any of Cobbett, Carlyle and Ruskin it would surely not be
misleading to substitute the name of Dickens? Dickens, after
all, does not keep out of the 'region of immediate practice in
the political, social, humanitarian sphere', and would indeed
have a properly contemptuous regard for Arnold's belief that
somehow the intellectual's speculative treatment of things
(what things?) may make itself felt in a natural and thence
irrisistible manner. I think, for example, of his letter to a young
Danish correspondent, written three years before Arnold's
Preface: 'Sympathise, not in thought only, but in action, with
all about you . . . do not let your life, which has a purpose in
it — every life upon the earth has — fly by while you are
brooding over mysteries'. Moreover, he takes on the infection
of language which Arnold believes to result from any kind of
engagement. To put the issue squarely: Arnold believes that
once the writer, as critic or creative artist, allows himself to
become a part of history he becomes one of the judged:
whereas his true rule — again as critic or creator — is to be the

judge and always, at least implicitly, to measure his age against the Platonic ideal which he constructs out of the free play of ideas with which he divinely deals. We might say that Arnold thinks that the writer — as critic and creator — must somehow be outside the historical moment at which he writes, and the proof of his success in attaining this condition will be the evidence provided by the innocence of his language, the purity of his intentions, and the maintenance of a free speculative play of ideas. In short, the artist will answer to Shelley's description of power, which 'dwells apart in its tranquility, / Remote, serene, and inaccessible' [Mont Blanc].[26]

II

Now all this is admittedly familiar, or ought to be. And certainly Arnold's notionalising of the elite in *Culture and Anarchy* takes for starting-point precisely the same assumptions as underlie all he says of the true artist. Yet though these points *are* obvious, their implications have hardly been grasped, at least if I may judge from critics who write about both Arnold and Dickens. For the plain fact is that such critics invariably give assent to Arnold's assumptions and definitions and at the same time try to allow for Dickens's greatness. And it can't be done. You cannot — if you are serious — find equal room for both of them, for the very good reason that Dickens embodies all that Arnold despised and rejected. Dickens is always *within* the situation he is writing about (and this is as true of the overtly historical novels quite as much as of the others); his language is very clearly and self-consciously an infected language; and far from providing an art that can console by directing our attention towards permanent perfections beyond the 'present age', his truest work insistently and unremittingly unsettles, discomforts, discomposes. His art, in other words, is the very opposite of Platonic. That is why an Arnoldian critic such as Lionel Trilling is absolutely and not accidentally wrong when, trying to accommodate Dickens to Arnold's prescriptiveness, he remarks of *Little Dorrit* that it is 'directed to the transcending of the personal will, to the search for the Will in which shall be our perpetual peace'.[27] Trilling's claim is in fact directly opposed to a true recognition of *Little Dorrit*'s greatness which, as William Myers has finely said, 'establishes

instead grounds for our perpetual disquiet'.[28] And because, as
that remark implies, Dickens in his major work has a highly
problematic and fully conscious relationship with his audience,
we need to recognise that his art is much concerned with the
offering of consolations that cannot console, affirmations that
are contradicted, certainties that are mutually exclusive.

The enacting of conflicts is at the very heart of Dickens's
great novels — and he himself is importantly present within
them as an essential part of the conflict. (I think, in comparison, of Arnold's remarking that Dickens's knowledge of
the middle class made him 'bone of its bone, flesh of its flesh',
and want to protest that it would surely have been more honest
for Arnold to have said 'our' rather than 'its', and to suggest
that his inability to do so is a part of his effort of withdrawal
that finally enacts a lie.) Of course, Dickens's presence, his
readiness to identify with his audience, means that his prose
can engage with specific abuses and confidently challenge and
condemn them — and this is a recurring feature of the novels
from the attack on Dodson and Fogg through to his anger at
Fascination Fledgeby. To take an instance from *Little Dorrit*:
Dickens is clearly incensed by the nepotism and debased form
of patronage of government whereby the Edmund Sparklers of
the world are appointed to office, and he clearly expects his
audience to be every bit as incensed as himself. There is a very
striking and swift contempt about the following passage:

In a day or two it was announced to all the town, that Edmund Sparkler,
Esquire, step-son of the eminent Mr Merdle of world-wide renown, was
made one of the Lords of the Circumlocution Office; and proclamation was
issued, to all true believers, that this admirable appointment was to be hailed
as a graceful and gracious mark of homage, rendered by the graceful and
gracious Decimus, to that commercial interest which must ever in a great
commercial country — and all the rest of it with blast of trumpet.

It is not difficult to see how Arnold would object against the
'infected language' of that passage, with its repeated phrase
'graceful and gracious', which makes a calculated appeal to
exactly that middle-class contempt for social etiquette and
breeding that can become the token for a crude jeering phil-
istinism. But compare Arnold on the English Divorce Court:

When one looks, for instance at the English Divorce Court, — an institution which perhaps has its practical conveniences, but which in the ideal sphere is so hideous; an institution which neither makes divorce possible nor makes it decent, which allows a man to get rid of his wife, or a wife of her husband, but makes them drag one another first, for the public edification, through a mire of unutterable infamy; — when one looks at this charming institution, I say...one may be permitted to find the marriage theory of Catholicism refreshing and elevating.[29]

That prose hardly represents a 'more free speculative treatment of things... which may perhaps make its benefit felt... in a natural and thence irresistible manner.' Manner, after all, is badly compromised by such phrases as 'public edification' and 'charming institution'. In their pecularly affected drawing-room style — a sort of combination of donnish acidity and polite raillery (Mark Pattison out of Lady Dorothy Nevill) — those phrases clearly indicate that Arnold is directing his criticism from within a particular situation, even if he is aiming at 'purer' style. And in so far as he achieves the purity it leads him into limp clichés, such as 'mire of unutterable infamy'. Arnold comes off worse than Dickens not simply because Dickens is a greater prose stylist but because, fully accepting contamination (if we take that to mean existence within his situation), he is able to use his presence as Arnold not only cannot but would think inimical to the creation of great art. The point is that Arnold's prose is made oddly pallid by his effort of distanced aloofness, and although we are customarily asked to see the effort as noble even in failure, both effort and attempted justification for it represent the kind of indulgence that warrant a sterner response. The drama of the liberal conscience to which Arnold's prose offers partial testimony is really a kind of farce.

In contrast, of course, Dickens's attack on patronage may look at first glance like melodramatics. He is working on his audience's rage and contempt, making the sort of identification with them that prohibits any very keen inquiry into the adequacy of what he says. Or so it may seem. Yet in fact the audience which can identify itself so untroublingly with Dickens's contempt for patronage is also the audience which finds itself confronted with the inadequacies of Mr Meagles, who both loathes patronage and supports it, and with whom it is both natural (one almost wants to say inevitable) and

terribly disquieting for Dickens's audience to have to identify.
Disquieting because Meagles's limitations, which at first seem
amiably philistine — the sort of things that might endear him
to Dickens's readers — turn out to be severe indictments.
Meagles, that is, becomes a person with whom sympathetic
identification seems both necessary and impossible. In other
words, Meagles is one of those characters by means of whom
Dickens confuses his readers' allegiances. And although the
art with which this is done reaches a new level of attainment in
Little Dorrit, we can easily point to earlier examples.

One of the most brilliant is Uriah Heep. Heep is odious in his
false humility, his dank and slimy deference, his repulsive
cringing manner. David hates him. Dickens is clearly very
close indeed to David, and we have no reason to doubt the
adequacy and rightness of their revulsion. Indeed we share it.
But then Uriah speaks these words:

> But how little you think of the rightful umbleness of a person in my station,
> Master Copperfield! Father and me was brought up at a foundation school
> for boys; and mother, she was likewise brought up at a public, sort of
> charitable, establishment. They taught us all a deal of umbleness — not
> much else that I know of, from morning to night. We was to be umble to this
> person, and umble to that; and to pull off our caps here, and to make bows
> there; and always to know our place, and abase ourselves before our betters.
> And we had such a lot of betters! Father got made a sexton by being umble.
> He had the character, among the gentlefolks, of being such a well-behaved
> man, that they were determined to bring him in. 'Be umble, Uriah', says
> father to me, 'and you'll get on. It was what was always being dinned into you
> and me at school; it's what goes down best. Be umble, Uriah', says father,
> 'and you'll do'. And really it ain't done bad. (Chapter 39)

The upsetting of all our knowledge of Heep, the sudden acces-
sion to a view that humanises and explains him, his contemptuous hatred for those who have had nothing but
contemptuous hatred for him and have seemed in the right of
it: these are terribly disturbing matters to have thrown at one.
They remind one of the plain truth of W. E. Adams' remark,
made at the end of the nineteenth century when he was an old
man:

> fifty or sixty years ago...the whole governing classes...were not only
> disliked, they were positively hated by the working population. Nor was this
> hostility to their own countrymen less manifest on the side of the 'better
> orders'.[30]

But more than that they make clear how Dickens uses the relationship he has with his audience to defeat the kinds of consolation and certainty that they are encouraged to discover in his work. And this process of engaged exploitation grows through the novels until we arrive at perhaps the most shattering and dis-orientating of all the studies in problematic identification, Jaggers of *Great Expectations*.[31]

Yet the study of Jaggers, or for that matter of Eugene Wrayburn in *Our Mutual Friend*, might seem to support the least sophisticated of Marxist arguments about Dickens, which is that after 1850 he 'sank into a profound depression and hopelessness'.[32] In other words, the presentation of Jaggers and Wrayburn might seem *so* contradictory as to imply that Dickens has lost belief in any kind of reality that can give him cause for praise or allow him to glimpse affirmative possibilities. But though this thesis may look plausible it doesn't really take note of the fact that the contradictions on which Dickens's great art is built are themselves a creative achievement. They do not register his submission to historical forces in which he can see no room for the potentialities of living but instead provide the true images whereby potentiality struggles to realise itself. There is a world of difference between seeing Jaggers as a 'good' but defeated man — which is how he is often regarded and how he would fit a liberal interpretation — and Jaggers as we *should* regard him. For Dickens presents him as a man whose bitterness, frustrated energies, and vicious and scorching intellect are properly creative because they are properly human; they represent a very full and engaged response to the conditions in which he finds himself. And with inevitable modifications the same can be said of Eugene Wrayburn. For both of them, the genuine contradictions in their identities — those contradictions which make it impossible for the reader to be at ease with them — spring from the ceaseless tensions between the life they struggle to live and the life which lives them.

Even so, the Marxist case could re-assert itself in terms of a claim that Dickens's impulse is to celebrate private bourgeois virtues because they shine like good deeds in a naughty world, and that his celebration is, he knows, doomed, because the deeds will soon cease to shine, and will never be enough to pin back the surrounding darkness. 'The noisy and the eager, and the arrogant and the froward and the vain', of *Little Dorrit* will continue to fret and chafe and make their usual uproar. It is, of course, quite true that Dickens's greatest works mark a turning away from the kinds of 'solution' to difficulties which he had allowed into his early novels. We have only to compare Nicholas's beating of Squeers with Pancks's shearing of Casby to see how the blithely optimistic note struck in the early novel is lost to the later one. Pancks's action is essentially a forlorn, hopelessly limited gesture, shining very faintly indeed in a world too naughty to be affected by good deeds. It very obviously has none of the moral grandeur which Arnold in 1853 proclaimed as the condition out of which great actions could spring and which alone gave art its importance.[33] Not that Nicholas's beating of Squeers comes much closer to meeting Arnold's requirements, but at least it provides a way out of a problem, and is meant to be a grand and liberating gesture. Yet it is, of course, imaginatively insufficient. And not simply because it is unrepresentative, even though we perhaps ought to remind ourselves that the Yorkshire Schools weren't got rid of by isolated assaults on some of their headmasters. More significant of Dickens's failure is the fact that Nicholas is imagined as being 'above' the world which his actions condemn. Admittedly, there is one point where he is made to think of himself as truly identified with the mess in which he finds himself:

When he recollected that, being there as an assistant, he actually seemed — no matter what unhappy train of circumstances had brought him to that pass — to be the aider and abettor of a system which filled him with honest disgust and indignation, he loathed himself, and felt, for the moment, as though the mere consciousness of his present situation must, through all time to come, prevent his raising his head again. (Chapter 8)

Such a passage might well have important implications for Nicholas's subsequent development — and in a later novel it would have. We might, for example, imagine it applied to Pancks or to Jaggers. But of course we have then to admit an essential difference between the Dickens of the early novels and the Dickens of the masterpieces. In the cases of Pancks and Jaggers consciousness is a far more complex and troubling matter than it is with Nicholas. For his consciousness can be very simply appeased by his beating of Squeers and escape from the system of which he 'seems' to be the aider and abettor. But for Pancks and Jaggers there is no escape, and therefore no easing of consciousness. In so far as they are conscious — and they are *acutely* so — they exist in a condition which is not very far removed from mental torment. And it is that which makes them more fully human than Nicholas, as it also makes each of them a focus for the great and creative contradictions of Dickens's art. They are not given Nicholas's improper escape-hatch through prose that allows him to think of himself as *seeming* to be an aider and abettor of the system. They *are* aiders and abettors. But because they are shown as fully conscious of the fact and still manage to function, albeit with the cynicism, energy and acceptance of contradictory impulses that their resourcefulness and intelligence expose them to, they testify to Dickens's great perception that the 'system' is itself part of the historical process and not a metaphysical or socio-political constant. By contrast, if Nicholas finds it possible to pretend that he doesn't actually belong in or to the Squeers' world it is because he can present himself as a gentleman, which is meant to make everything come out right. In later novels, being a gentleman is, of course, no help; indeed, it is no excuse. But in *Nicholas Nickleby* it is meant to excuse just about everything. ' "I am the son of a country gentleman," Nicholas tells Sir Mulberry Hawk, "your equal in birth and education, and your superior I trust in everything besides" ' (Chapter 32). After which remark one is no doubt meant to murmur, 'Oh, that's all right, then'. That it is far from all right becomes very plain as soon as we glance at Dickens's previous novel. Admittedly, *Oliver Twist* also betrays contradictions rather than making use of them, but whereas in *Nicholas Nickleby* the contradictions are betrayed through the hero's sense of being superior to and therefore better than the world in which he is placed, in *Oliver Twist* the kind of values which Nicholas himself represents are shown to be at the very least partly responsible for a world in which Fagin lives and in which the innocent suffer.

I have twice written about the split nature of *Oliver Twist*, and it would be tedious as well as unnecessary to cover the ground once more.[34] For my present purpose it is sufficient if I note the evident discrepancy in the novel between the 'official' comments on the dark underworld of crime and immorality and the very obvious and uncontrolled sympathy which Dickens also reveals for that world. And I must note also how Dickens's 'official' approval of the novel's middle-class world is severely qualified not only by the callousness with which it regards the unfortunates of the underworld but also by its own limp inadequacies.

How far Dickens knew what he was actually up to in *Oliver Twist* is obviously an impossible question to answer and it may be an unfair one to ask. But certainly in both that very remarkable novel and in *Nicholas Nickleby* we find the uncontrolled because unacknowledged emergence of contradictions which in the great novels become, it seems to me, fully acknowledged and therefore productive of great art. Nor is it really possible to answer the question as to why the change should occur. The deepening horror of Victorian England, with its 'dirty and miserable tragedy';[35] Dickens's own situation; the mystery of his genius: each element contributes something. Yet it is in the nature of the case that the matter should finally remain one of speculation. What is plain fact is Dickens's emergence as a great novelist — in my estimation the greatest of all English novelists — because of his ability to cope with the contradictions to which his genius and his situation exposed him. The test of a first-rate intelligence, Scott Fitzgerald remarked, 'is the ability to hold two opposed ideas in the mind at the same time, and still retain the ability to function'.[36] It is a remark that could well be applied to Dickens, from *Dombey and Son* onwards.

III

And yet one hears Arnold murmuring his protest that because the age has no moral grandeur it cannot produce great art. I need therefore to move him and Dickens into open confrontation, and *Bleak House* is the novel that will serve my purpose. For *Bleak House* was published in the year that Arnold delivered his judgement on the age, and it might immediately seem proper to suggest that Esther, Charley, Snagsby, George Rouncewell, Phil Squod and young Turvey-drop exhibit a positive decency that stands out against the misery, squalor and depravity with which the novel also concerns itself, and which is honourable even if it does not amount to Arnold's conception of moral grandeur. But then such a remark serves to bring to mind Orwell's famous criticism that it was beyond Dickens to grasp that 'given the existing form of society, certain evils *cannot* be remedied'.[37] In short, Dickens's presentation of moral worth or, to put the matter less insistently, of human goodness is unwittingly but hopelessly compromised because he does not fully grasp what it and he are up against. And Arnold would therefore be wiser than Dickens in remarking that the age could not possibly supply the materials out of which great art could be made, just as he would be right in wanting the artist to banish from his mind all feelings of contradiction and irritation and impatience.

Contradiction, irritation, impatience. Not only are they demonstrably present in *Bleak House*, they are so important and so central that they have to be spoken of in any adequate assessment of the novel. They show themselves both in the novelist's informing presence and also in the kind of relationship he has with his audience. And it hardly needs saying that in both cases one notices how very middle-class Dickens is. What one might *not* notice is how a middle-class confidence in the author and his fiction is systematically betrayed. For example, everyone who reads the novel is bound to see the middle-class contempt that Dickens has, and encourages his audience to have, for the aristocracy. But we have also to accept Dickens's very real regard for Sir Leicester Dedlock. Again, there is no mistaking the novelist's middle-class impatience of idleness. But we have to place against that Dickens's keenness to reveal the degradation of work in the world with which his novel deals. Equally, his patronising attitude towards the working class has its roots in his middle-class allegiances. Still, Dickens's just and illuminating praise of Charley has, troublingly, to be set against his irritation at Rick. It is the same with idealism. There is the confident appeal to the audience's sense of the ridiculous and its jeering hatred of ostentatious idealism in the presentation of Mrs Jellyby and Mrs Pardiggle, and yet there is also the approval given to Esther's ideal of duty (and of course it isn't just hers). In short, the most preliminary glance at *Bleak House* shows that it is a novel full of certainties which are contradicted by other certainties, and which are presented by a novelist whose palpable impatience and irritation seem sure of themselves but disquieting to an audience trying to hold the novel in focus.

Here a comparison offers itself. To put the matter as I have is perhaps to suggest that I am trying to talk about Dickens in terms that would be better fitted to an account of Swift's techniques and methods. For in Swift there is typically an undermining of just those expectations which we are encouraged to build up, and Swift, perhaps as much as any English writer, shows in his writing those three elements that Arnold thought the serious artist must banish from his mind. You have only to think of the 'Digression on Madness' or the Fourth Book of *Gulliver's Travels* to be aware of the extraordinary degree to which Swift upsets his audience's grasp of the certainties he himself has provided. Yet there is a fundamental difference between the Swiftian and the Dickensian methods. Though they share an appalled and appalling sense of contradictions, Swift characteristically demonstrates this by a calculated betrayal of the trust which he builds up. (The most striking example of a device which is utterly central to his method is, I suppose, in the 'Modest Proposal'.) But Dickens does not betray trust. The kind of relationship he has with his audience is different from Swift's relationship with *his* audience because Dickens accepts rather than exploits the trust that he builds and yet nevertheless finds himself required to call the trust in question. In doing so he very courageously exhibits a vulnerability which can hardly be thought of as Swiftian. After all, in Swift's work you can never be quite sure just who is making and mocking recommendation, standing for and standing on values. There is a shifting series of personae or masks behind or through which Swift operates and as a result of which identification of the author with any one point of view is made highly problematical. (Hence, for example, the continuing and ultimately irresolvable arguments about where Swift actually 'stands' in relation to the Yahoos and the Houyhnhnms). But I cannot imagine that anyone reading *Bleak House* would think of questioning Dickens's identification with Esther's self-admonition, 'Esther, Esther, Esther, Duty, my dear'.

And yet among those who do their duty in the novel are

Vholes and the Policeman who moves Jo on. And we do not want to identify Dickens with *them*. Or take so apparently Swiftian a moment as the initial description of Sir Leicester Dedlock:

He is a gentleman of strict conscience, disdainful of all littleness and meanness, and ready, on the shortest notice, to die any death you may please to mention rather than give occasion for the least impeachment of his integrity. He is an honourable, obstinate, truthful, high-spirited, perfectly unreasonable man. (Chapter 2)

The tone of this of course could never be Swift's, but there is something Swiftian about the way the passage canvasses possibilities, enjoys unsettling its audience and exhibits a final ruthless certainty of judgement. It sees all round and straight through its subject. Yet the passage also gratifies in a way that is unlike Swift. It ends with the expected condemnation for which Dickens's audience has been waiting, and the phrase 'perfectly unreasonable man' is itself a deliberate mocking of polite speech. Dickens is confident not only of the adequacy of his judgement but of his audience's agreement with it. The audience is not bewildered out of certainty, as Swift's audience is. On the contrary, its own certainties are continually reinforced by Dickens's judgements. Consider, for example, Esther's attitude to Charley's efforts at writing:

Writing was a trying business to Charley, who seemed to have no natural power over a pen, but in whose hand every pen appeared to become perversely animated, and to go wrong and crooked, and to stop, and splash, and sidle into corners, like a saddle-donkey. It was very odd, to see what old letters Charley's young hand made; they, so wrinkled, and shrivelled, and tottering; it, so plump and round. Yet Charley was uncommonly expert at other things, and had as nimble little fingers as I ever witnessed. (Chapter 31)

Esther's affectionate condescension is untroubled by any suggestion of the possible inadequacy of her response to Charley's fumblings, so that even the reference to the girl's being 'uncommonly expert at other things' is as smoothly patronising as the suggestion released by the comparison of her pen to a 'saddle-donkey'. It is, in fact, very like Papa Meagles's attitude to Tattycoram. And as the comparison implies, Dickens's audience can hardly help being discomposed out of the ease with which it is encouraged to identify with Esther's view of

Charley. For her remark that Charley had 'as nimble fingers as I ever watched' inevitably recalls us to Esther's and our first view of her in Bell Yard, where she is looking after her orphaned brother and sister:

We were looking at one another, and at those two children, when there came into the room a very little girl, childish in figure, but shrewd and older-looking in the face — pretty-faced too — wearing a womanly sort of bonnet much too large for her, and drying her bare arms on a womanly sort of apron. Her fingers were white and wrinkled with washing....

What we notice here is how Charley is simply beyond Esther's condescension, so that phrases like 'pretty-faced too' and 'a womanly sort of apron', which blend sentimentality and genuine compassion in exactly the same proportions as Jarndyce does, are not allowed to blur our view of Charley's resilient, untroubled goodness. It seems to me inevitable that we respond to the sight of the girl as Esther and Jarndyce do — and their response is perfectly genuine and decent — and also see from Charley's point of view how absurd such a response is. Her integrity is entire and it is clear from what he shows of Charley that Dickens shares Blake's and Wordsworth's great understanding of the uncontaminated purity of the child's mode of experience:

'Is it possible', whispered my guardian, as we put a chair for the little creature and got her to sit down with her load: the boy keeping close to her, holding to her apron: 'that this child works for the rest? Look at this! For God's sake look at this!'

It was a thing to look at. The three children close together, and two of them relying solely on the third, and the third so young and yet with an air of age and steadiness that sat so strangely on the childish figure.

'Charley, Charley!' said my guardian. 'How old are you?'

'Over thirteen, sir' replied the child.

'Oh! What a great age!' said my guardian. 'What a great age, Charley!'

I cannot describe the tenderness with which he spoke to her; half playfully, yet all the more compassionately and mournfully.

'And do you live alone with these babies, Charley?' said my guardian.

'Yes, sir', returned the child, looking up into his face with perfect confidence, 'since father died'.

'And how do you live, Charley. Oh! Charley,' said my guardian, turning his face away for a moment, 'how do you live?'

'Since father died, sir, I've gone out to work. I'm out washing today.'

'God help you, Charley!' said my guardian. 'You're not tall enough to reach the tub!'

'In pattens I am, sir,' she said, quickly. I've got a high pair as belonged to mother.'

'And when did mother die? Poor mother!'

'Mother died just after Emma was born,' said the child, glancing at the face upon her bosom. 'then father said I was to be as good a mother to her as I could. And so I tried. And so I worked at home, and did cleaning and nursing and washing, for a long time before I began to go out. And that's how I know how; don't you see, sir?'

'And do you often go out?'

'As often as I can,' said Charley, opening her eyes and smiling, 'because of earning sixpences and shillings!' (Chapter 15)

The scene continues, but I have quoted enough, I hope, to show what a major accomplishment it represents. It is, I think, one of the most discomposing pieces of writing in our literature, because we are forced to share Jarndyce's response to Charley at the same time as being aware that Charley is beyond such compassion. Her untroubled confidence, the ease with which she sets Jarndyce right, her genuine ignorance of the effect she is producing, the simple naturalness as it seems to her of her life: it is Dickens's unerring sense of these things that makes for the most astonishing effect of this great and astonishing scene. And what we learn here of Charley's human achievement (the words are clumsy but what others will do?) inevitably throws an uncomfortably mocking light on Esther's condescension towards those 'nimble little fingers'. To know exactly how she and we are being caught out we have only to remember the fingers 'white and wrinkled with washing'.

Yet it was perhaps with Charley in mind that George Eliot made her famous complaint against Dickens's 'preternaturally virtuous poor children and artisans',[38] and though the criticism is less often invoked nowadays it is by no means entirely stifled. That it shouldn't be is testimony to Dickens's power to discompose, to disturb. For it is, after all, radically unsettling to have to take so seriously committed a view of Charley as we are forced to take in *Bleak House*. It challenges exactly the class-consciousness which we like to think of as providing sure insight into other classes, other modes of experience. Yet the challenge is not to truth. As social commentators in the nineteenth century discovered, there actually were people like Charley, for all that George Eliot might not like it. Consider, for example, this passage from the *Bitter Cry of Outcast*

London (the author has just instanced examples of suffering among the poor):

It is heart-crushing to think of the misery suggested by such revelations as these: and there is something unspeakably pathetic in the brave patience with which the poor not seldom endure their sufferings, and the tender sympathy which they show towards each other. Where, amongst the well-conditioned, can anything braver and kinder be found than this? A mother, whose children are the cleanest and tidiest in the Board School which they attend, was visited. It was found that, though she had children of her own, she had taken in a little girl, whose father had gone off tramping in search of work. She was propped up in a chair, looking terribly ill, but in front of her, in another chair, was the washtub, and the poor woman was making a feeble effort to wash and wring out some of the children's things. She was dying from dropsy, scarcely able to breathe and enduring untold agony, but to the very last striving to keep her little ones clean and tidy.[39]

It is a miserable fallacy, George Eliot said, to believe that 'high morality and refined sentiment can grow out of harsh social relations, ignorance, and want; or that the working-classes are in a condition to enter at once into a millenial state of *altruism*, wherein everyone is caring for everyone else, and no one for himself'.[40] That so intelligent, sympathetic and magnanimous a person as George Eliot should commit herself to such a remark helps to demonstrate, I think, exactly how great Dickens is. And I am not wanting to demean the fineness of the *Bitter Cry of Outcast London* if I say that Dickens's effect is far greater, because though his opening of doors into strange lives has something of the crusading journalist about it, it has finally to be seen as great art in its power to upset, to confront us with contradictory certainties. Esther's certain 'placing' of Charley is very similar to George Eliot's condescension towards poor people and artisans. It offers a certainty with which we can find ourselves at ease. But we also are made to see Charley in a manner that upsets all our calculations and beliefs in human probability.

The contradictions in *Bleak House* are given dramatic force nor merely because Dickens unsettles our view of a character by the sudden fresh perspective that discomposes, but also because he uses the two narratives to complicate the certainties that belong to each. To take an obvious example. The view of Jo that we are offered in the omniscient narrative is not the view we gain through Esther's narrative. There are inevitable discrepancies, not just because Esther sees less than the omniscient narrator but because, being what she is, she cannot understand what she sees. And what is true for Jo is true for many of the other characters. But, in addition, I think any honest response to *Bleak House* will have to admit the sheer uneasiness which we are forced into when we want to respond to a character in an uncomplicated way (the way that we are so often told is the appropriate one in which to respond to Dickens's characters). To take another obvious example. We are certain of Vholes's predatoriness, his unhealthy and radically inhuman attitude to his clients. Indeed, our certainty of response to these things is actively encouraged by Dickens's prose and by the images of disease and death which constantly attend Vholes. Vholes is physically revolting and morally repulsive. But Vholes also has a father and three daughters dependent on him in the Vale of Taunton. And although his references to them are mealy-mouthed (given Vholes, what else should they be?) we cannot doubt that he is doing duty in caring for their welfare. The result is that an audience eager to see Vholes plain in order to treat him dismissively is forced to the uncomfortable awareness that his 'confiding eye of affection' *cannot* easily be dismissed, and that even he is too complicated to be comfortably coped with. To be sure, his pustular face is the obvious and strong indication of a radical infection. But then who can escape such infection? Life in Victorian England is a contaminated and contaminating condition. ' "You brought your interests with clean hands sir, and I accepted them with clean hands" ', Vholes tells Rick (Chapter 39). The irony implicit in that remark is most massively investigated in *Great Expectations*, but it is properly present in *Bleak House*. For nobody can stay clean, no man is an island entire unto himself, even the respectable reader is implicated in Jo's death (as the shattering end to Chapter 47 testifies) and even the most plangent of moral maxims, 'doing duty', is itself hopelessly compromised and corrupted. Neckett, pursuing bankrupts even to their death, does his duty; the policeman who moves Jo on does his duty; Bucket does his duty, and in the process brings suffering to the brick-makers' wives, to George Rouncewell, to Jo and to others; and Vholes does *his* duty, both by Rick and in the interests of his own dependents.

Almost, one feels, duty is what ought to be abandoned, since doing it can seem a vicious constriction of exactly those generous and humane forces of anger and indignation which would threaten the system that appeals to duty.

But then that is too simple. For although the concept of duty can be destructive it can also be creative, as it is for Charley and for Snagsby and for the Bagnets. Yet against *that* it has to be said that the creativity of personality and freedom is only partial. In the world that *Bleak House* explores there can be no possibility of a full and completely satisfying life. (There is no doubt that Dickens's presentation of Jarndyce strikingly rebukes those earlier untroubled pictures of goldenhearted philanthropists whose touch could transform the sordidness of contemporary life into the timeless world of Dingley Dell.) The central image of Tom all Alone's disease is crucial to the novel's meaning because of the way it is shown to reach out everywhere, to contaminate everyone. (Nor is it wrong to say that hidden disease implies just those contradictions of certainties that I have been mentioning, nor that the most aggressively and uncomplicatedly certain of Dickens's later novels, *Hard Times*, is also the worst.)

Finally, I want to note that the very language of *Bleak House* is contaminated. Dickens makes no pretence to an innocent language. The great moment when he turns on his audience, at Jo's death, owes its extraordinary effect to our necessarily precise sense of the author's own rage, his ready identification with the novel's rhetoric — which is often the rhetoric of fully-engaged anger, disgust, contempt. *Bleak House* has, I feel, hardly yet been studied with the sort of critical awareness that is needed if we are to see how fully Dickens understands and accepts the contamination of language in his society, the ways in which it expresses modes of seeing and thinking that are themselves traps, so that to speak is nearly always to be guilty. I think for example, of that amazing, emblematic incident when Krook refuses well-intentioned offers to help him with his reading and writing: "'They might teach me wrong.... I don't know what I may have lost by not being learned afore. I wouldn't like to lose anything by being learned wrong now'" (Chapter 14).

It would take a separate and very long essay to try to do

justice to Dickens's way with language in *Bleak House*. For the present I merely want to take the novel's opening sentences as an example of how Dickens uses the language of contamination to express his concerns:

London. Michaelmas Term lately over, and the Lord Chancellor sitting in Lincoln's Inn Hall. Implacable November weather. As much mud in the streets, as if the waters had but newly retired from the face of the earth, and it would not be wonderful to meet a Megalosaurus, forty feet long or so, waddling like an elephantine lizard up Holborn Hill. Smoke lowering from the chimney-pots, making a soft black drizzle, with flakes of soot in it as big as snow-flakes — gone into mourning, one might imagine, for the death of the sun. Dogs, undistinguishable in mire. Horses, scarcely better; splashed to their very blinkers. Foot passengers, jostling one another's umbrellas, in a general infection of ill-temper, and losing their foothold at street-corners, where tens of thousands of other foot passengers have been slipping and sliding since this day broke (if this day ever broke), adding new deposits to the crust upon crust of mud, sticking at those points tenaciously to the pavement, and accumulating at compound interest.

Place and description of place. A well-tried convention for the opening of novels. It might, on the face of it, seem trite enough. But there are odd features. Take, for example, the apparently arbitrary way that the reference to the Lord Chancellor is slipped between London and its weather, as though he is linked with the 'implacable' weather. (Why is he still sitting if Term is lately over? Doesn't he obey the due process of the calendar? Is he above law?). And then from weather to mud, and the fancifulness of meetings with prehistoric animals (as though the sculpted monsters at the Crystal Palace have somehow come alive and have taken over the city swamp, the imitation turned into truth). How seriously do we take the suggestions? Not at all, perhaps. Yet later in the novel mud and slime become powerful and even key words to suggest the radical dehumanising of society, the inversion of all contemporary dreams of progress. Clearly, such language creates a disturbing range of confusions: of natural with man-made (snow-flakes and soot); and of time (a day which may be a perpetuation of night). It also makes proleptic use of metaphor which confuses because we do not know how or with what degree of seriousness to take it: a 'general infection of ill-temper', for example, or mud deposited and 'accumulating at compound interest'. The language of Capital, the language of disease: they come together in describing the human and the natural, as though the world is made meaningful only through such languages.

The above remarks do no more than hint at the kinds of confusion that the opening paragraphs of *Bleak House* open up. They may, however, have done enough to suggest that Marxist critics, among others, are essentially right when they criticise what they take to be Dickens's ultimate failure to make sense of his world. Yet it is not mere paradox to insist, as I want to, that Dickens's readiness to seize on infected language is a sigh of his own health, nor to say that it allows him to explore truths that none of his contemporaries could possibly admit to, just because they hoped to 'keep apart' — which meant among other things maintaining an indissoluble purity of language. Nor is it trite to say that Dickens's willingness to deal in contradiction is an act of the greatest imaginative intelligence, an extraordinarily courageous immersion in the flux of history which earns him the right to speak truthfully and centrally in a way that Arnold cannot match. For Arnold, as I have remarked, wants to be outside history, 'dealing divinely with... ideas, presenting them in the most effective and attractive combinations'.

Of course, if you believe Arnold's prescription to be just then it follows that you have either to deny to Dickens the status of a great artist, or to locate his greatness in areas that are marginal to his characteristic achievement. But if, on the other hand, you think that Dickens's readiness to accept contradiction is crucial to his greatness then you have to find Arnold precious, limited, and in ways he would hardly appreciate, a victim of his society.

Notes

1 *Letters of Matthew Arnold, 1848-1888*, collected and arranged by G. W. E. Russell, 2 vols (1895) ii, 184.
2 The essay, 'The Incompatibles', first appeared in the *Nineteenth Century IX* (1881) 1034-42. It was re-printed in *Irish Essays* (1882).
3 Matthew Arnold, *Lectures and Essays in Criticism*, ed. R. H. Super (1962) p. 538.
4 F. R. Leavis, *The Great Tradition* (1948) p. 19.

5 *Little Dorrit*, i, Ch. 13. All quotations come from the Oxford Illustrated Edition.

6 Clay, MP for Hull, made the attack in a speech to his constituents in November 1864. Arnold, *Lectures and Essays*, ed. Super, *op. cit.,* p. 488.

7 Michael St John Pack, *The Life of John Stuart Mill* (1954) p. 311.

8 M. Trevor, *Newman: The Pillar of the Cloud* (1962) p. 421.

9 First given as a lecture from the Chair of Poetry at Oxford, 29 October 1864. Published in the *National Review* in November; and re-published, as had always been intended, as the Introductory Essay to *Essays in Criticism* (1865).

10 Arnold, *Lectures and Essays*, ed. Super, *op. cit.*, p. 285.

11 Serialisation began in May 1864, and was completed in November 1865.

12 Arnold, *Lectures and Essays*, ed. Super, *op. cit.*, p. 261.

13 *Ibid.*, p. 263.

14 Arnold, *Lectures and Essays*, ed. Super, *op. cit.*, p. 263-4.

15 *Ibid.*, p. 264.

16 *Ibid.*, p. 265.

17 *Ibid.*, p. 263.

18 See, for example, lines 171-87 of 'Rugby Chapel'.

19 *Poetical Works of Matthew Arnold*, ed. Tinker and Lowry (1957) p. xxix.

20 For Victorian attitudes to Voltaire see Chapter on W. H. Mallock, 'Tilting at the Moderns'.

21 *Poetical Works*, ed. cit., p. xxviii.

22 *Ibid.*, p. xxix.

23 W. Pater, *The Renaissance* 3rd edn (1888).

24 *Poetical Works*, ed. cit., pp. xxix-xxx.

25 Arnold, *Lectures and Essays*, op. cit., p. 275.

26 In a recent review article of Paul Harris's biography of Arnold, Denis Donoghue puts the same point rather differently.

> Arnold's programme seems innocent, and perhaps noble. But it contains, I believe, an impurity of motive. In a benign light you could say that ideas are the certainties by which the chaos of facts is rendered intelligible. But in a sharper light you would say that Arnold wanted ideas to deliver him from the bewilderment and the insecurity of experience. He wanted not experience but release from it into a world characterised by the free play and currency of ideas. *Times Literary Supplement* 28 August 1981, p. 972.

Ideas, in other words, are a substitute for experience, mark an unreadiness to confront the chaotic present. I think now that there is more to exonerate Arnold than I did when I originally wrote the essay — in 1972 — but I was exasperated by the orthodox view, which still prevails, that somehow Arnold was a more *reliable* or more dispassionately truthful judge or commentator on his age than Dickens. Such a view finds a natural home in the academic world and I admit that my essay deliberately set out to ruffle academic plumage.

27 See his essay on the novel in *The Dickens Critics*, ed. Ford and Lane (1961) p. 293.

28 See his essay on *Little Dorrit* in *Literature and Politics in the Nineteenth Century*, ed. John Lucas (1971) p. 103.

29 Arnold, *Lectures and Essays, op. cit.*, p.281.
30 *Memoirs of A Social Atom* (1903) i, p.237.
31 See my pages on him in John Lucas, *The Melancholy Man: A Study of Dickens's Novels* (1970) pp.307-10.
32 G.Lukacs, *Studies in European Realism* (1964) p.98.
33 Preface to the *Poems*; *Poetical Works*, ed. cit., p.xxix.
34 See my essay on Dickens in *Tradition and Tolerance in Nineteenth Century Fiction*, ed. D.Howard and others (1966); and also the chapter on *Oliver Twist* in *The Melancholy Man*.
35 Wm. Morris, *News from Nowhere*, in *Three Works by William Morris*, ed. A.L.Morton (1968) p.320.
36 *The Crack-Up and Other Essays* (1956) p.69.
37 George Orwell, *Collected Essays* (1970) i, 456.
38 *Essays of George Eliot*, ed. Pinney (1963) p.271.
39 W.C.Preston or Andrew Mearns, *The Bitter Cry of Outcast London* (1883) p.17.
40 *Essays of George Eliot op. cit.*, p.272.

Chapter 7

The Victorians and Water

In this essay I want to set myself to answer a simple question: what happened to the Victorians when they discovered that they had no clean water? Behind that question lurks another one, of course: what did they do about it? Now one might want to ask why the questions should be put in the first place. What is so strange about having to accept the fact of pollution? We live in a world of dirty water, and there's an end on't, as Dr Johnson might well have observed. Yet as it happens Johnson did not observe, or perceive, this fact, nor did the generations that came immediately after him. And this isn't so much a matter of whether they had clean rivers, streams, ponds and lakes, as of whether they were conscious of the possibility of pollution. For consciousness is all, and what interests me is a radical change that occurred in the consciousness of Victorian people once they perceived that their waters were not clean.

The change in consciousness is inseparable from the perception. I can put this simply enough if I remark that by the eighteenth century the Thames was a decidedly dirty river, but — Swift apart — that few perceived of it as being so. Certainly such a perception did not intrude on the more usual assumption that the river could still be accommodated to Spenser's 'Sweet Thames'. And the literature that the Augustans wrote typically depended on taking this assumption for truth. How otherwise could Pope invoke the Thames as a river whose mythic properties teasingly but properly take their place in 'The Rape of the Lock'?

> But now secure the painted vessel glides,
> The Sun-beams trembling on the floating Tydes,
> While melting Musick steals upon the Sky,
> And soften'd Sounds along the Waters die.
> Smooth flow the Waves, the Zephyrs gently play,
> Belinda smil'd, and all the World was gay.[1]

116

And we may also note that Pope's contemporaries saw nothing odd in calling upon Canaletto and Handel to celebrate the Thames, in paint and music. The Thames is the modern Tiber or Euphrates: it is to be identified with trade, beauty, wealth and the civic and social arts. No wonder, then, that most Augustans should choose not to notice that it was actually dirty.[2]

Yet the symbolic properties of water have less to do with its capacity to evoke a sense of the triumph of the city, than with its cleansing, purifying powers. Water washes away grime, it purges the sins of the world; and it absolves the corruptions of the flesh. In other words, water has a crucial role to play in both secular and religious literature, the literature which the Victorians inherited, and which they attempted to write. They sang in their churches hymns and psalms which referred to and celebrated the cleansing powers of water, and for many of them washing away the world's taints was almost inextricably interwoven with ridding themselves, at least by vicarious means, of the inequities of the social order and the dirt of labour and circumstance. They encountered in their bibles and in secular literature, whether prose, poetry or drama, celebrations of water's purifying properties; and they looked at paintings which equally celebrated such properties. In short, their imaginative experience was to an extent we can only guess at conditioned by the idea of clean water. So what happened when they found that in fact there wasn't any? What happened, for example, when Victorian congregations listened to Isaiah's words, promising that for him 'that walketh righteously ... his waters shall be sure' (Isaiah, 33:16)? What went through their minds when they heard or read Ezekiel's account of how the Lord God said to his chosen people, 'Then will I sprinkle clean water upon you, and ye shall be clean: from all your filthiness, and from all your idols, I will cleanse you' (Ezekiel, 34:25)? What did they think when they sang together Cowper's hymn, 'O Lord, I will praise Thee,' in which the following verse occurs: 'Here, in the fair gospel-field, / Wells of free salvation yield / Streams of life, a plenteous store, / And my soul shall thirst no more'?

These questions have to be asked, simply because by Victorian times those waters to which Isaiah referred were anything but sure, Ezekiel's had become incapable of cleansing, and the wells which Cowper confidently invoked as yielding streams of life in plenteous store were in fact much more likely to produce haphazard runnels of water clogged with ordure, offal, débris and industrial filth. In short, the majority of people who listened to and read the bible, who sang their churches' hymns, who read or saw *The Tempest*, or who quoted Spenser's *Prothalamion*, lived in a country where, no matter what the resonance of appeal to clean water might be, it was becoming impossible to believe that such water existed.

Given that suddenly-enforced perception, what would Victorians have made of Blake's 'The Chimney Sweeper', from *Songs of Innocence*?

> When my mother died I was very young,
> And my father sold me while yet my tongue
> Could scarcely cry weep weep weep weep.
> So your chimneys I sweep and in soot I sleep.
>
> There's little Tom Dacre, who cried when his head
> That curl'd like a lambs back, was shav'd, so I said,
> Hush Tom never mind it, for when your head's bare,
> You know that the soot cannot spoil your white hair.
>
> And so he was quiet, and that very night,
> As Tom was a sleeping he had such a sight,
> That thousands of sweepers Dick, Joe, Ned and Jack
> Were all of them lock'd up in coffins of black,
>
> And by came an Angel who had a bright key,
> And he open'd the coffin and set them all free.
> Then down a green plain leaping laughing they run
> And wash in a river and shine in the Sun.
>
> Then naked and white, all their bags left behind,
> They rise upon clouds, and sport in the wind.
> And the Angel told Tom, if he'd be a good boy,
> He'd have God for his father and never want joy.
>
> And so Tom awoke and we rose in the dark
> And got with our bags and our brushes to work.
> Tho' the morning was cold, Tom was happy and warm.
> So if all do their duty, they need not fear harm.[3]

One might, of course, say that the Victorians wouldn't have

made much of it for the very good reason that Blake was not well known to them. Yet this ceases to be true by the 1850s, and it is surely the case that one of the things they made of it found expression in Kingsley's *The Water Babies*. The boy hero of Kingsley's tale is called Tom, and he escapes from his brutal master and falls into a river, in which he is miraculously cleansed. (The master's name, by the way, is Grimes, a good name for a chimney-sweep, but surely owing most to Crabbe and his drunken, brutal master of terrified apprentices?) There are, it almost goes without saying, important differences between Blake's poem and Kingsley's tale. As we might expect, *The Water Babies* is more explicitly moral, and its tone is often hectoring. (Children's literature was becoming big business by mid-Victorian times, and with that went an increased desire to preach *at* innocence rather than speak *of* it.) In the second place, Kingsley will have nothing to do with the radical political implications of Blake's poem. For those children who 'wash in a river and shine in the sun' embody a potentially revolutionary force, as one can see not merely from the poem but from the illustration which Blake made for it. Their upstretched arms, the dance-like, if badly drawn, glory of the children, tell of energies which are innocently good, and whose exuberance inevitably threatens the world which seeks to constrain them. Each child is an emblem of those qualities associated with 'Glad Day', an image which Blake had first produced in 1780, where it bore the legend 'Albion Rose' or 'The Dance of Albion', and where it can be related to the dramatic fragment 'King Edward the Third', which was published in Blake's *Poetical Sketches*, in 1783, but which had almost certainly been written some years previously. 'Good morrow, brave Sir Thomas; the bright morn / Smiles on your army, and the gallant sun / Springs from the hills like a young hero / Into the battle, shaking his golden locks / Exultingly; this is a promising day.'[4] The sweepers' baptism is the prelude to their overthrow of old corruption. (So much for those, like E. D. Hirsch, who believe that there is no revolutionary intention in *Songs of Innocence*.)

There is no such intent in *The Water Babies*. Indeed, as we can see from the illustrations to the text, after his baptism Tom becomes a model Bengers' baby, on whose skin Pears' soap could hope to make no improvement. The message of *The Water Babies* is one of conformity, not revolutionary force. The great unwashed have only to wash or to be washed in order to take their place within society, which is precisely what you would expect from the author of *Alton Locke*.

But for my present purpose the most important difference between Blake and Kingsley is this: that whereas the river in which Blake's Tom Dacre and his fellow-apprentices bathe and from which they emerge to shine in the sun could easily be the Thames — it is simply 'a' river, and Blake is after all very much a London poet — the river into which Kingsley's child-hero tumbles runs through countryside in and around Wharfedale, in west Yorkshire. And Tom hears the river singing this song:

> Clear and cool, clear and cool,
> By laughing shallow, and dreaming pool,
> Cool and clear, cool and clear,
> By shining shingle and foaming weir;
> Under the crag where the ouzel sings,
> And the ivied wall where the church-bell rings,
> Undefiled, for the undefiled.
> Play by me, bathe in me, mother and child.

Undefiled when it runs beneath Godale Scar, perhaps, but not further on, for the river also sings:

> Dank and foul, dank and foul,
> By the smoky town in its smoky cowl;
> Foul and dank, foul and dank,
> By wharf and sewer and slimy bank;
> Darker and darker the further I go,
> Baser and baser the richer I grow;
> Who dare sport with the sin-defiled?
> Shrink from me, turn from me, mother and child.[5]

Money, dirt and squalor have now become the visible signs of 'sin' — Kingsley's Christian socialism is of course in evidence here. And as a result the unthinkable has happened. That which should cleanse from defilement has itself become defiled. The baffling horror of such a paradox hardly needs to be spelt out. 'If the salt has lost its savour...'

Songs of Innocence was published in 1789, *The Water Babies* in 1863. Long before then, however, the Thames had become perceived as a river of such filth that it could not possibly serve the purposes of Kingsley's fiction. And, to repeat, it is the perception that counts. Wordsworth, lover of clean streams and lakes, stood on Westminster Bridge in 1802 and proclaimed that 'Earth hath not anything to show more fair: / Dull would he be of soul who could pass by / A sight so touching in its majesty.' 'The river', he added, 'glideth at his own sweet will.' And one hears how the Spenserian 'sweet' falls snugly, even inevitably, into place. Fifty years later you could still find pictorial images of London which self-consciously attempt to endorse the Wordsworthian claim that 'all that mighty heart is lying still'. An example is Henry Pether's night-time view of the Tower of London from the Thames, which was painted sometime between 1850-1855. Yet the truer and certainly more widely-shared perception is that which Dickens provides at the opening of *Bleak House* (1853). 'Fog everywhere. Fog up the river, where it flows away in green aits and meadows; fog down the river, where it rolls defiled among the tiers of shipping, and the waterside pollution of a great (and dirty) city.' Kingsley's river became 'sin-defiled' as it passed into a town (presumably Leeds). Dickens's Thames is similarly 'defiled'; and one has only to take the major meanings of the word 'defile' to realise how powerful were the implications intended by both writers. For the *Oxford English Dictionary* offers us these then current definitions: ' "defile": to violate the chastity of; to debauch. To corrupt, taint, sully. To render morally foul. To render ceremonially unclean.' Thus, to speak of the river as being defiled is to imply strong ethical, metaphysical and religious objections to what has happened to it.

It should come as no surprise, therefore, to discover that there were some who pretended that the worst had not happened, who as it were muttered to themselves, 'this is *not* the promised end, nor image of such horror', and who claimed a true perception of water's retained cleanliness. One might, for example, consider in this context Millais's 'The Death of Ophelia' painted 1851-2, which hints at the possibility of a watery, but purgatorially cleansing death, and whose inevitable nostalgia may be linked to a painting by F. W. Watts, 'A Suffolk Landscape', which looks for all the world as though it must be a Constable, and yet which was painted some twenty to thirty years later. And one might also consider the clear-running Thames in Matthew Arnold's 'The Scholar Gipsy', which is set back some two centuries before its date of publication, in 1853. The pastness of the past has become complete, and not merely because of the town's steady and inevitable invasion of the countryside, as exemplified in Cruikshank's famous cartoon. There is also now that reason to fear death by water to which *Punch* got around to paying attention in 1858, by which time the connections between foul water and typhus and cholera were well known. (*Punch* as usual led from the rear.) Certainly Dickens had linked the river with death at least since *The Old Curiosity Shop*, where the malignant dwarf, Quilp, is drowned in the Thames. And Quilp has an appropriately foul, tumble-down summer house on its banks, evidence of an anti-pastoral that decisively inverts that Augustan view of the river as associated with Spenserian and other pastoral values, and typified in Zoffany's companion-piece pictures of 'Mr and Mrs Garrick taking Tea on Their Lawn at Hampton', and 'Mr and Mrs Garrick at the Shakespeare Temple'. In stark contrast, Quilp's house is in 'an advanced state of decay, and overlooking the slimy banks of a great river ... ' (Chapter 51). The taking of tea in Quilp's house wickedly opposes the values Zoffany celebrates. And Dickens's linking of the river with death continues through to his last complete novel, *Our Mutual Friend,* which opens with that unforgettable account of Gaffer Hexam fishing a dead body out of the Thames's foul waters.

Dickens was not alone in this perception. Indeed, by the 1840s the view from the bridge was not likely to endorse Wordsworth's sense of the river gliding at his own sweet will. Thus, when in 1843, Engels stood on Ducie Bridge in Manchester and looked down on the River Irk, what he saw was

a narrow, coal-black, foul-smelling stream, full of *débris* and refuse, which it deposits on the shallower right bank. In dry weather, a long string of the most disgusting, blackish-green, slime pools are left standing on this bank, from the depths of which bubbles of miasmatic gas constantly arise and give forth a stench unendurable even on the bridge forty to fifty feet above the surface of the stream. But besides this, the stream is checked every few paces by high weirs, behind which slime and refuse accumulate and rot in thick masses.[6]

I have quoted a few sentences of what is in fact a very long, precisely insistent account of the horrific spectacle that the Irk presented, but I do not need to quote it all. For the major point is clear enough: that you couldn't hope to wash in *that* river and then shine in the sun. Nor could you hope to do so in the stream which Ruskin saw, a few years later, just outside Rochdale, 'black as ebony, and thick with curdling scum; the bank above it trodden with unctuous, sooty slime'.[7]

In short, evidence of the newly perceived foulness of England's rivers was all around, once you started to look. And if one asks *why* people looked, *why* they began to perceive what the rivers were truly like, the answer is both that the evidence thrust itself at their eyes and nostrils, and also that Chadwick's famous reports of the 1840s made it inevitable that the Victorians were forced to come to terms with the fact that their rivers were no longer typically 'sweet', and couldn't be described or imaged in terms that had been possible in earlier ages. So that what happened to the Victorians when they discovered that they had no clean water was that they went out of their way to insist that this was so, even though some of them sought refuge in a past of clean water, and indulged that nostalgia which is, I think, inevitable in any society where change happens with the rapidity it did in the middle years of the nineteenth century. There is, in other words, an orgy of self-condemnation, an eager readiness to accept that England's rivers are not so much part of a worldly paradise as a worldly hell.

And yet at the same time there is the determination to try to reverse circumstances, to do something about the newly-perceived foul waters. For the discovery that one couldn't invoke images of its cleansing, purgatorial and purifying qualities did not lead to a kind of imaginative or intellectual paralysis: on the contrary, it spawned an enormous creative endeavour which was put at the service of recovering paradise. I do not think there is any need to spell out the practical details involved in working for this recovery, but they are certainly stupendous and deserve our admiration. We may, of course, say that it was appalling that so many cities should have been allowed, like Topsy, to just grow: but given the fact of the growth and the effect on their inhabitants of precisely that lack of sanitation and clean-water supply that could have made life more bearable and, literally, livable, it is nonetheless astonishing how much was achieved, how quickly, how efficiently, and how ingeniously. Suppose, for example, one says that it does not speak well for Liverpool, a great and notoriously overcrowded city with regular and appalling outbreaks of typhus, that it appointed its first medical officer, Dr William Henry Duncan, only *after* the publication of Chadwick's Report. And suppose we add that even doing that much was probably influenced by the fact that Duncan's own 'Report on the Sanitary State of the Labouring Classes in the town of Liverpool' was one of the appendices to Chadwick. We must surely add that the appointment of Duncan was a very proper move. It hurried up legislation for the sanitary regulations of clean water supplies, and by the 1850s Liverpool was well advanced in making such supplies available to the vast majority of its inhabitants. And that is a very impressive achievement, especially when one realises that clean water had previously been available only for a small minority who could afford to pay for it, and who therefore did pay for it — to private water companies.

And when we recall that many large towns, Manchester for one, simply didn't have a charter and therefore because they were not incorporated lacked any of the municipal powers which could enact the necessary legislation, must we not be impressed by the speed at which charters were secured and legislation introduced? Of course, there were delays and there were examples of the kind of thick-skinned insensitiveness that one might expect from government anywhere, at any time. (The case of Leeds is a good example, for its conservative council in the 1860s objected to the levying of rates to obtain the water supply and changed their minds only after a particularly nasty outbreak of cholera which threatened everyone's health, their own included.)[8] But given all that, we have still to admire the passion and power which went into the largely successful efforts to supply clean water and so get rid of plague and with it much of the sheer horror of city life.

The Victorians had every right to be proud of what they achieved and they were indeed proud of their achievement. The evidence of that pride can be seen in the pumping stations that were built throughout England during the second half of the nineteenth century and which are still regular features of our landscapes. They have been called temples to steam and they might even more properly be called temples to clean water.

You couldn't call earlier stations — or sheds — temples. They were purely functional buildings, of no architectural merit: plain, unambitious, as best self-effacing, at worst boring. One has only to look, for example, at the shed of Botallack, Cornwall, built in the very early years of the nineteenth century, or of Tregurtha Downs, Cornwall, of roughly the same date, and then to compare them with the station at Bilston, 1895, or that at Ryehope, built in 1860, to see the extent of the change. Ryehope is indeed something in the manner of a temple, as its interior reveals: because its four support columns, which are a design necessity, controlling as they do the space and movement of the beam engines housed within the temple, become also an opportunity for embellishment, for decoration, for architectural ingenuity and inventiveness: in a word, an opportunity for the display of civic pride. The entire entablature, architrave, corbels, capitals, all speak of it, though Ryehope is comparatively chaste, even severe, by comparison with others.

Not all the evidence of that pride has survived. Take Whitacre pumping station, for example. Whitacre was opened in 1884, and it served a large area of Birmingham. It was vast, and probably the most impressive building created by the city. The privately owned Birmingham Water Works company had been set up in 1826 and not until 1875 were the various stations brought under the control of the municipal authorities. As Derek Fraser points out in his *Power and Authority in the Victorian City*, Birmingham was decidedly sluggish in initiating municipal reform, though not as sluggish as some, and it was only in the 1870s that what he calls its civic renaissance really began. The city's private water company vigorously defended its rights in Parliament, but 'Public health triumphed over private commerce . . . ' On 2 August 1875 'the royal assent was given to the Birmingham Corporation's gas and water bills, establishing the city as a centre of municipal collectivism, or as it was soon to be called "gas and water socialism".'[9]

The outstanding result of this assent was Whitacre. Indeed, the *Engineer* was sufficiently impressed by its splendour to devote several issues to it, running from July through to September 1885,[10] including illustrations of the design drawings for the Station.

In his study of *Thomas Hardy and British Poetry*, Donald Davie remarks that there is an analogy to be drawn between Hardy's poetry and 'Victorian civil engineering, which topped off an iron bridge or a granite waterworks with Gothic finials'.[11] The absolute wrongness of this remark comes about not merely because hardly any waterworks were built of granite; nor is it to be indicated by Davie's dismissive phrase about 'topping off', which I think I can show to be absurdly demeaning. No, the crucial error is in implying that those waterworks were typically Gothic. Of course, there were pumping stations whose architects had obviously been influenced by Pugin, and by Pugin's epigoni; and Ryehope is a perfectly good example of that. Pugin's *Contrasts* appeared in 1841, and if we do as we are always enjoined by architectural historians and allow twenty years for the news of the latest fashion to hit the provinces, we shall see that Ryehope fits perfectly well with that revival of Gothic which was so marked a feature of mid-Victorian architecture. But Gothic was by no means the only style in which such stations were built, and I very much doubt whether it was the dominant one. Consider the pumping station of Hopwas, for example, which was built ten years later than Ryehope, and which served the town of Tamworth. Hopwas is by no means a spectacular example of architectural achievement; it is on a modest scale, and is not particularly successful. Nonetheless, it plainly owes much more to the 'Queen Anne' Style, which Mark Girouard has written about in his definitive *Sweetness and Light: The 'Queen Anne' Movement, 1860-1900*, than it does to Pugin.

I don't think it matters that Girouard should make no mention of Hopwas in his study. As I say, it is not particularly successful, although it has attractive features, including the mouldings of the windows; and the interior is not without style and a well-judged sense of proportion. I do, however, think it extraordinary that he should have nothing whatsoever to say about any pumping-station built in the Queen Anne style, especially since among the number that were is one that is something of a masterpiece: Hatton, near Stone, built in 1890. One might, I suppose, call Hatton a kind of bastardised Palladian, rather than Queen Anne, given its use of the central building supported, almost equally, by the outer-buildings on either side (in Palladian domestic architecture they would be the wings of the house). Yet what I find truly remarkable is the fact that this is an entirely functional building, and even so has a grace and pride of execution which makes the functionalism of Bauhaus seem very thin beer by comparison. There is a justifiable confidence about the building to which one is invited to respond. It confronts the road and the spectator with an unmistakable air of achievement, and spells out in large what Hopwas spelt out in little, with its fountain at which the people of Tamworth were invited to drink. (Unfortunately the invocation to drink of the *free* water has now been taken away for safe keeping.)

The name of Hatton's architect is not known. Nor is the architect of Hopwas. Of course, it will be possible to find out who they were by consulting the relevant County Records Offices. Yet I do not think the matter of great importance. For the fact is that the architects would have been appointed by the engineers, who themselves would have been appointed by the municipal bodies, so that one gets a very proper sense of genuine collaboration, in which architect is *part* of the achievement of clean water, and is content to identify his art with that achievement. In a review article about J. Mordaunt Crook's recent study of William Burges, David Brook remarks that 'the effort of believing in him as a great architect is made no easier by what appears to be the great man's alarming ignorance of his calling. One must worry about an architect who regarded the engineer as "the real nineteenth century architect" especially as his "aesthetic was essentially atectonic".'[12] Must one? Burges' regard seems to me entirely proper; and it was plainly shared by many of his less famous contemporaries. One sees the evidence of that not merely — or even so much — in Hatton's outer buildings, as in the interior work, though like Whitacre the interior of Hatton has been more or less gutted. But the most remarkable evidence of how the architect could express pride in the engineering achievement of clean water is to be found in the decoration, which is certainly to be linked with the Queen Anne movement.

The Queen Anne style was, of course, ideal for expressing such decoration. For it specialised in work that made use of flower motifs, of swags that in their genteel way recalled a classical concern with natural fruitfulness; and so on. The finest of all architects working in the style, Norman Shaw, favoured the use of sunflowers — as Girouard says, he may have got them from Burne-Jones; and he used them almost as a personal signature: for example, at 196 Queen's Gate, Kensington, which he built between 1874 and 1876; and again at 68 Cadogan Square, Chelsea, 1877-8. But it caught on: one can see it in the decoration to a house built at Leek, in 1885, the architect possibly being L. Sugden. Leek, of course, is not far from Stone; and if one considers the decoration at Hatton, built five years later, one finds that among other features there is a shell-like cusp supported by the fish-head; sporting dolphins; a swan and water-lily; and a cornucopia above the main entrance. All these motifs are part of that Queen Anne style which is in fact much more important than Gothic during the second half of the nineteenth century, in England at all events. But the really important point is surely this: that they are precise expressions of the achievement of clean water. Fish, flower and fowl all bespeak the achievement, and it is above all signalled by the cornucopia which promises that because of what's within — the great beam-engines which pumped out thousands of gallons of pure water by the hour — the citizens of the town of Stone could be promised boundless fruition, health, foison. It is as though the country-house ideal has been revived, but now its health and vitality are not the property of private individuals or families, who scatter beneficence upon the land. And one might claim for it in a degree which is hardly true even of Penshurst that it was 'reared with no man's ruin, no man's groan'. The house is therefore a justifiable expression of civic pride.

I suspect that the same might be said of most pumping-stations, but I have no wish to provide a detailed account of what they looked like. I want merely to note that one of the important expressions of the Victorian imagination lay in those stations, whether they were country-house style, such as Hatton, or castle-keep style, such as Sandfields, originally built in 1858 and then re-built in 1872, and whose majestic interior suggests a cathedral perhaps more than a temple. There is point to such analogy. For if we think of Kingsley's phrase 'sin-defiled' or Dickens's 'defiled' we surely recognise that the Victorians were apt to think that they had destroyed not just England's but God's green and pleasant land, and their ability to recover that land, to undo the defilement of the waters, would inevitably have for them subdued but genuine religious overtones. That is why it seems to me that those regularly repeated four columns had a significance we scarcely appreciate. For they suggest or provide an echo of the approach to the altar, the beam-engines being part of the choir, or perhaps congregation: the columns dividing choir from nave and implying even the transept. I don't think it in any way fanciful or blasphemous to suggest this, because it is precisely what those interiors themselves suggest, even insist upon. And they do so with an impressive solemnity and/or ebullience to which we must respond.

There is at least one occasion known to me when this transforms itself into a celebration that is akin to festival, and I wish to say just a little about the pumping-station at Papplewick, which is just outside Nottingham.

Like Whitacre, Papplewick was built in 1884, but unlike Whitacre it is small and has so far escaped the attentions of the Severn-Trent Water Authority that it has its own Trust and is in steam at regular intervals throughout the year. It may also be visited most week-ends. It is not all that prepossessing from the outside. A touch of Queen Anne, maybe, and the finials have the kinds of motif—birds leaving or returning to the procreant cradle — of which the Ruskin of the *Nature of Gothic* would have approved. But the wonder of Papplewick is its interior. For it is the most joyous celebration of the achievement of clean water that I know, and as a result of which joy is transformed into art; anonymous, to be sure. For although we know that the name of the engineer was Ogle Tarbotton, we do not know the architect's name, any more than we know the names of all those who must have assisted in the decorative work of the interior. But again, I do not think it matters: the anonymity is almost the point. This is a civic achievement. (All privately owned undertakings were transferred to the Corporation in 1880, by which time the water supply was in a very bad state.) Thus Papplewick is a kind of civic hymn to clean water.

Hymn is appropriate. For as you go in the main door you see the four columns / pillars ahead of you, and the beam-engines on either side, as though they pack the aisles and celebrate their own accomplishment. But look more closely at the pillars, and you see that the copper-work describes water plants with fish swimming through them. Let your eye travel up and it will be met by what might well appear as a pulpit lamp, let it move transversely and you see that the capitals are decorated with water-ibis, witty-mannerist-style corbels which recall the eagles of Whitacre but which have an iconographic resonance that the eagles lack; climb up to the first storey and you can look, as though from the choir's balcony, into the body of the station, in order to appreciate the lovely light sense of Papplewick's interior. Study the windows and you see that they are hand-painted glass, appropriate to a church. Look again, and you see that the paintings are of water-life: of flowers and bugs and all those things that thrive on and in clean water.

Look again at the detail of the machinery. Look at the handsome dishes that lie under the great arms of the engines themselves. They are both decorative and functional, for they are there to make sure that no speck of oil can fall 800 or so feet into the well which has been dug — by mining engineers — below Papplewick, so that Nottingham may have clean water. No boys are, or were, allowed into Papplewick, for fear that they might pee against trees and so infect the soil and then the water. And for that same reason staff were not allowed to keep pigs, and dogs were prohibited. In short, Papplewick is not only an expression of creative pride, it also testifies to an extraordinarily detailed thoroughness. It has about it that air which Dickens identified as belonging to Daniel Doyce:

There was something almost ludicrous in the complete irreconcilability of a vague conventional notion that he must be a visionary man, with the precise, sagacious travelling of his eye and thumb over the plans, their patient stoppages at particular points, their careful returns to other points whence little channels of explanation had to be traced up, and his steady manner of making everything good and everything sound ... His dismissal of himself from his description, was hardly less remarkable. He never said, I discovered this adaptation or invented that combination; but showed the whole thing as if the Divine artificer had made it, and he happened to find it. *(Little Dorrit,* Book 2, Chapter 8).

Doyce's self-abnegation is very like the anonymity of the architects of Victorian pumping-stations. Yet Dickens's celebration of Doyce's achievements brings me to my last point. For the truth is that literary people of the period were remarkable indifferent to the great engineering achievements that lay all around them. Dickens apart, we can point to Elizabeth Gaskell's depiction of the engineer Holdsworth in her wonderful story, *Cousin Phillis*, to the engineer Fergus Derrick, of Frances Hodgson Burnett's *That Lass O'Lowrie's*, published in 1887, and so far as I know, almost entirely forgotten; and we must of course mention Kipling's 'McAndrew's Hymn'. But that is about it.

It is perhaps because the literary world more or less conspired to ignore them that those who provided Victorian England with clean water felt themselves obliged to celebrate their achievements. If that is so, it is entirely proper, for it is a proud celebration of civic, *public* achievement; against which the efforts of the individual hardly count.

Notes

1   Twickenham edition of the *Poems of Alexander Pope*, Vol. II, p. 162.
2   It is only in satiric literature that the truth is admitted.
3   Blake, *Songs of Innocence and Experience,* Oxford University Press Reprint (1970).
4   See *William Blake* by Martin Butlin, Tate Gallery, (1978) p.30.
5   *The Water Babies*, Everyman edition, p.27.
6   F. Engels. *The Condition of the Working Class in England in 1844,* p.83.
7   Ruskin, *The Two Paths, Works* Vol. XVI, p. 338.
8   See Derek Fraser, *Power and Authority in the Victorian City,* Blackwell 1979.
9   *Ibid* pp. 107-8
10 *The Engineer*, Vol. XL, Pt. 2., July-December 1885.
11 Davie, *Thomas Hardy and British Poetry*, (1973) p.23
12 See David Brook, 'Builder of Dreams', *Quarto* (November 1981) p. 5.

Chapter 8

Tilting at the Moderns: W. H. Mallock's Criticisms of the Positivist Spirit

I

THE publication of *The New Republic* in 1877 made its author, W. H. Mallock, immediately famous. It was reviewed by almost the entire spectrum of the press, from the august quarterlies to the daily newspapers; and it was widely read. In a letter from Longleate, dated October 1877, Lady Paget remarked: 'People here rave about "The New Republic", although half of them don't understand it'.[1] T. H. S. Escott noted that 'No new writer of later Victorian days, following Laurence Oliphant, made more of a hit than Mr W. H. Mallock with his *New Republic*'.[2] And no less a celebrity than Disraeli was delighted with the book. In a letter to Lady Dorothy Nevill he said that 'It is a capital performance, and the writer will, I fancy, take an eminent position in our future literature'.[3] And on another occasion he told Violet Fane:

I place ... the 'New Republic' in a genuinely original trio, appearing within half a century. First in order of time came my own 'Popanilla' in 1828; then (looking towards Laurence Oliphant, who happened to be of the company) 'Piccadilly'; and now, 1877, the 'New Republic'. With these exceptions, in that department of satire and fantasy to which they belonged, I cannot recall any other works owing so little in idea and execution to other writers of the time.[4]

Mallock, of course, became a 'lion', as Augustus Hare recalled:

On Saturday night I was at a pleasant party at Lord Houghton's, meeting scarcely anyone but authors, and a very odd collection — Black, Yates and James the novelists; Sir Francis Doyle and Swinburne the poets; Mrs Singleton the erotic poetess ... ; Mallock, who has suddenly become a lion from having written a clever squib called The New Republic.[5]

132

The novelist referred to as 'James', is, presumably, Henry James, who recorded his own impression of Mallock. In the section of *The Conquest of London* concerned with James's entry into society, Leon Edel writes:

There is also W. H. Mallock, then the talk of London because his *New Republic* had just been published, 'a most disagreeable and unsympathetic youth, with natural bad manners increased by the odious London affectation of none. He strikes me as "awfully clever", but I opine that he will produce no other spontaneous or fruitful thing'.[6]

The tartness of James's judgement shouldn't blind us to the fact that he thought Mallock worthy of note. And just how wide Mallock's fame spread is suggested, I think, in a serial *Punch* ran throughout the latter half of 1877, called 'A Few Days in a Country House'.[7] The title and method — of dialogue between figures conceived as 'typical' — recall *The New Republic*, as by contrast does the matter of the dialogues: discussions of fishing, horse-racing, town-fashions are meant to show what really goes on in a country house.

In his *Memoirs* Mallock says that when he finished *The New Republic* he felt that his 'sense of the absurdities of current liberal philosophy had not even yet exhausted itself; and I presently supplemented that work by another — *The New Paul and Virginia,* or *Positivism on an Island*, a short satirical study in the style of Voltaire's *Candide'*.[8] And he adds:

The New Paul and Virginia was followed some two years later by *Is Life Worth Living?* a formal philosophical treatise, in which the values of life and their connection with religious belief, the methods of fiction being abandoned, were submitted to scientific analysis.[9]

Two other works naturally fit into the same area of Mallock's concerns. In 1881 he published a novel, *A Romance of the Nineteenth Century*. Of this, he notes that

a closer and wider acquaintance with the kind of life in question [social life in London and elsewhere], and the sorrows and passions masked by it, prompted me to translate the argument of [*The New Republic, The New Paul and Virginia* and *Is Life Worth Living?*] into yet another form, namely, that of a tragic novel — *A Romance of the Nineteenth Century.*[10]

Finally, in 1884 he brought out *Atheism and the Value of Life*, which contained five essays previously published in *The*

Edinburgh Review and *The Nineteenth Century*, all of which deal with the problems exercising him in the works mentioned above.[11]

These four books form a coherent body of work, and can properly be discussed together. They represent a sustained attempt on Mallock's part to justify the reputation of a considerable critic of Victorian society that *The New Republic* had earned him, and because they are intendedly polemical they engage with many famous names and important ideas. It is this that makes them peculiarly worth studying, and Mallock's conservative standpoint in religious, political, social and artistic matters, is firmly enough based to enable him to expose several limitations in his opponents' positions.

Mallock's adherence to his standpoint is well-nigh unbudgeable, so there is little point in exercising caution over comparison of the works with which I am concerned, because his ideas, as quotation will make clear, don't at all change from one to another; and though there may well be inconsistencies, not to say contradictions, this is to be attributed less to shifts of view-point than carelessness. The three main concerns of these works are: an attack on contemporary optimism and earnestness; a belief that positivism is an irrelevant answer to nineteenth-century problems; and a theory about 'modern love'. These concerns suggest how wide-ranging a controversialist Mallock is. Not a profound one, certainly, but he touches later Victorian life and ideas at so many points that an investigation of his works is one of the best ways to focus attention on the age. They not only light up several of its dark corners, they illuminate from unfamiliar angles what went on at the centre. To read Mallock is to become freshly aware of just how various and complex the period in fact was.

II

Although Mallock speaks of *The New Republic* being 'presently supplemented' by *The New Paul and Virginia*, this is a little misleading, for he was at work on the latter whilst *The New Republic* was appearing in *Belgravia*. Two letters in the Chatto and Windus office files show this.[12] The first is from the publishers to Mallock, and is dated 9 December 1876. It mentions an enclosed cheque for *The New Republic*, and continues: 'The "Belgravia" is already made up for the next few months, but we should like to see the concluding portion of your "The New Candide" before deciding upon it.'

Mallock's reply is from Bornehill, his father's house near Dartington in Devon, and is dated 12 December 1876. He acknowledges receipt of the cheque, and tells the publishers that

I will send you the concluding chapter of the short romance of which you have the beginning as soon as I have finished the complete edition of The New Republic. It — 'The New Candide' — would not take me, I find on looking on the MSS, more than a week or so to get finished. I could let you see the whole [illegible] about January 15th.

However, as matters turned out *The New Paul and Virginia* did not appear in *Belgravia*, but in *The Contemporary Review* for 1878.[13] The same year it was published without any alteration in book form by Chatto and Windus. In both cases it was called *The New Paul and Virginia*, and it is worth investigating a little this change of title, especially since in his *Memoirs* Mallock was to stress the kinship with *Candide*.[14]

In an essay on *The New Paul and Virginia* which he published in *Essays and Studies* (1955), P.M. Yarker notes:

Mallock twice referred to his debt to *Candide* for *The New Paul and Virginia*, but in neither case did he claim that the resemblance between the two books was more than superficial ... The book was not modelled on Voltaire, as *The New Republic* was modelled, for example, on Peacock. It was a trifle; it had none of the universal application of *Candide*, its depth or perennial relevance .... In writing it, Mallock simply selected certain features of Voltaire's satirical method which lent themselves to his purpose, and modified them to suit it better.

Yarker then makes a rather heavy-handed comparison of the two works, concluding that there are affinities of style, and that Mallock 'adapted Voltaire's method, rather than imitated it'.[15]

Yarker has missed the point here. For *The New Paul and Virginia* is a polemical work,[16] and the planned title is an important part of the polemic. That is, we can't really understand why the work was initially called *The New Candide* without understanding attitudes to Voltaire in the 1860s and

1870s. And these are significant enough to demand some investigation.

We may begin with Arnold:

A court of literature can never be very severe to Voltaire: with that inimitable wit and clear sense of his, he cannot write a page in which the fullest head may not find something suggestive: still, because, handling religious ideas, he yet, with all his wit and clear sense, handles them wholly without the power of edification, his fame as a great man is equivocal.[17]

And in his essay on Joubert, Arnold quotes approvingly his subject on Voltaire:

Voltaire is sometimes afflicted, sometimes strongly moved: but serious he never is. His very graces have an effrontery about them. He had correctness of judgement, liveliness of imagination, nimble wits, quick taste and a moral sense in ruins .... Those people who read him every day, create for themselves, by an invincible law, the necessity of liking him. But those people who, having given up reading him, gaze steadily down upon the influences which his spirit has shed abroad, find themselves in simple justice and duty compelled to detest him.

Of this, Arnold says: 'as the real definitive judgement on Voltaire, Joubert's is undoubtedly the true one'.[18] His lack of seriousness, his want of severity, and his handling of ideas without the power of edification: these are what worry Arnold about Voltaire. He doesn't seem to be in earnest.

Others were worried, too. 'The imaginative power', Ruskin says,

always purifies; the want of it therefore as essentially defiles; and as the wit-power is apt to develop itself through absence of imagination, it seems as if wit itself had a defiling tendency ... The *Candide* of Voltaire, in its gratuitous filth, its acute reasoning, and its entire vacuity of imagination, is a standard of what may perhaps be generally and fitly termed 'fimetic'[19] literature, still capable, by its wit, and partial truth, of a certain service in its way.[20]

That comes from a letter of *Fors Clavigera*, for October 1873, and it is clear that, like Arnold, Ruskin dislikes Voltaire's 'wit': it defiles rather than purifies, is, I think we may legitimately infer, opposed to the 'power of edification'.[21]

If we turn to the more specifically religious controversialists, we shall find that the same hostility shows itself. Of course we should expect the majority of the champions of the Church to dislike Voltaire intensely,[22] but it seems more surprising that those who see it as 'l'infame' should hesitate about their allegiance to him. Yet John Morley's study of Voltaire, which was first published in 1872, contains a highly revealing qualification of his general position of approval:

To admire Voltaire, cried a man who detested him, is the sign of a corrupt heart, and if anybody is drawn to his works, then be very sure that God does not love such an one. The truth of which that is so vehement a paraphrase amounts to this, that Voltaire has said no word, nor ever shown an indirect appreciation of any word said by another, which stirs or expands the emotional susceptibility, indefinite exultation, and far-swelling inner harmoney, which De Maistre and others have known as the love of God, and for which a better name, as covering most varieties of thought and manifestation, is holiness, deepest of all the words that defy definition. Through the affronts which his reason received from certain pretensions both in the writers and in some of those whose actions they commemorated, this sublime trait, in the Bible, in both portions of it, was unhappily lost to Voltaire. He had no ear for the finer vibrations of the spiritual voice.[23]

It isn't necessary to go to the lengths Basil Willey does in his *More Nineteenth Century Studies* and say that Morley shows himself in such passages to be essentially Christian;[24] it is enough simply to note that, by his pointing out Voltaire's failure to appreciate 'holiness', Morley places himself with Arnold and Ruskin.[25]

Now all three writers, in their accounts of Voltaire, share an attitude of mind which is readily accepted as dominant in Victorian thought: that is, earnestness. It hardly matters whether what they say of Voltaire is true or not, what *does* matter is how they agree to see him. Want of reverence, of seriousness, of earnestness, are seen as intolerable; they undermine all ideas of nobility, of striving for the truth. It is this catalogue of failings imputed to him that make even the agnostics feel uneasy about Voltaire, and it may be, too, that his persistent, caustic attacks on heroes and hero-worship aggravate their feelings.

The Victorian agnostics are forced to look uneasily over their shoulders at a previous age's great denier of Christian truth. But they cannot afford Voltaire's irreverent mockery because they are in the ascendancy, whereas he was very much an isolated figure. And since they *are* so important, they feel compelled to answer to charges that they are knocking the props from under traditional morality. Voltaire won't help them there. Indeed, a good deal of Victorian agnosticism answers to Huxley's description of Positivism as 'Catholicism minus Christianity'.[26] So the agnostics seek with an almost feverish eagerness to distinguish themselves from Voltaire and his spirit (which, by a quaint irony passes to some of the defenders of what Voltaire had condemned: orthodox Christians can afford to mock the pieties of Agnosticism, though the chance to do this is seized less often than might seem reasonable). And even where the name may be let alone, the spirit is under constant attack. So, for example, Arnold constantly urges a sense of seriousness on his contemporaries, and Ruskin complains to a captive audience: 'Our National mind and purpose are only to be amused: our National religion, the performance of church ceremonies, and preaching of soporific truths (or untruths) to keep the mob quietly at work, while we amuse ourselves. . .'.[27] The point I am making is well enough known, though it hasn't, I think, been noticed how Voltaire is used as a way of focussing it. But before going on I want to quote from what is perhaps the most considerable single attack on the Voltairean spirit: George Eliot's essay 'Debasing the Moral Currency', in the *Impressions of Theophrastus Such*. This appeared in 1879, and my feeling is that she has Mallock in mind in the attack she launches against Voltairean attitudes.[28] Certainly some of her terms are very close to those she used about *The New Republic*, in a letter to Mrs Ponsonby,[29] and since *The New Paul and Virginia* centres its attack on positivism, there is good reason to suppose she might be especially annoyed with him. She says:

The art of spoiling is within reach of the dullest faculty; the coarsest clown with a hammer in his hand might chip the nose off every statue and bust in the Vatican, and stand grinning at the effect of his work. Because wit is an exquisite product of high powers, we are not therefore forced to admit the sadly confused inference of the monotonous jester that he is establishing his superiority over every less facetious person, and over every topic on which he is ignorant or insensible, by being uneasy until he has distorted it in the small cracked mirror which he carries about with him as a joking apparatus.

A little later, she protests against

the burlesquing spirit which ranges to and fro and up and down on the earth, seeing no reason . . . why it should not appropriate every sacred, heroic and pathetic theme which served to make up the treasure of human admiration, hope, and love.

And later:

This is what I call debasing the moral currency: lowering the value of every inspiring fact and tradition so that it will command less and less of the spiritual products, the generous motives which sustain the charm and elevation of our social existence — the something besides bread by which man saves his soul alive.[30]

There can be little doubt that as a deliberate antagonist of positivism, Mallock chose initially to call his work *The New Candide*, and identified in particular its affinities with Voltaire's work, because he wanted to show that the seriousness of modern life was basically fraudulent, and that 'the treasure of human admiration, hope, and love' was fool's gold; we may note the motto on the title-page of *The New Republic*, 'All is laughter, all is dust, all is meaningless, for all the things that are arise out of the unreasonable', and see that for him the earnestness is silly because it is earnest about the wrong things. Once abandon God and the traditions of Christianity, and seriousness becomes a mockery. And, equally, optimism — which again suggests why he wanted to call his work *The New Candide*. The hope of which George Eliot speaks is, for Mallock, further delusion. Time and again he returns to these two points; and always to insist on the absurdity of holding fast by such earnest optimism. Thus *The New Candide* would be a highly relevant title for a work which satirises both attitudes.

This, however, brings us up against a problem. Why *didn't* Mallock call the work *The New Candide*, and why *did* he call it *The New Paul and Virginia* instead? The answer is, I believe, comparatively simple. He did not wish to be criticised for the wrong reason: that is, whilst his attitude was essentially Voltairean, explicit reference to Voltaire might only ensure the critical dismissal of his own work as not serious and therefore not worth serious consideration. If the attacks on optimism and the age's earnestness were to carry weight they must be freed from the taint of Voltaire: and of course it is always Mallock's claim to be deadly serious about what he attacks. I suspect that he changed the title in order to escape the wrong sort of criticism. *The New Paul and Virginia* suggested neatly enough a satire on Bernard St Pierre's sentimental optimism and yet freed him from the possible charge of levity. Or so he must have hoped. But in fact nearly all the reviews of *The New Paul and Virginia* were unfavourable, and most attacked its lack of seriousness.

The *Athenaeum* review strikes very much George Eliot's note: 'For such a writer to throw ridicule upon some of the most illustrious *savants* of the age is much as though he should write a satire upon the Indo-European theory of languages without a knowledge of Sanscrit.' And the same writer says sharply:

Suppose a true satirist had introduced, for the purpose of satirising Positivism, a male and female Positivist upon an uninhabited island to play Paul and Virginia there on altruistic principles. His notions of satirising the Positivist would not, we may be sure, have been like Mr Mallock's, which is as primitive and free from subtlety as that of a satirist of the Middle Ages — consisting, in short, of placing in absurd situations those with whose opinions he disagrees, and setting them to perform all sorts of buffooneries and repeat stock phrases.[31]

The *Westminster Review* is condescendingly cordial, and damns with loud praise:

Mr Mallock's 'New Paul and Virginia', will, like his 'New Republic', do good to the cause he ridicules. People who never before heard of the doctrine of evolution, and never knew the names of Tyndall and Clifford, will have their curiosity aroused. Nobody, we suppose, now fancies that ridicule is the test of truth . . . Scientific men believe too firmly in the doctrine of evolution to be disturbed by jokes, even good jokes. They can affort to laugh with Mr Mallock.

And the reviewer, affable to a degree, adds: 'We have certainly enjoyed the book. Mr Mallock's humour is refined and subtle. He possesses what is so rare in England — a light touch.'[32] It is a clever review, tricking the reader into admiring *The New Paul and Virginia* for quite the wrong reason.

The *Tablet* admired the satire for what Mallock no doubt took to be the right reason:

Perhaps no one but the author of the *New Republic* could have written this exceedingly clever paper. Mr Mallock has already shown how well acquainted he is with the writings of the whole modern school of philosophers, and how well qualified to criticise them. Those readers, but only those, who are conversant with the theories and the language of such men as Messrs

Frederic Harrison, Clifford, Tyndall, Herbert Spencer, Huxley and Darwin, will be able to appreciate the clever sarcasm of the present paper. We see on every page some sharp hit at one or other of these writers.[33]

And the reviewer goes to the extent of claiming that 'the whole paper is eminently readable, and will provide many a hearty laugh from those who understand its allusions and can appreciate the crushing severity of its blows.'[34] But this enthusiasm owes rather more, I think, to what Mallock was attacking than to how he managed it.

The notice in the *Nation* is the most balanced of all the reviews, perhaps because it was remote from the actual personalities attacked, and the particular ideologies involved. Reporting on the New York edition, published by Scribner and Welford, also in 1878, it begins:

'Positivism on an Island' pays the penalty of popularity by thus appearing in book-form. It was pre-eminently a *jeu d'esprit* that should have been allowed only the sparkle of a momentary existence. At first glance it seemed of doubtful value, and second thought is fatal to it.[35]

And the same point as the *Athenaeum* had made is also expressed, but with an interesting addition.

The impression deepens in the mind that Mr Mallock is not unlike the evangelical preacher ridiculing Popish mummeries of whose meaning he is ignorant — not unlike Diderot, whose wit played coarsely round the Immaculate Conception; in other words, that his satire has no sting of truth because he himself has no conception of the real significance of the doctrine he satirizes.[36]

The mention of Diderot is suggestive of how far Mallock failed to disguise the Voltairism of *The New Paul and Virginia*. Whether the criticisms made against this work are justified we must now attempt to discover; certainly they are united on this point, that Mallock attacks Positivism and that he does so in a spirit of burlesque. But we first have to tease out what he means by Positivism.

III

The *Westminster Review* closed its short and otherwise friendly notice of *The New Paul and Virginia* with a protest. Mallock should not ... have joined a Positivist head on to a Darwinian body in the person of his hero. Mr Harrison has little in common with the leaders of the evolutionist school. No critics have been so severe on the shortcomings of Comte as Tyndall, Huxley, and Herbert Spencer.[37]

It seems a fair criticism, even if Spencer is oddly placed. It is true that Huxley and Tyndall attacked Comte, and the former especially took great pains to separate his position from a positivist one. Equally, it is the case that Paul Darnley, the hero of *The New Paul and Virginia* combines elements of Huxley and Harrison. Yet, as I shall try to show, Mallock's handling of his hero has its justification; and it is subtler and more wounding than his treatment of Saunders in *The New Republic*.[38]

It will perhaps help if I set out the plot of *The New Paul and Virginia*. Professor Paul Darnley is on board 'The Australasian', homeward bound from a trip round the world which he has undertaken after completing 'three volumes on the origin of life ... five volumes on the entozoa of the pig, and two volumes of lectures, as a corollary to these, on the sublimity of heroism and the whole duty of man'. His wife, who is ugly, is not with him. Also on the boat is Virginia St John, a celebrated society beauty, who 'found herself at the age of thirty, mistress of nothing except a large fortune. She was now converted with surprising rapidity by a Ritualistic Priest, and she became in a few months a model of piety and devotion.' The Professor is in the middle of preaching a lay sermon when 'by a faithful conformity to the laws of matter, the boiler blew up, and *The Australasian* went down.' Of course he and Miss St John escape and get to an island which is ideally fitted to minister to their needs. From then on the Professor tries to convert the lady to altruism, while she tries to convert him to love. Two other characters show up but are summarily disposed of, and the tale ends with the arrival of Miss St John's bishop and the Professor's wife. Seeing her, the Professor exclaims:

'I do now indeed believe in hell.'
'And I', cried Virginia, with much greater tact, and rushing into the arms of her bishop, 'once more believe in heaven.'

As an appendix to the work, Mallock supplies a *sottisier* of statements by Tyndall, Huxley, Harrison, and Clifford; and these, or their equivalents, are at one time or another put into the mouth of Darnley. Without doubt, he is to be taken as an amalgam of these individuals, and this is what draws the *Westminster Review's* protest. Yet it is necessary to accept the fact of this amalgam if we're to justify Mallock; and certainly it does not help to limit the intended allusions to any one person, as A. J. Farmer does:

le professeur Paul Darnley, ne rappelle pas Darwin par la seule sonorité de son nom. Il est l'auteur de trois volumes sur *l'Origine de la Vie* . . . . Sa femme, en dépit de la figure bouffonne que lui donnent une robe vert pomme, et des papillottes, a, de Mrs Darwin, quelques traits . . . .[39]

In fact, Darwin seems to me the least suggested figure in Darnley's composite make-up, and it is difficult to see the attractive Emma Wedgwood in Mrs Darnley.

There may, of course, be reasons to suppose that Darnley represents an unlikely synthesis, and that he is a repetition of the mistake Mallock made with Saunders. Yet I think this isn't so. It is partly because he is less specific about Darnley's interests than he had been about Saunders'; his concern is with a general indictment of ideas of progress. As we shall see, this is what enables him in *Is Life Worth Living?* to treat Huxley and Harrison as 'positivists'. Indeed, Mallock adds a prefatory note to that work which is relevant to our present concern.

In this book, 'positive', 'positivist', and 'positivism' are of constant occurrence as applied to modern thought and thinkers. To avoid any chance of confusion or misconception, it will be well to say that these words as used by me have no special reference to the system of Comte or his disciples, but are applied to the common views and position of the whole scientific school, one of the most eminent members of which — I mean Professor Huxley — has been the most trenchant and contemptuous critic that 'positivism' in its narrower sense met with. Over 'positivism' in this sense Professor Huxley and Mr Frederic Harrison have had some public battles. Positivism in the sense in which it is used by me, applies to the principles as to which the above writers explicitly agree, not to those as to which they differ.[40]

This note shows that Mallock wants to link all those who are on the side of progress as 'positivists'; and that he is aware of the very interesting debates between Huxley and Harrison, about whether Huxley could be called a positivist. And this point seems to me sufficient justification for the way Darnley is presented in *The New Paul and Virginia*, and explains why the

Westminster Review tried to deny its validity. By having Darnley representative both of Huxley and Harrison, Mallock is making a neat contribution to the debate which had so engaged the two men for a decade.

Sydney Eisen has shown what trouble Huxley had in avoiding the tag of 'positivist', 'To [his] dismay, the public, and even some notable writers, were confusing Positivism with science itself; he was therefore determined to throw some light on the problem and thereby destroy the Positivists' claim that their views on religion and life were connected with science.'[41] But Harrison's constant reply was that he did not feel it necessary to accept all the teachings of Comte, that he agreed with Huxley that many of Comte's ideas were wrong, and that essentially he and Huxley were on the same side.[42]

Mallock's attitude is that these 'positivists' are *essentially* alike in their detestation of the past, of the old moral order, of Christianity; and he would be quick to seize on Huxley's discomfiture at Harrison's ready embrace. The differences between the two men, that is, are superficial. If we were to take account of the whole spectrum of their ideas, this idea of the 'essential' similarity of positivists and scientists couldn't survive, but Mallock is concerned with only one area: the consequences for human conduct, for moral sanctions; and here he is able to make some shrewd thrusts. His basic concern is with what is likely to happen to society if the existence of God is denied. And in his fears of the consequences he is on the side of Newman, when he wrote:

To one great mischief I have from the first opposed myself. For thirty, forty, fifty years I have resisted to the best of my powers the spirit of Liberalism in religion. [This] is the doctrine that there is no positive truth in religion, but that one creed is as good as another; and this is the teaching which is gaining substance and force daily. Religion is in no sense the bond of society. Hitherto the civil power has been Christian. Even in countries separated from the Church, as in my own, the dictum was in force when I was young that Christianity was the law of the land; now everywhere that goodly framework of piety which is the creation of Christianity is throwing off Christianity. The dictum to which I have referred, with a hundred others which followed upon it, is gone or going everywhere; and by the end of the century, unless the Almighty interferes, it will be forgotten. Hitherto it has been considered that religion alone, with its supernatural sanctions, was strong enough to ensure the submission of the mass of the population to law and order; now philosophers and politicians are bent on satisfying this problem without the aid of Christianity.[43]

Mallock's concern, in *The New Paul and Virginia, Is Life Worth Living?* and *Atheism and the Value of Life*, is to show the problem cannot be solved outside a Christian context. And in these three works — the last intermittently only — he aims to explode the alternative to the inner sense of charity conferred on man by Christianity: that is, altruism. Altruism is what is left when God is taken away; and though in its extremest form it is a positivist concept, it is generally asserted by agnostics in the latter half of the nineteenth century as the basic moral fact about humans in society. It would still be respectable as a moral concept to agnostics who distrusted positivism, since it is a central moral concept for Mill (who develops his ideas about it partly at least from Comte). Mill was England's dominant moral philosopher until the mid-1870s; only then did his influence begin to wane, and then not among those who had earlier accepted his ideas, but among younger people who began to turn to the idealism of which T. H. Green is the most influential representative. And even with them altruism retains its force, though it has moved back into a Christian context.

In the appendix to *The New Paul and Virginia*, Mallock quotes Huxley as saying: 'If it can be shown by observation and experiment, that theft, murder, and adultery, do not tend to diminish the happiness of society, then, in the absence of any but natural knowledge, they are not social immoralities.'

Yet 'assertion' is likely to be the key-word here: moral sanctions are found difficult of proof, as Huxley's remark suggests; and Sydney Eisen is correct to note that 'while he [Huxley] never doubted the validity of the moral principles he had learned as a child, he seemed unable to formulate a logical argument to support them.' Mallock sees this. He quotes a remark of Huxley's both in *The New Paul and Virginia* and in *Is Life Worth Living?*: 'For my own part, I do not for one moment admit that morality is not strong enough to hold its own.' That is very similar to George Eliot's famous statement as reported by F. W. H. Myers in his *Essays Modern*, 1883:

she, stirred somewhat beyond her wont, and taking as her text the three words which have been used so often as the inspiriting trumpet-calls of men, — the words, *God, Immortality, Duty,* — pronounced, with terrible earnestness, how inconceivable was the *first*, how unbelievable the *second*, and yet how peremptory and absolute the *third*.

And Frederic Harrison, in his important lay-sermon on *Science and Humanity*, makes a similar assertion:

> The true moving force of man's life, individual or social, is Affection: love of our kind, love of right, zeal for the good. Let us live for others, for the happiness of man is to live as a social being: let us live for self, only so far that we may live more truly for the whole, to which we belong by the very nature of man.

Harrison also announces the true business of modern man in a manner to which it is difficult to see that Huxley could object:

> Our business is to bring Religion once more to bear upon life and humanity by finding that key to life which will correlate at once life and humanity on all their sides, after all the vast development they have had in modern ages. And this, Theology cannot do, or at least does not do.[44]

Mallock burlesques this assertive optimism in *The New Paul and Virginia*, basing his attacks on the true Catholic pessimism: that 'natural' man is corrupt and can only be prevented from doing wrong by the coercive force of religion. He has some good fun at the expense of 'terrible earnestness', the mental pre-disposition that judged Voltaire as not serious. A curate who had been on *The Australasian* manages to reach shore and has, he claims, been converted by so much as the Professor's lay-sermon as was given before the ship sank.

> 'Do you believe', said Paul, 'in solemn, significant, and unspeakably happy Humanity?'
> 'I do', said the curate fervently. 'Whenever I think of Humanity, I groan and moan to myself, out of sheer solemnity.'
> 'Then two thirds of Humanity,' said the Professor, 'are thoroughly enlightened. Progress will now go on smoothly.'

That is, of course, angled at positivistic optimism, the tone of which Harrison revealed when he claimed that

> the final union of Love for the good with Knowledge of the true Order issues finally in one end — Progress: material, intellectual, moral: increased mastery over nature, wider knowledge, purer hearts, and loftier conduct.[45]

And yet the Professor's claim does not go beyond anything to which Huxley would give assent, because for him the discrediting of Christianity is enlightenment, and enlightenment progress, since through it men attain to a new human dignity. Later, however, when the curate catches sight of Virginia, he behaves in a most unenlightened manner, and kisses her. Paul puts an end to this by force, but not by argument, since the curate insists that

I do not care two straws about the highest good. What you call my lower nature is far the strongest: I mean to follow it to the best of my ability; and I prefer calling it my higher, for the sake of the associations.

Fortunately the curate then gets drunk, falls over a cliff and is smashed to pieces. The Professor asks Virginia: 'What event ... could be more charming — more unspeakably holy? It bears about it every mark of sanctity. It is for the greatest happiness of the greatest number.' Q.E.D. The curate's lower nature cannot be held in check once he gives up religion, and the Professor's optimistic belief in progress is, therefore, absurd: not altruism but selfish hedonism will result from the abandonment of Christianity; and, to return to Newman's words, 'the submission of the mass of the population to law and order', is thus seen to depend on the acceptance of 'religion alone, with its supernatural sanctions'.

Essentially, *The New Paul and Virginia* amounts to the making of that one point by a process of comic deflation; exact study of human behaviour undermines exact thought about it. And in this context not only the Positivists but J.S. Mill, too, are attacked for false hopes. Altruism is taken in a broad context. Thus, when Virginia tries to get Paul to kiss her, he refuses, saying:

'I perceive ... you are ignorant of one of the greatest triumphs of exact thought — the distinction it has established between the lower and higher pleasures. Philosophers, who have thought the whole thing over in their studies, have become sure that as soon as the latter are presented to men they will at once leave all and follow them.'

Mallock undoubtedly has in mind this statement of Mill's:

... there is no known Epicurean theory of life which does not assign to the pleasures of the intellect, of the feelings and imagination, and of the moral sentiments, a much higher value as pleasures than to those of mere sensations.

Mill, of course, accepts that some *do* choose the pleasure of sensation, but says:

... this is quite compatible with a full appreciation of the intrinsic superiority of the higher. Men often, from infirmity of character, make their election for the nearer good, though they know it to be the less valuable; and this no less when the choice is between two bodily pleasures, than when it is between bodily and mental.

But he is unable to show that men can be *made* to prefer higher pleasures. He says only: 'It may be questioned whether any one who has remained equally susceptible to both classes of pleasures, ever knowingly and calmly preferred the lower...'[46] And this is to give the victory to Mallock, for Mill has no way of preventing a man knowingly preferring the lower pleasures, even though he claims these are harmful. Indeed, he admits that men pursue 'sensual indulgences to the injury of health'. (In view of the attention given to Mill by Mallock we may have to revise our notions that Utilitarianism was a spent force by the 1870s. Still, Mallock undoubtedly over-values its contemporary significance. It is the price he pays for wanting to attack and condemn all forms of the modern spirit.) Mallock is bound to carry this point as long as his opponents identified the lower with sensual pleasures; a point I will return to when I come to discuss his treatment of love. That is, the 'philosophers who have thought the whole thing over in their studies' can do little about the brute fact of human nature, from which their study makes them absurdly remote.

IV

When we turn from *The New Paul and Virginia* to *Is Life Worth Living?* and *Atheism and the Value of Life*, we find that Mallock's essentially Catholic pessimism asserts itself as it hardly could in a work of comic burlesque. For example, in *Is Life Worth Living?* Mallock says that a code of morals 'is a number of restraining orders', and the moralist has to 'meddle with human nature mainly because it is inconstant and corrupted'. Such a statement, which he advances as undeniably true, suggests how fully in the grip of Christian assumptions Mallock is. In fact, he seems to be more explicitly Catholic in this work than his insistence on detachment will allow. Thus he claims: 'We are not our own; we are bought with a price. Our bodies are God's temples, and the joy and terror of life depends on our keeping those temples pure, or defiling them.' However, he adds that we can best retain our awareness of this, not through protestantism, which crumples at the positivists' attacks, but through the Church of Rome, 'the oldest, the most legitimate, and the most coherent' form of Christianity. In addition:

the Catholic Church . . . is a human organism, capable of receiving the Divine Spirit; and this is what all other religious bodies, in so far as they have claimed authority for their teaching, have consciously or unconsciously attempted to be like wise; only the Catholic Church represents success, where the others represent failure; and thus these, from the Catholic standpoint, are abortive and incomplete Catholicisms.[47]

No doubt it was passages such as this which caused the *Spectator* to qualify its praise for *Is Life Worth Living?* To attack irreligion was one thing; to defend Rome quite another. And so: 'while we are continually struck with the logical force and adequacy, as well as the literary power, of two-thirds of this volume, we are almost as much struck with the inadequacy, the logical weakness, and not infrequently even the literary feebleness, of the conclusion.'[48] and my own copy of the book has a furious annotation, 'I am glad the author of this book calls himself an R.C. as he seems to me to write in a very impious way.'

Yet the fact is that Mallock does *not* write as a Roman Catholic. For — and this is part of his specifically religious pessimism — having said the best for Rome that he can, he concludes: 'All this, of course, does not prove that Catholicism *is* the truth; but it will show the theist, that, for all that the modern world can tell him, it may be.'[49] The tragedy of the man who wants to believe is, however, that his intellect will not allow him to assent to dubious truths. So the only hope is that intellect will be used to restore the primacy of religious belief.

Intellect itself will never re-kindle faith, or restore any of those powers that are at present so failing and so feeble; but it will work like a pioneer to prepare their way before them, if they are ever revived otherwise, encouraged in its labours, perhaps not even by hope, but at any rate by the hope of hope.[50]

And this need for intellectual assent is what I take Mallock to be thinking of in his *Memoirs* where, speaking of his contempt for the liberal answers attempted to 'the riddle of life', he says that life would in 'the higher sense of the word' cease to be tolerable: 'unless the orthodox doctrines could be defended in such a way that in all their traditional strictness they could once more compel assent.'[51]

Thus there are two aspects to Mallock's religious pessimism: a belief in the corruptness of human nature which therefore needs religion; and a doubting of religion because of the intellect's scepticism. As such it links with pessimism in a broader sense, for in the works I am now considering Mallock sets himself in opposition to the optimistic hopes entertained for a future without faith. At its worst such pessimism degenerates into a callow pose, is faddish or simply immature; and it is at this level that the *Academy* represents Mallock. In the course of a highly intelligent review, Edith Simcox says:

> The phrase 'worth living' is ambiguous, and the whole subsequent argument is impaired by the want of a preliminary explanation as to whether the matter to be discussed is objective or subjective, positive or relative 'worth'. This is not merely a verbal criticism. The question, 'Do I feel as if *my* life were worth living?' is one, no doubt, of great importance to the youth who asks it, but the answer is of little moment to the rest of the world. We may feel some disinterested sympathy with the querist, and seek to provide him with materials for a satisfactory answer, while we shall think meanly of his moral and intellectual sanity if he remains indifferent to a life amply provided with normal sources of satisfaction.[52]

This touches on a very important point, and I shall have to say more about this facet of Mallock's pessimistic attitude. Before I do, though, I need to show that other critics took the pessimism more sympathetically. Madeleine L. Cazamian notes objectively:

> Le rapport qui relie l'abandon de la foi, et l'adoption du point de vue scientifique, au pessimism est donc très étroit dans le période qui nous occupe. Il est affirmé ou exposé dans d'innombrables textes par ceux qui croient encore, comme par ceux qui ne le peuvent ou ne le veulent plus.

W. H. Mallock appartient aux premiers; et dans un livre intitule *La vie vaut-elle d'etre vécue?* ... il depeint le remords, le dégôut de l'existence, l'indifference, la décadence, ces 'maladies du monde moderne et de notre civilisation, qui se traduisent a tout instant autour de nous, dans la conversation, la littérature, ou la législation', comme le résultat direct du positivisme et de la conception scientifique de l'univers.[53]

Cazamian's statement suggests that Mallock's attitude is commonly shared, and that this is so can be vouched for by the wide interest his book aroused. *Is Life Worth Living?* sprang initially from an invitation by James Knowles, editor of *The Nineteenth Century*, that Mallock should contribute to a symposium in his magazine on 'The Influence on Morality of a Decline in Religious Belief'. (The Symposium was conducted by members of The Metaphysical Society, and although Mallock wasn't a member, the fame of *The New Republic* gave Knowles the idea of asking him to contribute.) The articles, and later the book, were widely read and reviewed; and there were several lengthy answers.[54] Amy Cruse says that the articles 'gave rise to a newspaper correspondence which went on and on until the starting-point was lost to sight, and representatives of almost every section of the British public had given their answers to the question Is Life Worth Living?' And she further notes that 'Mr Mallock had a large following and was read even by those who disagreed with him most strongly. In 1879 his articles were collected and published as a book, which circulated widely.'[55]

As we might expect of such a subject, opinion was strongly for or against; and against the *Academy*'s disapproval we may set the support of the *Spectator*, which found *Is Life Worth Living?* a 'striking book', and claimed that 'it does show that apart from supernatural religion, the most ennobling and exhilarating of the motives of life shrink and dwindle to poor and wasted threads, insufficient to support men in prolonged suffering, or through the prospect of dreary and monotonous care.'[56] Its pessimism is thus justified. *The Athenaeum*, however, testy as always, allowed the pessimism only literary justification, not philosophical validity. 'This practical pessimism is the English form of the epidemic which has at last reached these shores. And it is evidently the prompting of personal experience that gives to Mr Mallock's denunciation of "liberal scepticism" its gloomy force and argumentative effectiveness.'[57] What the reviewer means by 'epidemic' is made clear in a review article on 'Pessimism', contributed to *The Edinburgh Review* for Spring 1879, the year of Mallock's book. In this article the writer says:

Few ages have been more prolific than our own in this resuscitation of forgotten modes of thought, or more disposed to cheat themselves with illusions of scientific, philosophic, or religious discoveries while really following in ways that have been beaten hard with the steps of former travellers.[58]

And having shown up some of these illusions, he concludes:

And now finally there comes an old and worn-out cry of Pessimism, transferred from the banks of the Ganges to the banks of the Spree, and caught up, as such cries always are in England, after they have begun their course, and even well nigh run it, in Germany. (p. 503)

I am conscious that the allusion here to Schopenhauer needn't be taken too seriously, and I am also well aware that although it was common for a type of English pessimist to think he was following Schopenhauer, in fact he was simply making him over in his own image. Yet I need to mention that Mallock may be (mis)using Schopenhauerian ideas in *Is Life Worth Living?*, and that when he speaks of 'will' at the end of the book, it is probably in an attempt to take over the German philosopher's concept. Mallock says that the first decision a man must make is whether or not he is a spiritual and moral being; and to make the decision requires an act of will.

Science and history are sullen, and blind, and dumb. They await upon our decision before they will utter a single word to us: and that decision, if we have a will at all, lies with our own will — with our will alone, to make. It may, indeed, be said that the will has to create itself by an initial exercise of itself, in an assent to its own existence. (p. 244)

Of course, this isn't really what Schopenhauer meant by the will, though it is true that 'will' for him is energy, a positive striving; and to the extent that a pessimistic outlook such as Mallock is concerned with lacks assertive energy — there being no good cause for assertion — it comes within hailing distance of what is understood as Schopenhauerian pessimism. Thus the *Tablet*, in its review of *Is Life Worth Living?*, begins by noting:

It is a profoundly true observation of St. Beuve's that in the present century moral energy of the will is one of the rarest spectacles... The number of people who will religious truth as they will riches or pleasure, or advancement in the world, is very small indeed. The number of people who are bent on attaining it at any expense or suffering or trouble is perhaps more restricted than at any other epoch. It is not that the age is wanting in earnestness. Far from it But —
> All its mind is clouded with a doubt.[59]

In other words, the energy required to make life worth living is not present in many men of the modern world. And clearly it is from, and about, this generally accepted area of experience that Mallock writes, as he himself says:

> The hypothetical pessimism that is contained in my arguments... makes no foolish attempts to say anything general about the present, or anything absolute about the future.... It deals with a certain change in human beliefs, now confidently predicted; but it does not say that this prediction will be fulfilled. It says only that if it be, a change not at present counted on, will be effected in human life. It says that human life will degenerate if the creed of positivism be ever generally accepted; but it not only does not say that it ever will be accepted by every body: rather, it emphatically points out that as yet it has been accepted fully by nobody. (p. 141)

And he also admits of modern men that

> Sin from which they recoil themselves they see committed in the life around them, and they find that it cannot excite the horror or disapproval, which from its supposed nature it should. They find themselves powerless to pass any general judgement, or to extend the law they live by to any beyond themselves. The whole prospect that environs them has become morally colourless; and they discern in their attitude towards the world without, what it must one day come to be towards the world within. (pp. 148-9)[60]

Mallock is here consciously putting himself forward as representative, in his pessimism, of modern man; and from this position he intends to examine critically the optimistic claim of the 'positivists'. ('Positivists', it will be remembered, are all those who are on the side of progress. For the rest of this section I shall use the word in Mallock's sense, unless I indicate otherwise.) I must now deal with Mallock's examination, but first I ought to add this warning note. At the end of his life he claimed that the argument of *Is Life Worth Living?* was to show

that without religion life is reduced to an absurdity, and that all philosophy which aims at eliminating religion and basing human values on some purely natural substitute, is, if judged by the same standards, as absurd as those dogmas of orthodoxy which the naturalists are attempting to supersede.

And he added that he 'elaborated this argument by the methods of formal logic'.[61] Of course this is absurd, and the best way to approach *Is Life Worth Living?* is as an interesting contribution to an important debate, which for all its inconsistencies, verbal muddle and repetitiveness, has still good individual charges to bring against the believers in progress.[62]

Mallock begins by saying that the worth of life 'is closely bound up with what we call *morality*, (p. 25), and he goes on to say that the positivists claim that their view of life 'does not destroy, but that on the contrary it intensifies, the distinction between right and wrong' (p. 26). Further, he claims that all men are agreed that the end of life is happiness. 'Now is such a happiness a reality or is it a myth? That is the great question. Can human life, cut off utterly from every hope beyond itself — can human life supply it? If it cannot, then evidently there can be no morality without religion' (p. 34). It is therefore necessary to investigate what the positivists believe 'happiness' to consist in, which they also call 'the highest good' (p. 29). And at this point Mallock makes what I think is a very astute criticism of the positivist case. It is by no means easy to find out what the positivist thinks happiness is. 'Thus they continually speak of life as though its crowning achievement were some kind of personal happiness; and then being asked to explain the nature and basis of this, they at once shift their ground, and talk to us of the laws and conditions of social happiness' (p. 35). Mallock returns a number of times to this charge of vagueness. He quotes George Eliot's famous hymn, 'Oh may I join the choir invisible', and says of it:

All the agony and the struggles ... that the positivist saint suffers with such enthusiasm, depend alike for their value and their possibility on the object that is supposed to cause them. And in the verses just quoted this object is indeed named several times; but it is named only incidentally and in vague terms, as if its nature and value were self-evident ....

Now the only positive ends named in these verses are 'the better self', 'sweet purity', and 'smiles that have no cruelty'. The conditions of these are 'beauteous order', and the result of them is 'the gladness of the world'. The rest of the language used adds nothing to our positive knowledge, but merely makes us feel the want of it. (pp. 56-7)

It is impossible not to feel a good deal of sympathy with Mallock over this. The claims of the positivists for the end of life so frequently slide into metaphor that it is difficult to believe they really have anything in mind, except the need to aspire. Thus Huxley:

The highest, as it is the only, content is to be attained, not by grovelling in the rank and steaming valley of sense, but by continually striving towards those high peaks, when, resting in an eternal calm, reason discerns the undefined but bright ideal of the highest good — 'a cloud by day, a pillar of fire by night'.[63]

Tyndall, of course, constantly has recourse to this sort of vision;[64] and even George Eliot's attitude isn't always to be excused as ironical. For example, what she says of later-born Saint Theresas in the prelude to *Middlemarch* may be nobly evasive:

Many Theresas have been born who found for themselves no epic life wherein there was a constant unfolding of far-resonant action; perhaps only a life of mistakes, the offspring of a certain spiritual grandeur ill-matched with the meanness of opportunity; perhaps a tragic failure which found no sacred poet and sank unwept into oblivion .... Here and there is born a Saint Theresa, foundress of nothing, whose loving heart-beats and sobs after an unattained goodness tremble off and are dispersed among hindrances, instead of centering in some long-recognisable deed.

However, accepting the force of Mallock's criticism here, we have also to acknowledge that positivists frequently meant something concrete by 'happiness' and 'the highest good'. And Mallock accepts it too. He knows they have in mind an identifying of personal and social morality, and that, in Harrison's phrase, this is the 'harmonizing principle of life', to be found in the

higher or unselfish instincts, in our feelings of Attachment, of Veneration, of Goodness; in those fine gifts of our nature which move us to devote ourselves to something outside us, to humble ourselves in awe before something that is greater than ourselves, to use our powers for good, for the benefit of our fellows and the common weal.[65]

Of course the terms are very near to those George Eliot used in describing her unknown Saint Theresas, and the 'something' before which we humble ourselves remains pretty vague, even when we know it is 'Humanity'. But Harrison does feel the ideal to be capable of concrete attainment, once 'Knowledge' — dispersal of the mists of Christianity — is coupled with 'Love'.

There was now a human Providence which watched over us, taught us, guided us, ruled us; there was a supreme Power which we might serve, but which we could not contend with; there was a Cause to which to devote our lives and which could inspire all the warmth of our souls. That cause was the onward march of the human race, and its continual rising to a better mode of life.[66]

Mallock has three arguments against this hoped-for worth to life. The first is to say that the 'Knowledge' promoted by the positivists does harm rather than good; 'truth, as the positivists speak of it, is plainly a thing to be worshipped in two ways — firstly, by its discovery, and secondly by its publication' (p. 116). But in fact, Mallock says, this can be shown as false; and he then offers a petulant analogy. 'A chattering nurse betrays his danger to a sick man. The sick man takes fright and dies. Was the discovery of the truth of his danger very glorious for the patient? or was its publication very sacred in the nurse?' (p. 117). Clearly this will hardly do, yet it is worth noting if only because it draws attention to what is frequently felt by the failed believer as a vindictive pleasure on the part of the positivist in causing him to lose his faith. It helps to explain why so many people thought Mallock was representing their cause.

Mallock's next argument is a good deal more interesting, at least in its mistakes. He claims that what makes for social happiness may not be moral at all, or that anyway there is no way of distinguishing degrees of pleasure. He says that both theist and positivist agree that the worth of life rests upon humanity's being capable 'of pleasures, of gratification, of enjoyment, or of happiness'.[67] But, he adds, the positivist regards all pleasures as equal provided that they are another person's.

Suppose two pigs, for instance, had only a single wallowing-place, and each would like naturally to wallow in it for ever. If each pig in return were to give his place up to his brother, and were consciously to regulate his delight in becoming filthy himself by an equal delight in seeing his brother becoming filthy also, we should doubtless here be in the presence of a certain moral element. (p. 45)

And Mallock says that on this analogy all pleasures are equal for the positivist, whereas the theist includes 'not only the subjugation of our own pleasures against others' happiness, but the subjugation of our lower pleasures, as warring against our own holiness'.[68] Again, it is clear Mallock's argument won't hold, as his analogy of the pigs should have told him. For he could hardly not have known Mill's famous dictum, that it is better to be a human-being dissatisfied than a pig satisfied; better to be Socrates dissatisfied than a fool satisfied. And Mill of course insisted that pleasures are qualitative as well as quantitative. But what Mallock fears is that with a reliance on a positivist pleasure principle, the lower human nature will quickly assert itself. Indeed, that is the point of the next part of his argument, which is to say that for the positivist anything that gives pleasure must be moral, whereas in fact it needn't be moral at all. 'But this supposition, from a moralist, is of course nonsense. For, were it true ... Sodom might have been as moral as the tents of Abraham...' (p. 42). And later:

Suppose that, on positive grounds, I find pleasure in humility, and my friend finds pleasure in pride, and so far as we can form a judgement the happiness of us both is equal; what possible grounds can I have for calling my state better than his? Were I a theist, I should have the best of grounds, for I should believe that hereafter my friend's present contentment would be dissipated, and would give place to despair. But as a positivist, if his contentment do but last his lifetime, what can I say except this, that he has chosen what, for him, was his better part for ever, and no God or man will ever take it away from him. (p. 76)

Yet once again the argument is well-nigh worthless, since Mallock simply identifies the immoral with the irreligious; and his confusion over the word 'pride' exemplifies the sort of error he all too easily commits.

His third argument against the morality of social happiness is really a quibble, and has to be noted only because he repeats it in the three works with which I have been so far concerned. As stated in *Atheism and the Value of Life* it is that for the positivist an act is morally valid only if social feeling of pleasure outweighs a personal one. Thus if a man goes to an opera his virtuous act is to give up his opera ticket to somebody else, so as to enjoy vicariously the other's pleasure; it isn't a virtue for him to enjoy the opera himself.

In *The New Paul and Virginia*, Mallock tries out the argument by having Paul give up the fat of his mutton, which he likes, to Virginia, while she gives up her lean, which she likes, to him.

> A few mouthfuls made Virginia feel sick. 'I confess', said she, 'I can't get on with this fat.'
> 'I confess', the Professor answered, 'I don't exactly like this lean.'

And he uses a similar *reductio ad absurdum* in *Is Life Worth Living?*

> Two rivals, in love with the same woman, would be each anxious that his own suit might be thwarted. and a man would gladly involve himself in any ludicrous misfortune, because he knew that the sight of his catastrophe would rejoice his whole circle of friends. (pp. 130-1)

Edith Simcox picked on this argument in her review, and says of it:

> Most human wants are more than arbitrary inventions; they have their source in the physical conditions of life, and while these conditions remain the same, men must either jointly pursue or severally renounce the desired end of social felicity.[69]

These then are the arguments by which Mallock tries to prove that the worth of life is not to be found where the positivists look for it. But he also produces an argument to show that even if, hypothetically, theirs *were* the ideal worth of life, in positivist terms it would in *fact* be unattainable. There are two stages to this argument: one is to deny the power of benevolence, or active social sympathy; the other is to insist on the need for morality being coercive, and therefore known 'inwardly' as absolute.

'Benevolence' is an important and complex idea in the latter part of the nineteenth century, and it would be beside the point to enter into a detailed discussion of it here. But I need at least to say that it is the active expression of the feeling of sympathy, and that although it frequently slides into sentimentality, it is at its best — as in George Eliot — an important concept of social morality. A famous passage from *Adam Bede* will suggest this well enough.

> These fellow-mortals, every one, must be accepted as they are, — you can

neither straighten their noses, nor brighten their wit, nor rectify their dispositions; and it is these people — amongst whom your life is passed — that it is needful you should tolerate, pity, and love ....

Mallock himself is, in his fiction, ready to demonstrate his characters' possession of sympathy and benevolence. Thus in *The New Republic* Miss Merton says: 'But what of those poor people ... who cannot be moral — whom circumstances have kept from being ever anything but brutalised? Still, this is a degenerate sympathy — sentimentality, in fact, since it merely shows off the goodness of the person speaking. In *A Romance of the Nineteenth Century*, on the other hand, Mallock employs the interesting tactic of divorcing the benevolent act from the sympathetic feeling. The novel's hero, Ralph Vernon, helps a lame little French girl to get proper attention, yet is revolted by her appearance. The point of this is to show that you don't have to be a positivist to do social good. What annoys Mallock is not a fear of the positivists having a monopoly of benevolence, but that they should think it dominates human conduct. He says:

> This is the fact in human nature on which the positive school rely for their practical motive power. It is this sympathy and benevolence that is to be the secret of the social union; and it is by these, that the rules of social morality are to be absorbed and attracted into ourselves, and made the directors of all our other impulses. (*Is Life Worth Living?* pp. 46-7).

And yet, Mallock insists, if we look at matters properly we will see that in matters of conduct selfishness is as much present as is selflessness.

> The sailor, for instance, who might struggle to save a woman on a sinking ship, will trample her to death to escape from a burning theatre. And if we will but honestly estimate the composite nature of man, we shall find that the sailor, in this latter case, embodies a tendency far commoner, and far more to be counted on, than he does in the former. No fair student of life or history will, I think, be able to deny this. (p. 47)

He then insists that if the positivists think otherwise it is because they do not know the world.

> Their strong intellects, their activity, and their literary culture, each supplements the power that it undoubtedly does give, with a sense of knowing the world that is altogether fictitious. They imagine that their own

narrow lives, their own feeble temptations, and their own exceptional ambitions represent the universal elements of human life and character; and they thus expect that an object which has really been but the creature of an impulse in themselves, will be the creator of a like impulse in others.... (p. 134)

But this sneer connects with that aspect of his pessimism about which I want to say more later, and so for the moment I need add only that this is all Mallock offers in the way of justifying his 'worldly' view of human nature.

The next stage of his argument against the ideal of positivism being realisable in practice is to say that, since benevolence is opposed by selfishness, it needs a coercive force if it is to hold sway over behaviour. Yet only religion can supply this coercion, because morality must be inward.

By calling the moral end inward, I mean that it resides primarily not in action, but in motives to action; in the will, not in the deed.... What defiles a man is that which comes out of his heart — evil thoughts, murders, adulteries. The thoughts may never find utterance ... the murders and adulteries may never be fulfilled ... yet, if a man be restrained, not by his own will, but only by outer circumstances, his immorality will be the same. (pp. 67-8)

But:

in the recesses of his own soul each man is, for the positivist, as much alone as if he were the only conscious thing in the universe.... No one shall enquire into his inward thoughts, much less shall anyone judge him for them.... It is evident, therefore, that one of the first results of positivism is to destroy even the rudiments of any machinery by which one man could govern, with authority, the inward kingdom of another; and the moral imperative is reduced to an empty vaunt. (p. 75)

To this Edith Simcox replies:

If a man proclaims that he would be a ruffian, a dullard, or a debauchee, if he were not half converted to Catholicism, we may hope and believe that he does himself injustice, but we can hardly argue with or contradict him. We do not see the logical necessity, and if he feels it it is a curious and unfortunate psychological peculiarity; but it is hardly necessary to argue at length that this idiosyncrasy cannot be raised into a rule, and that if other people wish (as is happily not uncommon) to cultivate the moral virtues without such half conversion, they may do so without insincerity of inconsistency.[70]

Edith Simcox isn't prepared to take account of Mallock's basic view of human nature; grant him his view, and what he says is perhaps more reasonable. Yet even so a problem is likely to remain. For he claims to write as a practical moralist, and he wants to accuse the positivists of nonsensical optimism in their hope that people will behave well without there being a coercive force to insist on it. (For the positivist — using the word more narrowly than Mallock — benevolence isn't merely action springing from good feeling, but intelligence. This is what it means for George Eliot, and Frederic Harrison also noted, 'we . . . are not content with unintelligent benevolence' (*The Choice of Books*, p. 187). Intelligence for the positivist goes with sympathy, a point Mallock neglects, I think.) People, he says, don't behave as the positivists would have us believe. And here is the difficulty. The 'people' he means by this certainly aren't the positivists themselves; for they *do* behave well, are interested in practical social problems: of education, housing, the trade unions, and so on. But they behave like this, Mallock suggests, because of their 'narrow lives, their own feeble temptations, and their own exceptional ambitions'. And yet since he himself insists on using the word 'positivist' in its widest sense, this has to include such very various individuals as: John Stuart Mill, George Eliot, Frederic Harrison, Huxley, Harriet Martineau, Tyndall, even Arnold. And it isn't easy to see how these can be dismissed as 'exceptional' and 'unworld-ly', at least not if the words are to be used consistently. As Edith Simcox said, 'it is not in the clauses of a confession of faith that the practical force and power of a conviction is to be found'.[71] That rests rather in how people live, and the people I have mentioned do, in practical terms, accept the inferences of their belief in social morality. Of course Mallock has some right to protest against their pietism. The religiosity of the following sentence, for example, undoubtedly rankles. 'After having thus exercised our powers to the full, and having given a charm and sacredness to our temporary life, we shall at last be for ever incorporated into the Supreme Being, of whose life all noble natures are necessarily partakers.'[72] Yet Harrison, from whom this quotation comes, did try to exercise his powers to the full on behalf of others, and it seems mean-minded of Mallock to put this down to his being an exception, and unworldly. On the other hand, it would hardly be to the point to try counting heads in order to see whether the majority of people behaved like Harrison, or as Mallock suggested; because to examine *Is Life Worth Living?* is to see very clearly what he means.

The truth is that Mallock uses 'unworldly' in two senses, but through a highly revealing muddle he doesn't see this. Thus he claims the positivists know nothing of the world, which is plainly nonsense until we realise that by the 'world' he means polite society. It that sense they *are* unworldly, but not in the broader sense to which Mallock passes without an awareness of the illegitimacy of so doing. As we have seen, he says that their 'sense of knowing the world is altogether fictitious', and here 'world' is being used in the widest sense. But then he adds:

> The religious moralist might well instruct the world, though he knew little of its ways and passions; for the aim of his teaching was to withdraw men from the world. But the aim of the positive moralist is precisely opposite; it is to keep men in the world. (p. 135)

Now here it seems as if the world from which the religious moralist withdraws is not the one in which the positivist keeps men; it is an altogether narrower world. And *this* is the world of which the positivist knows nothing. In his *Memoirs* Mallock admits as much. He says there that the writing of *Is Life Worth Living?*

> was largely due to that wider knowledge of the world with which social life in London and elsewhere had infected me. The bitterest criticism which that work excited was based on the contention that the kind of life there analysed was purely artificial, and unsatisfying for that very reason — that the book was addressed only to an idle class, and that from the conditions of this pampered minority no conclusions were deducible which had any meaning for the multitude of men. Some such objection had been anticipated from the first by myself. I was already prepared to meet it, and my answer was in brief as follows: 'If life without God is unsatisfying, even to those for whom this world has done its utmost, how much more unsatisfying must it be to that vast majority for whom a large part of its pleasures are, from the nature of things, impossible.' (p. 127)

Set this beside innumerable passages from *Is Life Worth Living?* and we see that Mallock's pessimism is, as it were, deeply shallow. The following example reveals as much:

> People cannot be always exclaiming in drawing-rooms that they have lost their Lord; and the fact may be temporarily forgotten because they have

forgotten their portmanteau.... And there are many about us, though they never confess their pain, whose hearts are aching for the religion they can no longer believe in. Their lonely hours, between the intervals of gaiety, are passed with barren and sombre thoughts; and a cry rises to their lips but never passes them. (p. 153)[73]

And, in a phrase that betrays him entirely, Mallock says that these people are characterised by 'general indifference' (p. 149). He means that his people who suffer can't escape from their misery as the unworldly positivists can, because positivist activity is largely concerned with attempting to bring about a state of affairs which, Mallock claims in the passage just quoted from the *Memoirs*, is 'in the nature of things, impossible'. Like James's Lord Warburton, the type of person with whom Mallock has most sympathy 'can neither abolish himself as a nuisance nor maintain himself as an institution.'[74]

Below the surface of *Is Life worth Living?* and *Atheism and the Value of Life* runs this fear: that once religion is abandoned the old order is threatened; the aristocracy, Mallock's 'world' may be superseded. Linking therefore with the specifically religious pessimism is the broader based one, social in essence; and the *ennui* which both works reflect and discuss is patently shallow, since Mallock can't show himself to be defending anything valuable. What he needs is a release into action, and this can hardly take a religious direction, for there seems little hope of Christianity regaining a firm hold on the nation. A would-be practical man must therefore do something other than complain about the relative triviality of the worth of life. He must try to defend that life by social arguments. And that is what Mallock does. In a group of works that he began to write in the early 1880s, he emerges as a political propagandist on behalf of the old order. It is beyond the scope of the present essay to follow him in these interests, but I want to investigate his discussion of what happens to love and personal relations when religion is abandoned because that will help show how imperative the need for political writing became to him.[75]

V

In *The New Republic* and the works that follow it, Mallock makes it his business to deal with love in the modern world. He has a very simple view of such love; without religion, it will quickly turn into the immoral 'ecstasy of the animals'. On one occasion after breakfasting with Mallock, Auberon Herbert noted in his diary: 'He feels that we shall all say with Gautier and Swinburne, "let the flesh be our mistress".'[76] the point is perhaps made most clearly in the essay on Tennyson where, speaking of the middle years of the nineteenth century, Mallock says:

> In proportion as [the progressive school] thought it hopeless to formulate what was divine, they sought to deify what was human. They preached a new gospel; we are not to check our nature, but to develop it. The delights of affection which had all along been permitted to man were no longer presented as concessions to our weakness, but as the chief elements of our strength. The allowed indulgence became an enjoined duty; we were to make it run away with us till it brought us to the gates of heaven. (*Atheism and the Value of Life*, pp. 121-2)

And at the end of the essay, he writes:

> Mr Tennyson has ever tried to discern God through the material universe. It is George Eliot's endeavour to show we can do without Him. Both treat the affections as the chief end of human life; but Mr Tennyson makes these the germ of faith, George Eliot makes them the end of it. (pp. 143-4)

It will be apparent, I think, that, consciously or otherwise, Mallock is here muddling up two senses of the words 'love' and 'affection'. He wants to say that the progressive school opens the way to sexual indulgence, even champions it; yet all he can legitimately say is that the positivists — to use the word in his sense — insist on the primacy of social love.[77] They say very little indeed of personal love, and where they do it is apt to be unfavourable. Thus, to refer again to Mill on the lower pleasures, 'Men often, from infirmity of character, make their election for the nearer good, though they know it to be less valuable.... They pursue sensual indulgences to the injury of health, though perfectly aware that health is good.' The schoolmasterish tone of that suggests that Mill is prepared to allow very little to sexual indulgence. And the same is surely true of George Eliot? Indeed, it seems to me that the *Athenaeum*, in its review of *Is Life Worth Living?*, was almost woefully accurate when it remarked that 'there is another failure to show any logical connexion between the Positivist ideal and "Les Fleurs du Mal" .... Mr Mallock fails to show that with George Eliot, who represents the new ideal of modern life, love is nought but lust.' Positivism, I think, could have done with some of Forster's belief in 'less chastity and more delicacy', but that wasn't its way and therefore Mallock's attack on 'the progressive school' is wrong-headed.

Elsewhere in his work, however, he does not make this mistake, and I think it arises out of his tendency to over-hasty conflation. More often, his position is that although the positivists attempt to deny what will happen to love and sexual relations when religion is abandoned, it is in fact happening. The idea is sketched out at its simplest in *The New Paul and Virginia*, in the scene where the curate wants to kiss Virginia, and the professor argues that he would be unhappy if he did.

> The curate, however, altogether declined to be convinced. He maintained stoutly that to kiss Virginia would be the greatest pleasure that Humanity could offer him. 'And if it is immoral as well as pleasant,' he added, 'I should like it all the better.'
>
> At this the Professor gave a terrible groan; he dropped almost fainting into a chair; he hid his face in his hands and murmured half-articulately, 'Then I can't tell what to do!' In another instant, however, he recovered himself; and fixing a dreadful look on the curate: 'That last statement of yours,' he said, 'cannot be true; for if it were it would upset all my theories. It is a fact that can be proved and verified, that if you kissed Virginia it would make you miserable.'
>
> 'Pardon me,' said the curate, rapidly moving towards her, 'your notion is a remnant of superstition; I will explode it by a practical experiment.'

The professor's dilemma here is, of course, that faced with worldly fact his theories crumble; it is another example of Mallock criticising the positivists' unworldliness. Now we have already seen that in *Is Life Worth Living?* he uses 'unworldly' ambiguously, and our sense of this will be sharpened if we turn to that book again, and consider its discussions of sex and love.

There are a good many of them. Indeed, in *Is Life Worth Living?* Mallock is obsessed with sex. It isn't only the chapter on 'Love as the test of Goodness', but throughout; almost always when he wants to give an example of the consequences of irreligion it turns out to be a sexual one. It is his persistent claim that, though morality must rest on the facts of sociology, 'it rests upon them as a statue rests upon its pedestal and the same pedestal will support an Athene or a Priapus' (p. 44). His central concern is to show that society soon will be governed by the morals of Priapus, if it isn't already.

There are three parts to Mallock's contention of society's imminent thralldom; the first is to say there is already a good deal of immorality; the second to suggest that this must be connected with a wave of literature which extols such immorality; and the third is to imply that somehow this is all the fault of the positivists. The first point is where, not surprisingly, we again encounter Mallock's confusions about 'society' and therefore the ambiguity about the 'unworldly' positivists. For it seems pretty clear that the society he has in mind is polite, high society, about whose goings-on the positivists might well be ignorant. We have already seen that in speaking of how men in the modern world regard each other, Mallock argues that

Sin from which they recoil themselves they see committed in the life around them, and they find that it cannot excite the horror or disapproval, which from its supposed nature it should. They find themselves powerless to pass any general judgment, or to extend the law they live by to any beyond themselves. (pp. 148-9)

Mallock is here thinking of himself and the society *he* lives in; and the betraying phrase is the one in which he admits that sin 'cannot excite the horror or disapproval, which from its supposed nature it should'. Interpreted most generously, this statement means that religious doubt produces moral *ennui*; taken more sceptically, it means that Mallock finds it difficult to disapprove of the behaviour of those people among whom he is permitted to pass his life, and with whom he wants to identify himself. As we shall see, this is how the phrase can be made to bear on *A Romance of the Nineteenth Century*, and since Mallock admits that he translated the arguments of *Is Life Worth Living?* into a novel because of 'a closer and wider acquaintance with the life in question', and this life is 'social life in London and elsewhere',[78] there is every reason to believe it is this he is referring to in the passage from *Is Life Worth Living?*: 'the life around' is 'social life'.

Having said this, I also need to say that the sin Mallock has in mind is sexual; and sexual sin is about to over-run the world.

Indeed towards the end of *Is Life Worth Living?*, the vision rises to one of an — unintentionally — comic apocalypse. Natural theism, Mallock says, is helpless against what is happening:

and in the dim and momentous changes that are coming over things, in the vast flux of opinion that is preparing, in the earthquake that is rocking the moral ground under us, overturning and engulfing former landmarks, and re-opening the graves of the buried lusts of paganism, it will show itself very soon more helpless still. (p. 210)

This is bound to be the case, because failure to believe in God leads to cynicism, and cynicism goes with profligacy: both are 'essentially the spirits that deny ... and profligacy is the same as cynicism, only it is cynicism sensualised' (p. 107). To demonstrate that this is the case, Mallock includes both a cynic and a profligate in *A Romance of the Nineteenth Century*.

The second part of his contention is that modern literature extols the immorality which daily gains ground in society. To establish this, he compares the love of Desdemona and Othello with that of D'Albert and Mademoiselle de Maupin, and naturally he draws attention to the comparison D'Albert makes between the Christian Madonna and his own. In fact here Mallock does no more than recapitulate Gautier's own programme: of making a diagrammatic opposition between the pagan and the Christian, and preferring the former because it is 'healthier' — the idea coming with the force of a paradox to a society accepting Mill's idea that the lower pleasures injure the health. (Of course, it isn't just Mill. Steven Marcus has shown in *The Other Victorians* how widely this was held in Victorian England; it was a medical as well as religious 'fact'. Quickly, though, a new paradox succeeded with the decadents: paganism was seen as unhealthy but preferred for that reason.)

In a previous attack on the modern age, Mallock had made use of *Mme de Maupin*, [79] and that he should return to it suggests how seriously he took, if not the novel itself, the spirit it threatened to release. That spirit is generally referred to as 'the decadence'. We have to tread very gingerly here because I don't think that Mallock's knowledge of this movement extends very far, or deep.[80] In so far as he does know about it, it is mainly through Swinburne, with whom he was personally acquainted and whose poetry he admired. (In his *Memoirs* he claimed an adolescent interest in the 'scandalous' *Poems and Ballads*, first series. And he met Swinburne frequently at Balliol, Mallock's college.) As Graham Hough has shown, Swinburne's attitutes continually parallel Gautier's: '... the spirit of the *Hymn to Proserpine* is precisely that of *Buchers et Tombeaux* .... Swinburne's conception of pagan antiquity as something nude, splendid, joyous, and cruel ... was picked up ... at the feet of Gautier.'[81] But in spite of his references to 'the buried lusts of paganism' Mallock understands very little of the ramifications of Swinburne's debt to Gautier — as they are tabulated, for example, in *The Romantic Agony*.[82]

However, this is to be less than just, because it suggests Mallock should have known more. Yet the movement to which Arthur Symons was later to give a name was only in its infancy in 1879, and perhaps it is fairer to remark on Mallock's shrewdness in noting it at all. It also seems that in *The New Republic* he had been acute in foreseeing that Pater's *Studies in The History of The Renaissance* would be interpreted as the holy book of the aesthetic movement which led on to the decadence, with Oscar Wilde as chief conductor. Of course, later commentators have joined in agreeing that the famous 'Conclusion' shouldn't have been interpreted as it was, but even if that is granted it has still to be said that Mallock showed remarkable prescience in seeing how it *would* be taken. He and 'the decadence' are frequently at one in accounts of what was happening in England; they differ only in the value attached to it; resurrection of 'the buried lusts of paganism' appals the one and delights the other, but both agree it is taking place.

And yet there is a steep problem in Mallock's account of the re-emergence of paganism. For it wasn't happening, certainly not to the extent he pretended. Indeed the idea of an England of the 1880s being given over to profligacy is so funny it is difficult to see why he himself failed to see the comedy of it. If he had been following the 'decadence' then his fears might become explicable; but as I have said, in 1879 the movement — in England at least — was in its infancy: if anything the decadents must have got encouragement from the vision of *Is Life Worth Living*? rather than Mallock being driven to his account by the evidence of the decadence itself. About all he has to go on is Swinburne's praise of Gautier and Pater's *Renaissance*. The problem is solved, however, once we remind ourselves of the intensity of Mallock's dislike of the positivists. And this leads us to the third part of the contention: that society is coming to be governed by the morals of Priapus. For Mallock wants to blame it on the positivists. The argument is extraordinarily naive, and suggests that he was so ready to pre-judge the matter that the inadequacy of what he was saying simply didn't occur to him. He claims that the positivists

observe, and quite correctly, that [love] is looked upon as a treasure; but the source of its preciousness is something that their system expressly takes from it .... [Their system does] not, indeed, confound pure love with impure, but it sets them on an equal footing; and those who contend that the former under these conditions is intrinsically more attractive to men than the latter, betray a most naive ignorance of what human nature is. (p. 91)

It is the old argument: without religion's coercive power, anarchy will rule; the positivists not only clear the ground for decadence, they actively encourage it.

My ultimate feeling about Mallock's arguments and visions concerning love in *The New Paul and Virginia* and *Is Life Worth Living?* is that they are decidedly unreal. And this is partly because the arguments are wrong: the positivists did not put 'pure and impure love on an equal footing'; besides, the decadence owes little to positivist ideas and what it does is in matters of opposition; and anyway the decadence is a very narrow, literary phenomenon, not something which engulfs England. But the visions are unreal, too. The truth is that Mallock has trapped himself in absurdity through his hatred of the moderns: in the interest of lamenting the failure of religion, of the old order, he commits himself to a vision of England which is mostly of his own making: and though he seizes on the few strands available to him, they aren't enough to weave a pattern: casual liaisons and a few divorce scandals among the rich, the poetry of Swinburne, and the moral arguments of the positivists, do not add up to an England governed by the morals of Priapus.

We can gain a clearer sense of the unreality of Mallock's vision if we look at *A Romance of the Nineteenth Century*, and in concluding this essay I need to say a little about that novel.

Its appearance certainly caused something of a disturbance, as Mallock himself recalls. Many critics of the time, he says, denounced the book: 'because it dealt plainly with certain corruptions of human nature, the very mention of which, according to them, was in itself corrupting, and was an outrage of the decorums of a respectable Christian home.'[83] If we turn to contemporary reviews, we can see at once that the book undoubtedly caused offence. The *Annual Register* contented itself with noting the novel's appearance, presumably having no words with which to describe it;[84] and the *Westminster Review* and the *Saturday Review* both dismissed it more or less contemptuously.[85] But the most savage attacks came, perhaps predictably, from the *Athenaeum* and the *Academy*. The former begins: 'In these volumes Mr Mallock introduces with much frankness scenes, situations, motives and sentiments which have long been strangers in English novels. The plot of this romance . . . is exceedingly simple, remarkably sensuous, but not at all passionate.' And it goes on to claim that the heroine, Cynthia Walters, 'may claim the proud distinction of being a new character in English literature, indeed, in a somewhat extended acquaintance with the fictitious literature of ancient and modern Europe, we are bound to say that we do not know her like.' In addition, the two central characters 'are supported by a body of accessories who would suffice to ruin any novel.'[86] The review ends by advising Mallock to give up novels altogether.

The *Academy* review suggests admiration for Mallock's literary skill, but distaste for his ideas. 'Brightly, cleverly as much as of it is written, there is nothing to lay hold of, either in the religious or secular elements, of which it is so strangely concocted, except what is perhaps best left alone.' And the review has fine fun with Mallock's picture of high society, considering that the Duchess couldn't really have said the things he puts into her mouth, not anyway in a restaurant at Monte Carlo. 'There is evidently some mistake here. It really must have been on some more private occasion — perhaps when her Grace and the other ladies were beating hemp in Bridewell.' In conclusion:

This painful story is developed with something of the unsparing directness of Rétiff la Bretonne, from whom, indeed, it may have been derived. That it is direct — that it deals with downright vice, and not mere equivocal suggestion — is a small matter; but the spirit in which it is handled is surely everything. We cannot feel that Mr Mallock has written with a wise, a good, or an earnest intention, or even with any intention at all.[87]

But these accounts of the novel tell more about the prudishness of the day than of *A Romance of the Nineteenth Century*.[88] Even so, Mallock was sufficiently impressed to revise the novel for its appearance in 1892, and he omitted or altered various passages, in the interest of making the hero and heroine more acceptable to what he thought contemporary taste required or would tolerate. We shouldn't, however, be misled by the shocked response with which reviewers greeted the book; they also thought it bad — apart, that is, from the *Academy*. And they were right. For it is a very bad novel, and the *Athenaeum* was quite right to speak of its 'peculiarly unpleasant mixture of devoutness and indecency.'[89]

Here is Mallock's version of the plot:

The heroine, who is young, but not in her first girlhood, has in her aspect and her natural disposition everything that is akin to the mystical aspirations of the saint; but, more or less desolated by the diffused scepticism of the day, she has been robbed of innocence by a man, an old family friend, and has never been at peace with herself or has wholly escaped from his sinister power since. The hero, who meets her by accident, and with whom she is led into a half-reluctant friendship, has at first no suspicion of the actual facts of her history, but believes her troubles, at which she vaguely hints, to be due merely to the loss of religious beliefs which were once her guide and consolation. He accordingly does his best, though deprived of faith himself, to effect in her what Plato calls 'a turning round of the soul', and hopes that he may achieve in the process his own conversion also. For aid in his perplexities he betakes himself to a Catholic priest.... But he feels as though he were the blind endeavouring to lead the blind, and the end comes at last in the garden of a Mediterranean villa, behind whose lighted windows a fancy ball is in progress. The hero, whose dress for the occasion is that of a Spanish pedlar, encounters the seducer in one of the shadowy walks and is shot dead by the latter, who believes that his life is being threatened by some genuine desperado; and the heroine, draped in white, like a Greek goddess of purity, witnesses this sudden event, is overcome by the shock, and dies of heart-failure on a marble bench close by.[90]

Mallock's memory is at fault here, for the ending isn't quite so farcically melodramatic as he makes out (Cynthia Walters has had her heart attack by the time that Vernon, the hero, encounters Stapleton); though perhaps the failure to recall his novel accurately suggests how forced it had been. His account also omits certain matters that are surely very important? One is that Ralph Vernon is a man with a past, and that just before he dies he has found a way out of his *ennui* by accepting a nomination to stand for parliament. Another is that the novel is as much concerned with society life as with individuals. And it is with this concern that my account must start.

As we saw in *Is Life Worth Living*? Mallock claims that it is difficult to make any judgement of the sin we see in the 'life around us', and it is clear that the life he has in mind is that led by high society. *A Romance of the Nineteenth Century* presents a fictionalised version of this life: the society at Monte Carlo is the best England can offer, yet is, if not corrupt, 'morally colourless', its spirit devitalised or subtly tainted. Now Mallock had already suggested this in *The New Republic*, where Mr Herbert had said of the planned society that 'the ways of polite life, and the manners of fine ladies and gentlemen, are beautiful only as the expression of a beautiful spirit.'[91] That speech can be traced to a long section in *Modern Painters* in which Ruskin deals with the idea of the gentleman.[92] In *Sesame and Lilies* he returns to this idea in the course of defining vulgarity, and one sentence in particular seems to me to suggest an authoritative version, if not the genesis, of Mallock's contention about society. What Ruskin says is this: 'it is in the blunt hand and the dead heart, in the diseased habit, in the hardened conscience, that men become vulgar'. True, he goes on to consider this vulgarity in a political context, and there Mallock would not want to follow him:[93] but I think it quite certain that Mallock's own feelings about the life with which he claimed close acquaintance took definitive shape from Ruskin's words. (Ruskin's idea, in its turn, reaches back to Carlyle, and *his* claim in *Past and Present* that modern society has gone dead because it has lost its sense of purpose as Christianity has lost its hold on men's lives. 'There is no longer any God for us! . . . man has lost the *soul* out of him; and now, after the due period, — begins to find the want of it! This is verily the plague spot; centre of the universal Social Gangrene, threatening all modern things with frightful death'. Again, Carlyle's attention is drawn to the political consequences of this loss of soul, but the 'frightful death' he prognosticates results from the failure of God, and that line runs clear to Mallock.) *A Romance of the Nineteenth Century* is meant to show society's blunt hand and dead heart, its diseased habit and hardened conscience. And it shows them in its attitude to sex.

Though Ralph Vernon aspires to better things, he intermittently falls into the dull routine of flirtation, of casual sex. For example, he meets a woman in the foyer of a Monte Carlo hotel and she asks him to secure a diamond pin in her hair.

> Vernon's hands lingered over the soft brown plaits. 'You are very lovely,' he said, 'though, of course, you don't need to be told that; and my words will let you play with my heart, though my prudence, I fear, will not let you play with my fortune.'(i, 66)

And much later he dallies with a married woman in a scene which comes as near as Mallock dare to actual seduction.

> 'If you were nice,' (Mrs Crane) said presently, 'you'd ask me to stop and dine with you . . . .'
> 'Very well,' said Vernon, still smiling down at her.
> She pulled a peacock's feather from a vase beside her, and began to touch his face with it. As she continued looking at him, he felt he was becoming magnetised. His face was drawn down to hers, and once more he kissed her. 'Naughty boy!' she murmured, patting his cheek tenderly. Vernon now felt as if a net had been thrown over him — a net of the coarsest kind, and yet he could not escape from it.[94]

Vernon's powelessness against the sin Mrs Crane represents is, we are to understand, directly attendant on his failure to believe in God; and it is not any action of his, but the fortuitous appearance of Mrs Crane's husband 'in very bad humour', which prevents seduction.

But it is through the Duchess and Lord Surbiton that Mallock tries most forcefully to reveal the squalor and *ennui* of society life. In the scene that caused the *Academy* to think the Duchess really belonged to Bridewell, she discusses the occupants of the restaurant other than her own party — which comprises Vernon, Lord Surbiton and another couple. And her equable tone is, I think meant to suggest how far she accepts that from which she ought to recoil.

> 'Now, look round, all of you, and take stock of the company. There are plenty of men one knows — of course, one expects that; but the women with them — did you ever see anything like it. Just observe the couple behind

you — they can't talk English, so we needn't mind discussing them — are they man and wife, do you think? Or that fine lady, with the hair sprinkled with gold-dust, whom Lord Surbiton seems to admire so — what relation should you say she was to the old Jew she is dining with? Upon my word, Mrs Grantly,' she added presently, 'I don't believe that, our two selves excepted, there's a single woman here you could possibly call respectable.' (i, 44-5)

In view of the fact that the *Academy* and the *Athenaeum* said they were shocked by this, Mallock can be said to have succeeded in suggesting the tainted spirit of society, even though the cause for such outcry seems trivial. But the point I want particularly to insist on lies in another direction, and is this: that it's difficult really to believe Mallock himself disapproves of the Duchess. Now it could of course be argued that to say as much proves his point: he fails to make up his mind how to take her because he shares the 'moral colourlessness' of his age. It wouldn't be a satisfactory argument, though, because while it may be all very well for Vernon to be evasive, Mallock not only very plainly doesn't disapprove of the Duchess, his descriptions of her make it clear that he approves of her and admires her intensely. And if this is true of the Duchess, it is much more obvious in his handling of Lord Surbiton. Mallock would need tact here, for Lord Surbiton is without doubt based on Lord Houghton. Vernon describes Surbiton as 'the first poet I ever knew; and when I was seventeen, he seemed to me little short of a god'; and we know this to have been true of Mallock's relationship with Houghton. (Mallock's *Memoirs* make clear his early admiration for Houghton.) Moreover, Surbiton is described as 'the poet, diplomat and dandy', and we are also told that he suffers from indigestion through eating too much.[95]

But Mallock models Surbiton on Houghton more deeply and significantly than the above details can suggest. For Houghton was also the possessor of a large library of erotica, and Mallock undoubtedly draws on this knowledge in his portrait of Surbiton. This is partly shown as a matter of Surbiton's conversational freedom. For example, when Mrs Grantly offers to bet him six to one in black silk stockings on a certain woman's having unimpeachable morals:

Lord Surbiton eyed Mrs Grantly with a look of somewhat sinister gallantry. 'If your feet and ankles,' he said, 'are as lovely as your hands and wrists, I shall proudly pay the bet, even if I have the sad fortune to win it.' (i,48)

More than this, however, Surbiton is repeatedly shown to be a connoisseur of women and erotic customs. This emerges in a discussion he has with Colonel Stapleton , the villain of the piece, about customs in the East.

'I often think,' said the Colonel, 'that the best meat I ever tasted was a piece of mutton in the desert, that was cooked for me by a young Coptic girl.'
Lord Surbiton turned to him with a keen glance in his eyes. 'The Coptic Church,' he said, 'shows a singular lenity, does it not, in its rule over human affections?' (i, 225)

And then Stapleton mentions that the previous year he had been in Jerusalem 'with a remarkably unrepentant Magdalene', who had wanted to see 'a certain dance in Damascus'.

Lord Surbiton's eyes shot with a fire of intelligence, and his mouth emitted the ghost of a hollow cackle. 'I know the dance you mean,' he said. 'I've seen it several times.'
'I mean this,' said the Colonel; and he gave a minute description.
'I must confess,' said Vernon, 'that I don't myself see the point of it.'
'Why, my dear fellow,' replied the Colonel in a slightly aggrieved tone, 'it's the most damned suggestive thing imaginable. Though . . . I don't know if it beats some of the plays in Paris. Have you, Lord Surbiton, seen — ?' and he named a certain play and theatre. 'You have? Well, in the second act, did you ever notice how the women's dresses were cut?'
Lord Surbiton with regretful interest confessed that he had not. The Colonel at great length enlightened him. It was now Lord Surbiton's turn to impart instruction, and he repaid the Colonel in kind; it may also be said with usury. His vivid power both of imagination and description made most of what he said quite unfit to be chronicled; and the Colonel's eyes, as he listened, swam with attentive moisture. (i, 226-8)

In detailing Surbiton's interests, Mallock is plainly alluding to Houghton's friendship with Richard Burton and their mutual passion for erotica, especially the sexual customs of the Middle East, on which Burton was an expert. Besides, Burton was the man who provided Fred Hankey — the anonymous English sadist of the de Goncourt journals and Praz's *Romantic Agony* — with mementoes of his travels, including, or so he claimed, human skin with which Hankey bound his books; and Hankey was the main supplier of Houghton's library of erotica.

It is even possible that Colonel Stapleton may have his real-life prototype. Pope-Hennessy quotes a letter written to Houghton by one, Colonel Studholme Hodgson: 'Have you

read Mlle de Maupin which the Parisian ladies rave about? . . .
It was recommended to me by quite a young woman — it is
beautiful French, but a perfectly bawdy book . . . .' Pope-
Hennessy remarks that the bulk of the letter is spent in 'describing the habits of an hermaphrodite'. Hodgson certainly sounds
like Stapleton, especially since Pope-Hennessy notes that Burton and Milnes 'spent many bachelor evenings together in
London, sometimes with Burton's crony Colonel Studholme
Hodgson, an elderly libertine who enjoyed describing his con-
quests and seductions, as a third'.[96] It would have been possible
for Mallock to have met Hodgson in Houghton's company,
and the use of him in the novel could follow.[97] And this would
be thematically right for, as I pointed out earlier, Surbiton and
Stapleton represent cynicism and profligacy; they are products
of a failed faith, and they are meant to suggest the moral
decadence beginning to overtake England. It may even be that
Mallock's own knowledge would allow him to link Houghton
fairly closely with the literary movement whose beginnings he
had attacked in *Is Life Worth Living*?, for he must have known
that Houghton was the friend, indeed patron, of the young
Swinburne, and it was Houghton who introduced the poet to
Burton and to Hankey.[98] Yet this has to remain conjecture
because it belongs only to the hinterland of *A Romance of the
Nineteenth Century*, and nothing is actually made of it in the
novel; apart from any other consideration it would have been
supremely tactless. And Mallock wants to be tactful — certainly as far as Surbiton is concerned.[99] He therefore makes him a
victim of the age. Shortly after the conversation with Stapleton
quoted above, Vernon studies Surbiton's expression:

> His furrowed face invested itself with a look of thoughtful gravity; and in
> his tone and gesture . . . there was the most perfect mixture of fitting respect
> and dignity. Vernon thought, as he watched him, that he had never seen a
> truer gentleman. (i, 232)

How can such a gentleman be friendly with Stapleton? The
answer emerges a little later. The Catholic priest, Stanley,
enters and he and Surbiton speak of the Church. For the latter
'a change is coming' so that the Church's power mostly
belongs to the past.

> 'She was once a perfect saint, and a perfect woman of the world, and she

could understand all men's lowest impulses, and yet still for ever lead him up to the highest. Me,' he went on sighing, 'she has taught at least one lesson — that there is little in this world worth a regret on losing it.'

'You are the last person, my lord,' said Stanley with politeness, 'one could expect to hear say that. You have fame, position, fortune — all that the world can give you.'

'It is these blessings,' said Lord Surbiton, 'that have made my heart so teachable. It may be wisdom to despise the world; but to despise it thoroughly you must first possess it.'

These words were uttered with a ghastly kind of impressiveness, and received the reward they courted — a moment's complete silence. (i, 239)

This just about sums up Mallock's case about 'the life around us'. Society is becoming progressively worthless as the grip of faith weakens; cynicism, the spirit that denies, grows out of the morally colourless world of the latter half of the nineteenth century.

And yet, as I imagine is clear, this passage is very awkwardly introduced into the book, to explain and defend Surbiton's behaviour which, thesis apart, I'm quite sure Mallock approves of. Or if that puts the matter too simply, this much at least is true: that Mallock cannot finally decide whether what for argument's sake he has implicitly to condemn isn't rather to be noted with approval as part of the 'tone' of society with which he had been so concerned in *The New Republic*. We can be certain that he disapproves of the profligate Stapleton; but then Stapleton isn't a true gentleman. He wears big checks on his coat, and though Mallock says of him that 'he held himself well and gracefully, and had an air about him of dissolute good breeding' (i, 45), it is clear that he is essentially vulgar. When Vernon is showing a party including the Colonel round his villa, the two men are left behind in the library.

'If you want,' (the Colonel) said, 'to see modern art, just look into that. I got it at Nice this morning.' Vernon looked, but for an instant only. The contents were a series of photographs, such as in England the police would seize upon; and he gave it back with a curt 'Thank you' to the Colonel. (i, 43)[100]

Later, the photographs turn up in Cynthia Walters' possession, proof of how far the Colonel has corrupted her. And it is clear that Mallock regards the photographs as evidence of the Colonel's vulgarity — Surbiton would never possess such things, or if he did wouldn't show them around. (This is perhaps because photographs are a plebeian — cheap — form of erotica. They belong to a democratic age. The true aristocrat would go for etchings, and Houghton possessed the famous Carracci and Giulio Romano illustratio s.)

My final impression of Mallock's treatment of society in *A Romance of the Nineteenth Century* is that he cannot really bring himself to believe in his own thesis. (The *Westminster Review* ended its criticism of the novel by saying: 'If English society were really so lewd, so gross, and so stupid as Mr Mallock has chosen to represent them, we ought to welcome a new '93 that would purge the world of them. Happily, we are not bound to believe Mr Mallock's picture'.) The corruption of this society is simply not convincing; indeed, Mallock is more liable to suggest the presumed fineness of high society's tone; and those individuals Mallock shows to be corrupt are either not truly members of the society, or at best are tolerated by the others — and here, I suppose, the notion of life being 'morally colourless' does apply. It would be possible to advance reasons for Mallock's hesitancy and equivocation. Perhaps it was due to his own uncertain claims of belonging to society, so that he wouldn't wish to give offence. ('The old leisured aristocracy of the past delighted in gathering together people of conversational power, and for this reason alone certain individuals whose sole credentials were their wit and mental cultivation were accorded a place in society.' *The Reminiscences of Lady Dorothy Nevill* (1906) p. 106. (Though this doesn't entirely fit Mallock's case, it was the success of *The New Republic* that guaranteed him his place; he had comparatively little money, and his family claims were not considerable.) More probably, he only believes his thesis in so far as he accepts Ruskin's analysis of what is happening to society; that is, in his dislike of all ideas of progress he needs to include an account of polite society's degeneracy. But then this poses a dilemma: he ought to abandon either society or Ruskin. And, as his career as a political propagandist shows, he chooses to abandon Ruskin. When he begins to devote himself to political matters, it is as spokesman for the old order, whose blemishes — if he still thinks they exist — he covers over, as though in seeking to justify himself to the old order, he has to justify the old order to himself.

If it is difficult to accept that Mallock believes in his thesis about society, this is still more the case with his hero and heroine. They are incredible. I don't think there is much point in showing this at length. What the *Athenaeum* found is true enough: 'with a remarkable tendency to indulge their bodies, they are still more remarkably cumbered about the state of their souls'.[101] So, for example, after Cynthia Walters has confessed the full truth about herself to Vernon, she kneels in front of him.

> With a movement of kindness that was then almost mechanical, he laid his hand upon her shoulder; her hands were folded before her face. Vernon was glad that she was not watching him. He felt that his thoughts were wandering far from hers, and that his face, rigid and melancholy, would at once have betrayed the fact. Presently a low sound broke from her, and he caught the familiar accents, as of a little girl's 'Our Father'. He meanwhile, in a bitter and blank wonder, let his eyes stare at the stars and the palm-beaches, as he thought, 'Does prayer mean anything?' (ii, 160)

A great deal of the book is taken up with that sort of prose, and although it is of course true that much great nineteenth-century literature is concerned with the psychology of self-destruction, this can hardly be said to constitute a realisable theme in *A Romance of the Nineteenth Century*. Instead we are offered two 'pure souls' who have been spotted. And to use that word is to point to the externality of it all. For instance, a little later than the passage quoted above, Miss Walters confesses that she has lain with men other than Colonel Stapleton: '... she said to him in a sad clear voice: "Do you think such affection as Colonel Stapleton gives a woman is of a kind that is likely to keep her faithful during his absence?"' (ii, 166). But this suggestion of degradation is merely tacked on, and it doesn't in the least modify her essential purity which is insisted on *ad nauseam*. (And actually, although Mallock says in his *Memoirs* that Cynthia Walters lets herself in for corruption because of her lack of faith, and although this is suggested in the novel itself, in fact in her confession she insists she was 'so young' when Stapleton corrupted her. Mallock, making her as innocent as he can, loses sight of the supposed cause of her corruption; she would have been too young for religious scepticism to have had much application to her case.)

A Romance of the Nineteenth Century quite fails, then, to

make good the claim hinted at in *The New Paul and Virginia*, and insisted on in *Is Life Worth Living?*, that England is coming to be governed by the morals of Priapus. How seriously Mallock believed his thesis I'm not sure, but it has to be said that he quite failed to realise it in his novel; as the *Athenaeum* noted, the romance is 'not at all passionate'. There is no sense of the rebirth of buried pagan lusts. There is merely talk of them, and persistent religiosity.

One last point. Towards the end of the novel Vernon receives a visit from Surbiton and a Conservative ex-minister.

The visit, it appeared, was one of more than ordinary compliment. There was something like business at the bottom of it, and of a very flattering nature. The ex-minister had just received intelligence that a relation of his own, who sat for a certain borough, was to accept the Chiltern Hundreds, and it was now suggested to Vernon that here was a new opening for him. (ii,229)

Now all through the novel we have had mention of Vernon's interest in public affairs and how that contrasts with the tedium of his private life. For example, at one of the Duchess's dinner-parties there is much discussion of politics.[102]

All this discourse put Vernon in better spirits. He began to feel he was waking up in earnest . . . he plunged with interest into various questions of politics; and the image of Miss Walters, which had been hitherto still watching him, seemed to melt at such magic words as *land, labour,* and *capital*. (ii, 221)

Vernon accepts political activity as a way out of his *ennui*. I said that in *Is Life Worth Living?* Mallock can't find the way out because political activity is mostly concerned with opposing the interests of the society with which he identified himself. The point arises in the novel, too. Stanley says:

a strong man's mind is like a corrosive acid. It eats through countless interests that suffice to absorb others. It even takes the gilt off vice, and it makes gambling vapid. What it asks is, 'Give me something to work for that I feel is worth the work'. Now for the bulk of mankind there is a ready answer to this. They must work to live, or at least to live in comfort; and all that they need do is to make a virtue of necessity. But the rich man's task is by no means as simple as this . . . . By an act of will and choice he must take that yoke upon him, that the larger number are born with. He must choose some line of action; he must devote himself to something. What makes a man is the sense that he has committed himself.

'True,' said Vernon, 'but the struggle lies in choosing.' (ii, 176-177)

At the end of the novel he chooses, and it would not be wrong to say that the decision to enter public life is also a resolution of his creator's. Mallock settled something in his own mind. The *ennui* which had characterised both Otho Laurence, the semi-autobiographical host of *The New Republic*, and Ralph Vernon, is replaced in the last pages of *A Romance of the Nineteenth Century* by a sense of commitment. The way out is through political activity, defending the old order of things. And for Mallock that is bound to be more satisfactory than having to argue that the old is as corrupt as the new. There is plenty of evidence to show he hoped for a parliamentary career, perhaps to emulate one of his heroes, Disraeli. Failing that, he would become a Tory propagandist. As matters turned out he had to content himself with the latter role.

Notes

1 Lady W. Paget, *Embassies of other Days* (1923) ii, 320.
2 T. H. S. Escott, *Personal Forces of the Period* (1898) p. 258.
3 *The Reminiscences of Lady Dorothy Nevill*, ed. Ralph Nevill (1906) p. 210.
4 T. H. S. Escott, *Great Victorians* (1916) p. 288
5 Augustus Hare, *The Story of My Life* (1896-1900) v. 16.
6 Leon Edel, *Henry James: The Conquest of London* (1962) p. 333.
7 It began on 4 August 1877. See LXXIII, p. 45.
8 *Memoirs of Life and Literature* (1920) p. 67.
9 *Ibid.*
10 *Ibid.*, p. 127.
11 The Essays which make up *Is Life Worth Living?* appeared initially as follows: *The Nineteenth Century*, (ii) September 1877, 'Is Life Worth Living?'; *ibid.*, (iii) January 1878, 'Is Life Worth Living?'; *ibid.*, (iv) October 1878, 'Faith and Verification'; *ibid.*, (iv) December 1878, 'Dogma, Reason and Morality'; *ibid.*, (v) January 1879, 'The Logic of Toleration'; *The Contemporary Review* (xxix) January 1877, 'Modern Atheism'; *ibid.*, (xxxi) March 1878, 'The Future of Faith'. *Is Life Worth Living?* was published in book form in 1879. There were several alterations to the essays, though none to the argument; Mallock altered to give the appearance of consecutive chapters. *A Romance of the Nineteenth Century* was first published in two volumes by Chatto and Windus, 1881. *Atheism and the Value of Life* was composed of the following essays: *The Edinburgh Review* (cl) October 1879, Review of *Impressions of Theophrastus Such*; *ibid.*, (cli) April 1880, Review of *Lectures and Essays by the late W. K. Clifford*; *ibid.*, (cliv) October 1881,

Review of Tennyson's *Ballads and Other Poems*; *ibid*., (clvi) October 1882, Review of *Natural Religion* by the author of *Ecce Homo*; *The Nineteenth Century*, (vii) 1880, 'Atheistic Methodism'. *Atheism and the Value of Life* was first published London, Bentley and Son, 1884. Mallock makes no alterations from the periodical form of the essays.

12 The letters are in the Chatto and Windus files, Mallock's in autograph.

13 *Contemporary Review* (xxxii), 1-29.

14 Apart from the comparison already quoted, Mallock later describes it as 'in the manner of Voltaire's *Candide*', *Memoirs*, p. 126.

15 P. M. Yarker, *Essays and Studies* (1955) pp. 35-8.

16 Yarker accurately calls it 'a contribution to a current controversy'. *Ibid*., p. 36.

17 Arnold, *Lectures and Essays in Criticism*, ed. R. H. Super (1962) p. 179. This passage, although it was inserted into 'Spinoza and The Bible', first appeared in an essay 'The Bishop and The Philosopher', published in *Macmillan's Magazine* (1863). The passage was grafted on in 1869.

18 Arnold, *Op. cit*., p. 205.

19 Ruskin's editors have a note, explaining that 'fimetic' is his coinage from an obsolete word 'fime' meaning dung.

20 *Works*, ed. Cook and Wedderburn (1903-12) xxvii, 630.

21 In a letter of 1886, Ruskin went much further, saying of Voltaire: 'Literary chemists cannot but take account of the sink and stench of him; but he has no place in the library of a thoughtful scholar'. *Works*, xxxiv, 587.

22 Jowett said that Voltaire 'has done more good than all the Fathers of the Church put together'. John Morley, *Recollections* (1917) i, 9. But then Jowett's was a unique position.

23 John Morley, *Voltaire* (1872) p. 229.

24 Willey, *More Nineteenth Century Studies* (1956), see pp. 263-7.

25 Only the more militant atheists would be likely to swallow Voltaire whole. See, for example, an essay on him by J. Watt in *Biographies of Ancient and Modern Celebrated Free-Thinkers*, by Charles Bradlaugh and others (1877). An interesting bibliography of writings on Voltaire during this period has been compiled by Mary-Margaret H. Burr, Institute of French Studies (1929).

26 Huxley's epigram, though normally accepted as original, was probably borrowed from the right-wing Anglican *Saturday Review*, which had called Comtism 'that strange parody upon religion which might be described as Popery conducted upon atheistical principles'. *Saturday Review* (15 April 1865) xix, 432.

27 *Sesame and Lilies*, xviii, 47.

28 However, Mallock himself doesn't seem to have noticed the possibility. His review of *Impressions of Theophrastus Such* appeared in the Edinburgh Review cl (1879) pp. 557-86. Later it became one of the essays in *Atheism and the Value of Life*.

29 See George Eliot, *Letters*, ed. Gordon Haight (1954-55) vi, 406.407. Haight has a footnote to one letter of George Eliot's to Mrs Burne-

Jones, thanking her for liking ' Debasing the Moral Currency'. The footnote says, 'Mrs Burne-Jones shared G.E.'s indignation over *The New Republic*, in which her husband is probably glanced at.' *Ibid.*, vii, 75. But there is nothing in this letter to show that Mallock was under particular attack; perhaps Haight knows what Mrs Burne-Jones's letter says. Anyway it isn't *The New Republic* but *A Familiar Colloquy* she must have had in mind, for it was there that her husband's paintings came in for adverse criticism.

30 George Eliot, *Impressions of Theophrastus Such* (1879) pp. 176-81.

31 *Athenaeum*, No. 2647 (20 July 1878), 69.

32 *Westminster Review*, n.s. liv (1878), 571.

33 *Tablet* (4 May 1878) p. 555. The review is of *The New Paul and Virginia* as it appeared in the *Contemporary Review*.

34 *Ibid.* (4 May 1878) p. 555.

35 *Nation*, No. 687 (29 April 1878) p. 133.

36 *Ibid.*, p. 134.

37 *Westminster Review*, art. cit.

38 Saunders was largely based on W. K. Clifford. But there are also elements in him of Frederic Harrison, and J. S. Mill, and the way these elements are developed quite disrupts the consistency of his development. For example, he is required to suggest anarchic possibilities in championing the trade unions; and Mallock is certainly thinking of Harrison here. Yet the Utilitarians, whose point of view Saunders is also meant to represent, are *against* unions. Mallock tries to make Saunders carry too large a bundle of ideas in progress — without seeing (or knowing) how mutually contradictory many of these ideas were.

39 A. J. Farmer, *Le Mouvement Esthétique et 'Décadent' en Angleterre, 1873-1900* (1931) p. 47.

40 *Is Life Worth Living?* (1879) p. xxiii. The note suggests that Mallock is taking account of the *Westminster Review* criticism of *The New Paul and Virginia*.

41 'Huxley and the Positivists', *Victorian Studies*, vii (1964) p. 389.

42 Nearly all these articles and replies appeared in the *Fortnightly Review*; the two key ones being Huxley's attack on Comte in 'The Physical Basis of Life', and Harrison's answer 'The Positivist Problem'.

43 Quoted by J. H. Bridges, *Five Discourses on Positivist Religion* (1882) p. 23.

44 F. Harrison, 'Science and Humanity', in *Five Discourses on Positivist Religion, ibid.*, pp. 3 and 12.

45 *Ibid.*, p. 4.

46 J. S. Mill, *Utilitarianism*, ed. A. D. Lindsay (1910) pp. 7, 9 and 10.

47 *Is Life Worth Living?* pp. 32, 106, 211-2, and 238.

48 *Spectator*, lii (1879) 885.

49 *Is Life Worth Living?* p. 239. The *Tablet*, in its review of the book, found it a very fine attack on positivism, and an equally fine defence of the Roman Church, and held that 'no Catholic could have discussed

the same subject quite in the same way. His very certitude would have been a hindrance to him.' xxii (1879), 74.

50 *Ibid.*, p. 242.

51 *Memoirs of Life and Literature, op. cit.*, p. 64. Mallock, it should be said, carried on a life-long flirtation with Rome — his cousins were the Froudes — and was given a Catholic burial. Many contemporaries thought he *was* a member of the Church, however, his sympathies were so apparent.

52 *Academy* (1879) xvi, 24. Edith Simcox, it should be said, was a worshipper (the word is the literal truth) of George Eliot, and her positivistic position demands she attack Mallock. But she does this with a high degree of wit and clear-sighted argument.

53 M. L. Cazamian, *Le Roman et les Idées en Angleterre: L'Influence de la Science (1860-90)* (1923) p. 253.

54 Among them were Edward Aveling's *The Value of this Earthly Life* (1879); an anonymous compilation of American essays, *The Value of Life: A Reply* (1879); (Herbert Spencer's *The Data of Ethics*, Mallock said, 'though in no way designed to be an attack on myself, has yet turned out to be so practically' (*Atheism and the Value of Life*, p. 307)); and two essays by L. S. Bevington, under the general title of 'Modern Atheism and Mr Mallock', which appeared in *The Nineteenth Century*, vi (October and December 1879).

55 Amy Cruse, *After the Victorians* (1938) p. 24. And of John Burns we are told that, forced to choose between a new pair of boots and Mallock's book, he chose the latter. See W. Kent, *John Burns: Labour's Lost Leader* (1950) p. 54.

56 *Spectator*, lii, 584.

57 The reviewer adds that 'when . . . he comes to the actual dialectical encounter, his blows hit the air as ineffectually as any country parson's, who descends from his pulpit with an inward satisfaction at having demolished "the late Mr Hume's argument against miracles". The reader feels that Mr Mallock has taken upon himself a task too mighty for his powers . . . .' *Athenaeum*, No. 2695 (1879) pp. 786 and 787.

58 *Edinburgh Review*, cxliv (1879), 500-1.

59 *Tablet*, art. cit., p. 73.

60 This statement can be paralleled by many in *Atheism and the Value of Life* especially in the essay on Tennyson, whom Mallock sees as living out of optimism into something far other, and who keeps going only because of a residue of his earlier self in the older man. 'It is hard to believe . . . that the world, as for the last twenty years he has looked on it, has not in many ways been growing a darker sight to him. His faith in progress may still be firm, but the fact of it has not been visible to him' (*Atheism and the Value of Life*, p. 132). In general this section concentrates on *Is Life Worth Living?* as the better, more influential, more widely noticed book.

61 *Memoirs of Life and Literature, op. cit.*, pp. 126 and 127.

62 It may be that Mallock was encouraged to speak of his 'methods of

formal logic' since Ruskin, in *Fors Clavigera* (September 1877), told his working-men: 'Respecting the real position of the English mind with respect to its former religion, I beg my readers' accuratest attention to Mr Mallock's faultlessly logical article in the *Nineteenth Century* for this month, "Is Life Worth Living?"'. In fact, Mallock dedicated his book to Ruskin, and aligns himself with him against the Positivists. And this alignment has a context, because in his *Fors* letter of June 1876, Ruskin had attacked Harrison's article of the previous month 'Humanity — A Dialogue', which had appeared in the *Contemporary Review*. Ruskin claimed that, contrary to Harrison's optimism, 'the entire system of modern life is . . . corrupted with the ghastliest forms of injustice and untruth'. Harrison replied in the July number of the *Fortnightly Review*, and his essay was subsequently reprinted in *The Choice of Books* (1886). He maintained that, in spite of all Ruskin could say, 'the human race is worthy of our regard' (*The Choice of Books*, p. 122).

63 Quoted by Mallock, *The New Paul and Virginia*, p. 142.

64 Some of the funniest moments in *The New Republic* are in the absurdly sentimental speeches of Mr Stockton — based on Tyndall — who on one occasion urges the others, 'Let us beware, then, of not considering religion noble; but let us beware still more of considering it true.' And some of the best attacks in *Is Life Worth Living?* are at Tyndall's expense (see esp. pp. 169-85). The *Academy* was quick to recognise this: 'Positivists [using the word still in Mr Mallock's sense] are quite as far from accepting Prof. Tyndall as an inspired doctor of their Church, as the Church of Rome is from endorsing the opinion of Bellarmine as to the place of purgatory. Popular lecturing and profound philosophy do not necessarily go together . . . (*op. cit.,* p. 25).

65 *Five Discourses on Positive Religion, op. cit.,* pp. 16-17.

66 *Ibid.,* p. 24.

67 *Atheism and the Value of Life*, p. 315. The remark comes from the essay 'Atheistic Methodism', a reply to the critics of *Is Life Worth Living?*.

68 *Ibid*, p. 350. I use these texts interchangeably because the argument is the same, and I want to employ the pithiest quotations I can.

69 *Academy*, p. 24.

70 *Ibid.,* p. 25. It is a curious fact that Mallock appears not to recognise that the positivists allowed for defective individuals in their concept of progress; he seems to think that if he can prove one man would not behave morally outside a coercive system he has wrecked their case.

71 *Ibid.,* p. 35.

72 'Science and Humanity', in *Five Discourses on Positive Religion, op. cit.,* p. 26.

73 A very similar passage occurs in *A Romance of the Nineteenth Century*, ii, 272, where the hero, dressed for a fancy-dress ball, wonders: 'How could he bear to be making a fool of himself outwardly, when his whole inward being was as dark as death itself, and concerned with as serious issues?'

74 'The Victorian gospel of work, derived from both its religious and economic life and preached the more earnestly because the idea of progress called for dedicated action, found further support from an unexpected quarter. As the difficulties of belief increased, the essence of religion for Christians — and for agnostics "the meaning of life" — came more and more to lie in strenuous labour for the good of society. That was not only a rational alternative to fruitless speculation but also a practical means of exorcising the mood of ennui and despair which so often accompanied their loss of faith' (W. E. Houghton, *The Victorian Frame of Mind* (1957) p. 251). Houghton's statement shows that for Mallock and *his* society there could be no accepting this gospel, which is closely connected with the positivists he hated. For, of course, 'the good of society' was socially and politically quite unacceptable to them.

75 For a full discussion of Mallock's political writings in the 1880s see my essay in *Literature and Politics in the Nineteenth Century* (1971-and 74) ed. J. Lucas.

76 S. A. Harris, *Auberon Herbert: Crusader for Liberty* (1943) p. 214.

77 'Placing our highest happiness in universal Love, we live, as far as it is possible, for others', Frederic Harrison, *Five Discourses on Positive Religion, op. cit.*, p. 26.

78 *Memoirs of Life and Literature*, op. cit., p. 127.

79 'A Familiar Colloquy', *The Nineteenth Century* (August 1878). Gautier's novel is there called 'the foulest and filthiest book that ever man put pen to. It is the glorification of nameless and shameless vice' (p. 298).

80 For example, Yarker's statement that *A Romance of the Nineteenth Century* 'belonged to the "decadence"', exploiting the juxtaposition of innocence and vice' won't at all do, because whatever awareness Mallock has of the decadence leads him to combat it: he doesn't belong to it in any meaningful sense, nor can he be said to 'exploit the juxta-position of innocence and vice'. 'W. H. Mallock's Other Novels', *Nineteenth Century Fiction*, xiv, 195. On the evidence of his essay Yarker does not fully understand either the nature of the decadence, nor the significance of Mallock's novel.

81 'The Hymn to Proserpine' appeared in the 1st series of *Poems and Ballads* (1866). Hough quotes these highly relevant lines:

> Thou hast conquered, O pale Galilean; the world has grown
> grey from thy breath,
> We have drunken of things Lethean, and fed on the fulness of death.

Graham Hough, *The Last Romantics* (1947) p. 190.

82 M. Praz, *The Romantic Agony* (1933), esp. pp. 239 and 243. Mallock's ignorance is because he wasn't a member of the Swinburne circle; there is reason to believe that only in that circle were the full details of Swinburne's 'paganism' known.

83 *Memoirs of Life and Literature*, op. cit., p. 127.

84 *Annual Register* (1881) p.449.
85 *Westminster Review*, cx (1881); *Saturday Review*, lii (1881). The *Westminster* noted that Mr Mallock has 'tried to be indecent — he has succeeded in being dull', p.565. And though the tone is morally very shrill, the review repeats the charge of dullness. In the *Saturday Review*, the notice of *A Romance in the Nineteenth Century* ends with these words: 'It has one failing which from any point of view is unforgivable. It is desperately dull'. The review also speaks of the novel's 'nauseous and quasi-religious sentimentality', pp.81, 80.
86 *Athenaeum*, No. 2804 (1881), 109-10.
87 *Academy*, p.103.
88 In *Literature at Nurse*, George Moore complained that whereas the circulating libraries had rejected *A Mummer's Wife* they had accepted Mallock's novel, which is certainly odd, given the tone of the reviews (*Literature at Nurse* (1885) p.3).
89 *Athenaeum*, No. 2804 (1881) p.110.
90 *Memoirs of Life and Literature, op. cit.*, p.128.
91 *The New Republic, op. cit.*, p.112. Herbert is basically a very sympathetic portrayal of Ruskin.
92 Ruskin, *Works*, vii, 343-62.
93 *Ibid.*, xviii, 80.
94 *Ibid.*, ii, 4. In fact the passage beginning 'She pulled a peacock's feather ...' was cut from the edition of 1892. See p.158.
95 *A Romance of the Nineteenth Century*, i, 37. For Houghton's gluttony in old age, see James Pope-Hennessy, *Monckton Milnes: the Flight of Youth* (1951) p.250.
96 See Pope-Hennessy, *ibid.*, pp.117-24, 116, 125.
97 Mallock claims the portrait of Stapleton is founded on 'Lord —'. But he admits that 'Lord —' was known to Houghton, so he may be covering up, or simply have forgotten Hodgson's true status. In which case, being Mallock, he'd be far more likely to elevate than depress it. See *Memoirs of Life and Literature, op. cit.*, p.129.
98 See Pope-Hennessy, *op. cit.*, pp.113-28 and 129-60.
99 In His *Memoirs* (p.129) he says he received a letter from Houghton after the publication of the novel, saying that *A Romance* 'required no apology'.
100 In the 1892 edition the photographs were changed to 'A French Romance, written during the last century' (p.147).
101 *Athenaeum*, pp.109-10.
102 I have a strong suspicion that the Duchess is based on Lady Dorothy Nevill, who greatly busied herself in party politics, and round whose dinner-table the idea of the Primrose League was born. See *The Reminiscences of Lady Dorothy Nevill*, pp.284-8.

Chapter 9

From Naturalism to Symbolism

I

NATURALISM came to England at the end of the nineteenth century. It flourished in a pallid sort of way for a few years, and was more or less dead by the turn of the century. In what follows I want to comment on these facts and also suggest why naturalism brought about the rise of the symbolist movement. I am not concerned with anything like an exhaustive account of the two: we have the documents and we have quite enough monographs to be going on with. The reader who wants to enquire more deeply into the nature and causes of naturalism and symbolism may be referred to — among others — Becker's *Documents of Modern Literary Realism*, Stromberg's *Realism, Naturalism and Symbolism,* Stern's *On Realism*, Powers's *Henry James and the Naturalist Movement*, and Lehmann's *Symbolist Aesthetic in France, 1885-1895*. In this brief essay I shall largely concern myself with four writers: George Moore and George Gissing, and Arthur Symons and W. B. Yeats.

We start, however, with a French novelist. Zola is the undisputed father of naturalism, and his preface to *Thérèse Raquin*, added to the second edition, 1868, is a key text for an understanding of the movement. Zola sets down there his ideas of the artist's role and responsibility:

I had only one desire: given a highly-sexed man and an unsatisfied woman, to uncover the animal side of them and that alone, then throw them together in a violent drama and note down with scrupulous care the sensations and actions of these creatures. I simply applied to two living bodies the analytical method that surgeons apply to corpses.... The human side of the models ceased to exist....

It is a highly contentious statement and one that begs a number of crucial questions. But it would be beside the point to quarrel

188

with Zola's account of his task. All that need concern us here is the seriousness with which he insists on dispassionate observation, and the fact that this is bound to imply some crippling limitations (though it is only fair to add that the limitations often don't apply to Zola himself, simply because he is frequently more than a naturalistic writer). Once you decide to see human beings or a social situation in the manner Zola describes, they become exotic, strange, and not fully known at all. The naturalist programme is immensely ambitious: the novelist acts as a kind of Baconian scientist, recording, reporting, listing. Yet the end result of the enterprise is to make the whole add up to less than the sum of the parts. It must be so, I think. For the novelist who follows Zola is reduced to working with the strictly contemporary, which at the very least means not understanding, or not seeing as relevant or taking account of, the complicated meshings in which human beings and social situations gain their identity, and which have a great deal to do with the past and perspectives onto the past. These matters are closed to the naturalist writer since observation and reportage have to be of the present. History shrinks to now.[1]

This is not to say that the naturalist programme has no concept of history. It has one all right, but unfortunately it is hopelessly reductive. Unwavering, gimlet-eyed scanning of the contemporary world will reveal or find clues to the important truth that individuals are determined by environment and circumstance. Whatever socio-economic process there may be indifferently condemns the vast majority of human beings to lives of pointless suffering. These are the beliefs on which a naturalist concept of history is built.

Naturalism: pessimism: determinism. The three terms go together and between them they provide a defeatist, glumly pessimistic fiction. (Optimistic naturalism is a contradiction in terms.) The struggle for survival, the reduction of a person to his elemental, 'animal' level, success or failure depending on how well adaptation is made to given circumstances: this is the very stuff of the naturalistic novel, and its terms spread wide. In William Hale White's *Revolution in Tanner's Lane*, the hero, Zachariah Coleman, finds himself in the alien world of Manchester:

These men treated him not as if he were a person, an individual soul, but as an atom of a mass to be swept out anywhere, into the gutter — into the river. He was staggered for a time. Hundreds and thousands of human beings swarmed past him, and he could not help saying to himself as he looked up at the grey sky, 'Is it true then? Does God really know anything about me? Are we not born by the million every week, like spawn, and crushed out of existence like spawn?' (Chapter 9)

Zachariah does not finally lose his dissenting faith (this part of the novel is after all set in the early years of the nineteenth century). But Hale White was writing in the 1880s and the language of atoms and spawn has much more to do with that decade than with any earlier one.

Grant the possibility of being crushed out of existence, like spawn, and you are faced with an account of the historical-social process which invites you to set aside all moral considerations in the interests of survival. One of the most rigorous expressions of this in English fiction is to be found in Gissing's *New Grub Street*. Characters may be presented as apparently bad in a conventional sense (to call someone Jasper is certainly to invite your reader to think badly of him), yet moral judgement is warded off, or made irrelevant. Consider the account of Mrs Edmund Yule:

She kept only two servants, who were so ill paid and so relentlessly overworked that it was seldom they remained with her for more than three months. In dealing with other people whom she perforce employed she was often guilty of incredible meanness; as, for instance, when she obliged her half-starved dressmaker to purchase material for her, and then postponed payment alike for that and for the work itself to the last possible moment. This was not heartlessness in the strict sense of the word; the woman not only knew that her behaviour was shameful, she was in truth ashamed of it and sorry for her victims. But life was a battle. She must either crush or be crushed....

But whilst she could be a positive hyena to strangers, to those who were akin to her, and those of whom she was fond, her affectionate kindness was remarkable. One observes this peculiarity often enough; it reminds one how savage the social conflict is, in which these little groups of people stand serried against their common enemies, relentless to all others, among themselves only the more tender and zealous because of the over-impending danger. (Chapter 18)

At first glance it might look as though Gissing is being ironical: Mrs Yule's defence of herself — crush or be crushed — could be mere sophistry. But Gissing's own underlining of the savagery of the social conflict makes it plain that as far as he is concerned Mrs Yule isn't to be condemned as a moral hypocrite. And her struggles to survive are matched by others in this grim novel of London life in which the ultimate winners are those who fight meanest, understanding the need to do so, and having the right kind of toughness for the battle.

Yet here it is important to note that a particular kind of complacency underlies Gissing's bleak account of contemporary life, and I think it is one that inevitably belongs to the naturalistic movement. It surfaces in an early description of Mrs Yule:

Mrs Yule's speech was seldom ungrammatical, and her intonation was not flagrantly vulgar, but the accent of the London poor, which brands as with hereditary baseness, still clung to her words, rendering futile such propriety of phrase as she owed to years of association with educated people. In the same degree did her bearing fall short of that which distinguishes a lady. The London work-girl is rarely capable of raising herself, or being raised, to a place in life above that to which she was born; she cannot learn to stand and sit and move like a woman bred to refinement, any more than she can fashion her tongue to graceful speech. (Chapter 7)

One notes here the entirely spurious use of terms derived from evolutionary biology, as though to suggest that class is immutable and that refinement is more than the name for a blood sport of arbitrarily framed rules. ('We see Blood in a nose, and we say "There it is! That's Blood!" It is an actual matter of fact. We point it out. It admits of no doubt.' But Dickens's wonderful satire didn't kill the sport off.)

The naturalistic writer in England relies heavily on assertions about 'types', as though he is providing scientifically exact observations. We may place beside the passage from Gissing one from Moore's *A Mummer's Wife*:

The hearts of the people change but little — if at all. When rude work and misery does not grind and trample all feelings out of them, they remain for ever children in their sentiments, understanding only such simple emotions as correspond to their daily food...in the woman of the people there is no intellectual advancement; she never learns to judge, to discriminate.... (Chapter 8)

There are similar passages scattered about Moore's 'Realistic' trilogy (the term is his own choice).

Moore and Gissing are without doubt the most important

naturalistic writers in England. Frank Swinnerton remarks that they 'alone, or almost alone were trying in the published novel to tell the world something about life at first hand'; and he considers that the success of their efforts was such that they gave rise 'towards the end of the nineties, to a new school of naturalistic writers'. Yet Swinnerton later calls this school 'a vogue for tales of mean streets', in which the 'very poor [were used] as literary material'.[2] That gives the game away with a vengeance. To speak of a movement as a vogue is to imply that in the final reckoning it simply isn't authentic. And in one respect at least Moore and Gissing are every bit as vogue-ish as their imitators. They work from stock assumptions which are hardly ever put to the test, and this is especially true for what they have to say about class.

This brings us to a crucial point. The naturalist differs absolutely from the realist in believing that class is somehow a given fact of — well, of nature. People *naturally* belong to one class or another. It's a matter of genes, or blood, of evolved characteristics: of anything but money. The possibilities of class mobility are therefore outlawed. You find your natural place, and you stay there. (The exceptions only serve to prove the rule.) In which case the very poor can be treated merely as literary material. And of course it is material which illustrates the naturalistic writer's proper pessimism. Or so it is assumed. The poor are doomed to suffer and there is nothing much that anyone can do about it. It's the way, not of the world, but of nature. When Gissing remarks that the accent of the London poor still clings to Mrs Yule's words, 'rendering futile such propriety of phrase as she owed to years of association with educated people', he doesn't simply mean that those educated people recognise that she is no lady, but that she is doomed to eventual defeat, that she'll go under. For in the world of Gissing's novels if someone isn't capable of raising herself, or being raised, to a place in life above that to which she was born then she must fall into the limbo world of the scarcely human. (And of course such raising is finally impossible. Mutimer in *Demos* cannot sustain his marriage with the gentle Adela because he is too near the condition of beast.[3]) In the struggle for survival 'the people' and the 'London poor' will always lose.

II

London is very important. By the 1880s it had become the City of Dreadful Night, grinding out 'death and life and good and ill: / It has no purpose, heart or mind or will'. (Thomson's poem was first published in 1878.) The city is an appalling, oppressive fact of modern life, an uncontrollable growth which feeds on millions and to whom all but the strongest are thrown as victims. In *Mark Rutherford's Deliverance* (1885), Mark and his journalist friend, M'Kay, try to relieve the meaningless lives of people who exist in and around Drury Lane. But it is a hopeless task, and Mark reflects that:

To stand face to face with the insoluble is not pleasant. A man will do anything rather than confess it is beyond him. He will create pleasant fictions, and fancy a possible escape here and there, but this problem of Drury Lane was round and hard like a ball of adamant. The only thing I could do was faintly, as I was about to say, stupidly hope — for I had no rational, tangible grounds for hoping — that some force of which we are now not aware might someday develop itself which will be able to resist and remove the pressure which sweeps and crushes into hell, sealed from the upper air, millions of human souls every year in one quarter of the globe alone. (Chapter 5)

Hale White is not a naturalist novelist, but he is writing at the same time as Gissing and Moore, and his feelings about London are shared by Gissing at least. Hopelessness is the keynote; and it is echoed by Arthur Symons, walking along the Edgware Road in the 1890s, wondering at the people he passes, wondering:

why these people exist, why they take the trouble to go on existing. As I passed through the Saturday night crowd lately, between two opposing currents of evil smells, I overheard a man who was lurching along the pavement say in a contemptuous comment: 'Twelve o'clock: we may all be dead by twelve o'clock'. He seemed to sum up the philosophy of that crowd, its listlessness, its hard unconcern, its failure to be interested. Nothing matters, he seemed to say for them; let us drag out our time until the time is over, and the sooner it is over the better.[4]

London is the fact and the type of what existence means in the last decades of the nineteenth century. Its growth, size, complexity, all indicate that the majority of men are unable to control their own fates. Individuals triumph, but at the expense of shared humanity. This is undoubtedly the view that Gissing takes from *Demos* onwards, and it marks something of a departure from the argument put forward in the 'Hope of Pessimism', an essay which he had written in 1882. There, he had presented the struggle for survival as an unacceptable concept with which to identify, a fact to be resisted. He imagines its champion claiming that:

the competitive system, depend on it, is the grandest outcome of civilization. It makes us robust and self-reliant: we expect no mercy in the battle, and accordingly give no quarter; the strong man will make his way; for the weak are there no workhouses and prisons? We are a growing population; our great problem is, how to make the food of two keep three alive; it is patent that we cannot stand upon ceremony, must e'en push our best to get us a place at the board. Does not science — the very newest — assure us that only the fittest shall survive? If we tread upon a feeble competitor and have the misfortune to crush the life out of him, we are merely illustrating the law of natural selection. A man must live we suppose?

To which rhetorical question Gissing returns the answer, but not by bread alone. And he asks us to give our approval to the pessimist, the man whose habit of life is the conquest of instinct. 'Life is no longer good to him; he is a Pessimist. And this is the final triumph of mind, the highest reach of human morality, the only hope of the destruction of egotism.'[5]

Variations of this form of pessimism abound in the literature of the period, but what matters to us is the fact that by the time Gissing came to write *The Odd Women* and *New Grub Street* he had more or less abandoned it. Instead, he creates his heroes out of those who are determined to save themselves. Admittedly, he preserves an ambiguity of tone towards those heroes: there is a saving irony in the way in which he writes about Rhoda Nunn and Jasper Milvain. But it is a protective irony. What else could they do? It isn't *their* fault if triumphant survival requires unscrupulous behaviour. Pessimism is now directed at history — history according to a naturalistic reading, that is. The individual or small group of individuals is pitted against society at large, 'the common enemy'. If you belong to the middle-class, so much the better for you. You have more chance of surviving, but not because of economic factors. No, it is because nature has created certain breeds to be middle-class and hence more likely to succeed (economic advantage is the effect, not the cause). In *The Odd Women*, Rhoda and Miss Barfoot are quite clear that their status as middle-class women gives them an advantage they would be fools to throw away. Which means that they feel contempt for weaker — lower-class — women who cannot find ways to survive. In *New Grub Street* Reardon and Biffin throw away their advantages and so inevitably go down.

I realise that this may look like the grossest parody of Gissing's position, and yet it is not really unfair to him. For Gissing is in the tradition of nineteenth-century English thought whose typical expresion is melioristic humanism; only for him the tradition has turned sour. The humanism I have in mind found its most eloquent expression in positivistic ideology, with its idea of historical progress from which any serious possibility of conflict has been excluded, and its thoroughly decent but mistaken insistence on the doctrine of altruism. (Gissing's hope for pessimism is a last despairing flare-up of the doctrine.) As all commentators have recognised, positivism and liberalism run parallel courses in the nineteenth century, so far at least as their theories of history go. In both cases progress is seen as fundamentally evolutionary and unilinear; it is not to be marred by radical upheaval or conflict, and it will promote the general good of humanity. But by the late 1880s matters seemed not to be working out that way. The result was that as it became increasingly apparent that progress didn't guarantee an improvement in the general good, positivism ceased to be a vital force in English thought.[6] The hope for altruism passed into its opposite: a belief in the necessity or inevitability of egotism. George Eliot had been sustained by her belief that history steadily unfolded possibilities, realised promises and potentialities. A later generation of writers took over her belief in history as an unfolding, but they saw no promise in it. Pessimism replaces optimism, ardour gives way to cynicism: realism turns into naturalism.

In 1896, John Jacobs noted that:

It is difficult for those who have not lived through it to understand the influence that George Eliot had upon those of us who came to our intellectual majority in the seventies. Darwinism was in the air, and promised, in the suave accents of Professor Huxley and in the more strident voice of Professor Clifford, to solve all the problems of humanity. George Eliot's novels were regarded by us not so much as novels, but rather as applications of Darwinism to life and art. They were to us *Tendenz-Romane*, and we studied them as much for the *Tendenz* as for the *Roman*. Nowadays ... their *Tendenz* is discredited .... [7]

Jacob's remarks hint at the fact that by the 1890s the typical 'applications of Darwinism to life and art' were in no sense offering to solve all the problems of humanity. It is the opposite. Only the most cynical solutions were on offer. Survival is for the few. For the rest: 'Let us drag out our time until the time is over, and the sooner it is over the better'. This is the essence of English naturalism.

III

Four years after Jacob's regretful account of the discrediting of melioristic humanism, W. B. Yeats asked himself, 'How can the arts overcome the slow dying of men's hearts that we call the progress of the world, and lay their hands upon men's heart-strings again, without becoming the garment of religion as in the old times?'[8] Yeats is the greatest spokesman for the symbolist movement in English literature as it developed at the end of the nineteenth century, just as he is its greatest (some would say only) practitioner; and it is no accident that he should set symbolism up as the supreme antagonist of naturalism. 'The scientific movement', he wrote in the essay from which I have already quoted, 'brought with it a literature which was always tending to lose itself in externalities of all kinds, in opinion, in declamation, in picturesque writing, in word-painting, or in what Mr Symons has called an attempt "to build in brick and mortar inside the covers of a book".'[9] Symons may well have derived his figure from a memory of Clough's famous championing of high-Victorian novels as ones that give us 'a real house to be lived in'; but Yeats's grandly vague reference to the 'scientific movement' serves to remind us that Symons's remark was directed at Zola himself,[10] and that both men were on the attack against the naturalism of their own day.

Yeats set his face against an art which deals in 'externalities'. It is more than probable that when he used the word he was recalling George Moore's *A Modern Lover*, in which the art we are asked to approve of is concerned with the painting of 'housemaids in print dresses, leaning out of windows, or bar girls serving drinks to beery-looking clerks'. On the studio walls of one of the approved artists are canvasses filled 'not with the softness of ancient, but with the crudities of modern life' (*A Modern Lover*, Chapter 7).[11] Yeats hated such art. 'I was in all things a Pre-Raphaelite,' he famously remarked, and he mourned his father's readiness to take up the cause and practice of realist painting:

its defence elaborated by young men fresh from Paris art schools. 'We must paint what is in front of us', or 'A man must be of his own time', they would say, and if I spoke of Blake or Rossetti they would point out his bad drawing and tell me to admire Carolus Duran or Bastien-Lepage.[12]

It was precisely this art for which Moore had beaten the drum in *A Modern Lover*: an art 'of truth, unpopular and created by men of integrity'.[13] But Yeats would have none of it, and by the 1890s Moore had also withdrawn his approval. Indeed, in an essay called 'Our Academicians', he does a complete about-turn and belabours the very art which he had earlier both championed and professed. In this extraordinary performance he picks out 'Mr Stanhope Forbes, the last elected Academician, and the most prominent exponent of the art of Bastien-Lepage', for particular criticism. According to Moore, Stanhope Forbes 'continues at the point where Bastien-Lepage began to curtail, deform, and degrade the original inspiration'. And then he goes on:

Mr Stanhope Forbes copied the trousers seam by seam, patch by patch; and the ugliness of the garment bores you in the picture, exactly as it would in nature.... A handful of dry facts instead of a passionate impression of life in the envelope of mystery and suggestion.

Realism, that is to say, the desire to compete with nature, to be nature, is the disease from which art has suffered most in the last twenty years.... Until I saw Mr Clausen's 'Labourers' I did not fully realize how terrible a thing art becomes when divorced from beauty, grace, mystery, and suggestion....

Mr Clausen has seen nothing but the sordid and the mean, and his execution in this picture is as sordid and as mean as is his mission. ... Mr Clausen seems to have said, 'I will go lower than the others; I will seek my art in the mean and the meaningless'. But notwithstanding his very real talent, Mr Clausen has not found art where art is not, where art never has been found, where art never will be found....

The mission of art is not truth, but beauty....[14]

As the language of that passage sufficiently reveals, Pater has replaced Zola as Moore's lawgiver. In Chaikin's words, 'It was Pater who convinced Moore that repose and evenness were in tune with his genius rather than the dynamism of Zola ... and that it served the cause of Art better to wander in the flowered field than to roll in the mud. Naturalism was putrid; Zola was vulgar; and it came to him that the artist preferred the refined to the vulgar'.[15] It is worth noting that after his conversion Moore used the word 'externality', as did Yeats and Symons, to define and damn naturalism. For example, in an essay on Turgenev, written in 1888 and collected in *Impressions and Opinions* (1891), Moore complained that Zola 'was too much concerned with the externalities of life.'[16]

I cannot take Moore's conversion very seriously — he seems to me nothing if not unserious — but at least it shows that symbolism is the reverse side of the coin from naturalism. Moore trivialises the matter by setting 'truth' and 'beauty' in opposition, but his sudden and spectacular rejection of the naturalistic mode offers at least initial comparison with Yeats's much more serious criticism of *A Doll's House*. 'I was divided in mind, I hated the play; what was it but Carolus Duran, Bastien-Lepage, Huxley and Tyndall all over again? I resented being invited to admire dialogue so close to modern educated speech that music and style were impossible.'[17] Yeats's concern with music and style may be linked to some remarks of Symons's in his Introduction to the *Symbolist Movement in Literature*. (Who knows but that they came from Yeats?)

after the world has starved its soul long enough in the contemplation and the re-arrangement of material things, comes the turn of the soul; and with it comes the literature of which I write in this volume, a literature in which the visible world is no longer a reality and the unseen world no longer a dream.

For in the art of the symbolist may be found:

an attempt to spiritualize literature, to evade the old bondage of rhetoric, the old bondage of exteriority. Description is banished that beautiful things may be evoked, magically.... Mystery is no longer feared.... We are coming closer to nature, as we seem to shrink from it with something of horror, disdaining to catalogue the trees of the forest. And as we brush aside the accidents of daily life, in which men and women imagine that they are alone touching reality, we come closer to humanity, to everything in humanity that may have begun before the world and may outlast it.

As I imagine is clear from these passages, Symons's language owes a good deal to Pater, but it would be quite wrong to think that he is therefore championing a literature of escapism — such as Pater may well look to be championing at the end of *The Renaissance*. On the contrary: Symons makes no break between 'truth' and 'beauty'. But he does insist that the more true-to-fact art is the less truthful it becomes, because it is then less able to penetrate beneath accident and casual phenomena ('exteriority') to the 'essence' or 'soul' (favourite words of his and of Yeats).

The point needs some stressing, I think, because we may otherwise be tempted to dismiss Yeats's concern with 'music and style' as mere sterile aestheticism. This is not to deny that the concern can and does sometimes lead in that direction, as Yeats's own early verse amply reveals. But there is a good deal more to it than just that. We need to recall and to take seriously Yeats's insistence that the arts should be 'the garments of religion' and to link the phrase with a famous and crucial passage in the *Autobiographies* where he remarks that:

I was unlike others of my generation in one thing only. I am very religious, and deprived by Huxley and Tyndall, whom I detested, of the simple-minded religion of my childhood, I had made a new religion, almost an infallible Church of poetic tradition.... I wished for a world where I could discover this tradition perpetually....[18]

He is properly wry about this youthful attempt to overthrow the dominant presence of the 'scientific movement'; but there can be no doubt that in this passage we have the seeds of Yeats's deep and abiding concern with symbolism. For he sees in symbolism a way of reading the universe that will discover permanences and, by extension, purpose and design. It provides for an unfailing recognition of mysteries that once again bring alive the possibility of religious faith. This is made absolutely clear in his note on 'The Body of the Father Christian Rosencrux', written in 1895, and published in *Ideas of Good and Evil*:

I cannot get it out of my mind that this age of criticism is about to pass, and an age of imagination, of emotion, of moods, of revelation, is about to come in its place; for certainly belief in a supersensual world is at hand again; and when the notion that we are 'phantoms of the earth and water' has gone down the wind, we will trust our own being and all it desires to invent; and when the external world is no more the standard of reality, we will learn again that the great passions are angels of God, and that to embody them 'uncurbed in their eternal glory', even in their labour for the ending of man's peace and prosperity, is more than to comment, however wisely, upon the tendencies of our time, or to express the socialistic, or humanitarian, or other forces of our time, or even 'to sum up' our time, as the phrase is; for art is a revelation, and not a criticism....[19]

Such a passage makes plain the reasons for Yeats's hatred of naturalism. Naturalism, dwelling on the surface of things, is anti-visionary, whereas for Yeats the true function of art is to be visionary. The externalities of the world are to be rejected. They spread a thick crust of accidentals which prevent the artist from seeing into the underlying structure of things. Of course naturalism has its own structure of things: the scientific movement means progress of a kind, means reducing human beings to jostling atoms in an unending fight for survival. But Yeats fiercely rejects the adequacy of such a structure, for 'I am very religious'. It will take him a lifetime's effort fully to develop his own reading of the universe — *A Vision* is its most elaborate expression — but already, in the 1890s, he finds it natural to identify with such system builders as Blake and Shelley, and he writes magnificently of both. What he says of Blake in particular applies to himself. 'He was a symbolist who had to invent his symbols .... He was a man crying out for a mythology, and trying to make one because he could not find one to his hand'.[20]

Yeats's genuinely religious temperament explains the need he felt to create his own mythology. It also explains why he found it impossible to take socialism seriously. He flirted with it, largely because he fell under the influence of Morris's writings, but he soon abandoned it. He attended a number of meetings at which Morris was in the chair (presumably they were meetings of the Socialist League), but:

gradually the attitude towards religion of almost everybody but Morris, who avoided the subject altogether, got upon my nerves, for I broke out after some lecture or other with all the arrogance of raging youth. They attacked religion, I said, or some such words, and yet there must be a change of heart and only religion could make it. What was the use of talking about some new revolution putting all things right, when the change must come, if come it did, with astronomical slowness, like the cooling of the sun, or it may have been like the drying of the moon? Morris rang his chairman's bell, but I was too angry to listen, and he had to ring it a second time before I sat down .... I never returned after that night ....[21]

It is hardly surprising. For a symbolist reading of history can have little in common with a socialist one. Yeats's own version was not of course fully elaborated at this time, though both its inevitable assertiveness and its necessary indifference to fact are implied in his claim that 'certainly belief in a supersensual world is at hand again'. But the point to make is that Yeats the symbolist is at one with Gissing the naturalist in rejecting a socialist interpretation of history. For both a 'change of heart', either through a realised pessimism or acceptance of belief, will accomplish social change. Nothing else will do. In the 'Trembling of the Veil' Yeats asked rhetorically, 'Had not Europe shared one mind and heart, until both mind and heart began to break into fragments a little before Shakespeare's birth?'[22] The mission of the true artist is to restore the fragments to a condition of wholeness (at least among his own people).

IV

The symbolist says that art cannot be 'criticism'. The naturalist agrees. The naturalist writer is, after all, necessarily debarred from doing anything other than record the facts: he has to tell it as it is, or as the Marxist critic, Ernst Fischer, puts it:

Naturalism revealed the fragmentation, the ugliness, the surface filth of the capitalist bourgeois world, but it could not go further and deeper to recognize those forces which were preparing to destroy that world and establish socialism.

That is why the naturalistic writer, unable to see beyond the patchwork shoddiness of the bourgeois world, was bound — unless he moved towards socialism — to embrace symbolism and mysticism, to fall victim to his desire to discover the mysterious whole, the meaning of life, behind and beyond social realities.[23]

I do not know what writers, if any, Fischer may have had in mind when he came to write that passage; but Moore obviously fits the case, and Fischer could point to Yeats as an example of the writer whose hatred of naturalism led him 'to embrace symbolism and mysticism'.

One can hardly think of naturalism as a powerful literary movement in England, and as I have said by 1900 it was more or less a spent force. The only novels that we can reasonably put beside those of Moore and Gissing already mentioned are Arthur Morrison's *A Child of the Jago* (1896) and Bennett's *A Man from the North* (1898).[24] In both novels London is presented to us in terms that strictly echo Gissing's fiction: it is vast, menacing, indifferent to the lives it feeds on. Indeed, as Peter Keating has pointed out in his introduction to *A Child of the Jago*, Morrison was to endorse a proposal by the Rev. A. Osborne Jay 'for the establishment of Penal Settlements which would solve the problem of heredity by wiping out the entire strain [of Jago Rats]'. Keating comments:

At first it seems incredible that so humane a man as Jay could advocate building Penal Settlements in isolated parts of the country where the inmates would be well treated but 'actually sentenced to remain there for life, and will not under any conceivable circumstances be allowed to propagate their species and so perpetuate their type'. But the seemingly contradictory mixture of profound humanity and unbelievable inhumanity or stupidity, was a common characteristic of many late-Victorian slum-workers; an ambivalence created by their fear of failing at the vast work of character transformation they had eagerly undertaken.[25]

Keating has put his finger on a crucial matter, but without properly understanding its cause. For it is surely the fact that a naturalistic writer, such as Morrison, comes up against a hopeless contradiction: if he is right about society, then only the exceptional individual escapes from the abyss, that nether world in which the 'very poor' and the 'people' dwell? Morrison shares with Gissing and Moore a complacent assertiveness about the immutability of class. And since that is so he has also to rule out 'character transformation' or a 'change of heart' on any large scale.

Now in writing his novel Morrison relied heavily on Jay's *Life in Darkest London* (1891). Jay had concentrated his attention on the Old Nichol, one of the worst London slums (Morrison's Jago); and the sardonic title of his work alerts us to the fact that he sees London as containing life at jungle level: nature red in tooth and claw. And it may also perhaps remind us that *Heart of Darkness*, written some eight years later, is about London, at least in part. As Conrad's story opens we are on board a cruising yawl, at anchor in the Thames. It is evening and our narrator tells us that:

the air was dark above Gravesend, and farther back still seemed condensed into a mournful gloom, brooding motionless over the biggest, and the greatest, town on earth.

The sun finally sinks, and as it does so the narrator fancies that it is about to go out, 'stricken to death by the touch of that gloom brooding over a crowd of men'. And then Marlow speaks. ' "And this also", said Marlow suddenly, "has been one of the dark places of the earth." ' Has been? Still is.

Heart of Darkness is a symbolist tale. It uses language as a way of evoking terrible and final truths that lie somewhere beneath the surface of things. (The word 'dark' in particular threads through its pages, connecting London and Africa, past and present.) For Conrad as for Morrison there can be no large-scale 'character transformation', but in Conrad's case pessimism is not confined to a single class of men. It applies to all. The heart of man is dark.

Most commentators have felt that there is something evasive in Conrad's persistent use of this word. It is as though he is about to deliver some final truth, but cannot or will not do so. I share the feeling, but am surprised that nobody — to my knowledge — has suggested that the explanation for Conrad's evasiveness can be traced to the same source as the naturalistic pessimism which saw London as a place of final darkness. History is reduced to a set of timeless absolutes — 'the horror, the horror' — freed from any sense of complex actuality and presented with the symbolist's concern for evocation rather than argument. Conrad's reading of history is as absolute as Yeats's, although it is only fair to acknowledge that the story permits this to exist as a tactful suggestiveness, one that cannot operate in a full-scale novel, so that *Nostromo* and *Under Western Eyes* have to be more concerned with actualities, and are undoubtedly great works, just because they resist an overwhelming reliance on a symbolist reading of history.

It was left to Forster to lighten the darkness by showing London as grey. The London of *Howards End* spreads uncontrollably and with no concern for individual lives:

bricks and mortar rising and falling with the restlessness of the water in a fountain, as the city receives more and more men upon her soil. Camelia Road would soon stand like a fortress, and command for a little, an extensive view. Only for a little. Plans were out for the erection of flats in Magnolia Road also. And again a few years, and all the flats in either road might be pulled down, and new buildings, of a vastness at present unimaginable, might arise where they had fallen. (Chapter 6)

Leonard Bast belongs to this world, just. He is poised perilously above the abyss, knowing of people who had 'dropped in, and counted no more'. Above him are the Schlegels, 'still swimming gracefully on the grey tides of London'. Forster comments:

To speak against London is no longer fashionable.... Certainly London fascinates. One visualizes it as a tract of quivering grey, intelligent without purpose, and excitable without love; as a spirit that has altered before it can be chronicled; as a heart that certainly beats, but with no pulsation of humanity. (Chapter 13)

Forster clearly knows all about late-Victorian attitudes to London — he could hardly not have known. But, decent-minded and liberal by persuasion, he cannot bring himself to see it as a heart of darkness, or as providing the raw material for a blackly apocalyptic reading of history. Grey, yes it is grey all right; and at the end of the novel its advancing tide is moving steadily nearer to Howards End itself. Yet the house is meant to be an assertion of the connected and connective human spirit, of love triumphant: of fruition and hope.

'The field's cut!' Helen cried excitedly — 'the big meadow! We've seen to the very end, and it'll be such a crop of hay as never!'

The confident ring of Helen's words has Forster's blessing. After all, the symbolist claims to be able to see to the very end, and *Howards End* is a symbolist novel. But the long-sighted vision of such art proved sadly defective. Four years after Forster finished his novel a very different kind of darkness blotted out his reading of history.

Notes

1   In his essay on Zola in *Studies in European Realism*, Lukacs shows how Zola's 'reporting' inevitably limits his achievement, and at its worst makes him anti-realistic.

2 Swinnerton, *The Georgian Literary Scene* (1938) pp. 132-3, 152. Arthur Morrison's *Tales of Mean Streets* was first published in 1894.

3 For a fuller account of this, see my essay on 'Conservatism and Revolution in the 1880s', in *Literature and Politics in the Nineteenth Century*, ed. J. Lucas (1971).

4 Arthur Symons, *London: A Book of Aspects* (1909) p. 66. The passage was written in the 1890s. I owe my discovery of it to Martin Wood's as-yet unpublished thesis on *Darwinism and Pessimism in Late-Victorian Life and Literature.*

5 George Gissing, *Essays and Fiction*, ed. Coustillas (1970) pp. 90-1.

6 As far as I know, W. H. Mallock was the only man of opinion to think that Positivism was still alive and well and to be attacked in the 1890s. In 1895 he published a volume of essays, *Studies of Contemporary Superstition*, an attack on Positivistic ideas. See also Chapter 8 above.

7 *Jewish Ideals and Other Essays*, quoted by V. Cunningham, *Everywhere Spoken Against: Dissent in the Victorian Novel* (1976) p. 281.

8 'The Symbolism of Poetry', in *Essays and Introductions*, New York (1968) pp. 162-3.

9 *Ibid.* p. 155.

10 The phrase comes from the introduction to Symons's *The Symbolist Movement in Literature*, published in 1899 and dedicated to Yeats, who 'will sympathize with what I say in it, being yourself the chief representative of that movement in our country'.

11 For a fuller discussion of this and other novels in the trilogy see my *Arnold Bennett: A Study of his Fiction* (1975) pp. 31-40.

12 Yeats, *Autobiographies* (1955) p. 115.

13 Milton Chaikin, 'George Moore's Early Fiction', in *George Moore's Mind and Art*, ed. Graham Owens (1968) p. 26.

14 *Modern Painting* (1898) pp. 116-19.

15 Chaikin, *op cit.*, p. 26.

16 Chaikin, *ibid.* Cf. Yeats's complaint against literature which 'was always tending to lose itself in externalities of all kinds'. Behind both statements is Pater's phrase about 'the flood of external objects'.

17 Yeats, *Autobiographies*, *op. cit* p. 279.

18 *Ibid.* pp. 115-16.

19 Yeats, *Essays and Introductions*, p. 197.

20 *Ibid.*, p. 114.

21 Yeats, *Autobiographies*, *op. cit.* pp. 148-9.

22 *Ibid.* p. 191.

23 Ernst Fischer, *The Necessity of Art*, Harmondsworth (1963) p. 80.

24 Maugham's *Liza of Lambeth* is not so much a genuine naturalistic novel as one that 'took its place in the fashion', in Swinnerton's apt phrase (*The Georgian Literary Scene* p. 153).

25 *A Child of the Jago*, ed. P. J. Keating (1971) p. 21.

Chapter 10

Wagner and Forster: *Parsifal* and
A Room with a View

I

You cannot read very far in Forster's work without realising
the potency of music's hold over him. Not only does he employ
it in various of his novels as something integral to his thematic
concerns, he also writes about it with a particular affection:
composers, he is never tired of suggesting, tell the truth in a
manner and with a purity impossible to the literary or graphic
artists; music, he says, 'seems to be more "real" than anything,
and to survive when the rest of civilisation decays.'

His greatest love is reserved for Beethoven, and when
Forster speaks of music it is to him that he most readily turns.
But Beethoven is one among several, of whom none is more
important than Wagner. Wagner, indeed, is a passion that
begins with Forster's youth and continues at the very least
until 1939 and the famous *What I Believe*, in which he writes:

the strong are so stupid. Consider their conduct for a moment in the
Niebelung's Ring. The giants there have the guns, or in other words the gold;
but they do nothing with it, they do not realise that they are all-powerful,
with the result that the catastrophe is delayed and the castle of Walhalla,
insecure but glorious, fronts the storm. Fafnir, coiled round his hoard,
grumbles and grunts; we can hear him under Europe today; the leaves of the
wood already tremble, and the Bird calls its warnings uselessly. Fafnir will
destroy us, but by a blessed dispensation he is stupid and slow, and creation
goes on just outside the poisonous blast of his breath. The Nietzschean
would hurry the monster up, the mystic would say he did not exist, but
Wotan, wiser than either, hastens to create warriors before doom declares
itself. the Valkyries are symbols not only of courage but of intelligence; they
represent the human spirit snatching its opportunity while the going is good,
and one of them even finds time to love. Brünnhilde's last song hymns the
recurrence of love, and since it is the privilege of art to exaggerate, she goes
even further and proclaims the love which is eternally triumphant and feeds
upon freedom, and lives.[1]

206

Of course, since that *was* written in 1939 one's immediate
reaction is to suspect that Forster is cheering himself up.
Perhaps he is — a little. But there's also a confidence about the
passage which suggests that he is not merely spinning metaphors and refusing to face the reality of the catastrophe. (There
is, after all, a modest good sense in the championing of Wotan
who 'hastens to create warriors before doom declares itself'.)
Just before the words I have quoted Forster has been saying
that all society rests upon force, and he regards this choice of
the *Niebelung's Ring* to prove the validity of his contention not
as fanciful but unavoidable: music is 'real' because it embodies
the essential truth of so vastly complex a situation as that
existing in the Europe of 1939; the threat Hitler represents is
part of a reality that art, and especially music, fully contains.
Art tells the truth, and we can see in Forster's use of the
Wagnerian myth a habit of mind that looks to discover in art
the enduring elements of any situation which may come to
exist in the temporal world.

Now Forster is prepared to admit that not all music yields
such explicit meanings: its truths may resist any attempt at a
discursive revelation; they may be too allusive, too deep, too
purely themselves. But however that may be with some composers, it is not the case with Wagner. In an essay called *Not
Listening to Music*, which he also wrote in 1939, Forster wryly
confesses that his delight in Wagner springs from the fact that
his music *is* explicit.

I used to be very fond of music that reminded me of something, and
especially fond of Wagner. With Wagner I always knew where I was; he
never let the fancy roam; he ordained that one phrase should recall the ring,
another the sword, another the blameless fool and so on; he was as precise in
his indications as an oriental dancer.[2]

Not Listening to Music is, in fact, concerned largely with
distinguishing between music 'that reminds me of something'
and 'music itself', and Forster goes to some pains to confess his
readiness in earlier years to put Beethoven in the former
category — under Wagner's influence. And although he does
not in fact mention it, he almost certainly has in mind *Howards
End*, and the use that is there made of Beethoven's fifth
symphony.

It is in the famous description of the concert at the Queen's Hall that Forster, for the first time in the novel, uses music to remind us of something.

> ... the music started with a goblin walking quietly over the universe, from end to end. Others followed him. They were not aggressive creatures; it was that that made them so terrible to Helen. They merely observed in passing that there was no such thing as splendour or heroism in the world. After the interlude of elephants dancing, they returned and made the observation for the second time. Helen could not contradict them, for, once at all events, she had felt the same, and had seen the reliable walls of youth collapse. Panic and emptiness! Panic and emptiness! The goblins were right.[3]

Forster's tactic with Helen Schlegel in the scene calls for some comment. For her, Beethoven's music provides an explanation of her own personal experiences, its truths validate the significance that, dimly enough, she had felt lay beneath the mess of her abortive engagement to Paul Wilcox. And there is nothing in the passage to suggest that Forster thinks she is wrong; indeed the point is that, for him, the music is right, and she is his way of focussing its truths and of making them available to the reader. Now Forster is offering in *Howards End* an account of English society that is intendedly comprehensive;[4] and although he came to describe the novel in deprecating terms as a 'hunt for a home', there is no doubt that it has an apocalyptic note to it. So 'panic and emptiness' is necessary, because it helps to sustain that note, it is what the Wilcox 'outer world' of 'telegrams and anger' finally comes to. And that is why Helen is made to recognise it in Beethoven's fifth symphony; for the music is truthfully apocalyptic.

Forster's confidence that the music *is* telling this kind of truth leads him to introduce the identical phrases taken from the experience of the music into episodes essential to the central themes of *Howards End*: of past and present, the rural against the urban, personal relationships and the business world. And we begin to develop a resistance to the phrases simply because they are so obtrusively fed in — we are too insistently prodded in the right direction. In fact this method, which is essentially symbolist and takes for granted an uncritical contentment with the 'truths' of art, is responsible for most of what is unsatisfactory with the novel; potentially intricate and troubling matters are too neatly slotted into the overall pattern: 'truth' produces a crop of improbabilities. It is difficult to take seriously, for instance, the denouement of Henry Wilcox's liaison with Jackie Bast, or of Helen's with Leonard Bast because — and this is to Forster's credit — they are well enough realised as individuals to make the formal requirements of their being coupled seem damagingly intrusive. In fact it is legitimate to wonder whether this type of novel can ever deal adequately with the sort of theme that *Howards End*, for all Forster's subsequent disclaimers, aspires to. Can an artist expect of another art-work that it should perform the platonic function of revealing the coherence subsisting in his own work's deliberately chosen confusions? It is asking too much; and what I think survives as finest in Forster's novel is not the pattern of connection but the confusions themselves, which have a vitality and integrity that are merely stifled by the constricting demands of 'only connect'.

Yet if this is true of *Howards End* what is to be said for *A Room with a View*, the first novel at which Forster had tried his hand? For in this novel music is of the utmost importance. We learn a great deal about the heroine, Lucy Honeychurch, through the music she plays; for example, we are meant to take her transition from Beethoven through Schumann to Mozart as pre-figuring her decline into a probable future of middle-class sterility. And since so much is made out of these three names it is unfortunate that the truths their music carries should seem suspiciously to reflect particular limits to Edwardian taste; Lucy, we learn, 'tinkles' a Mozart sonata: it is all either of them is good for. On the other hand, Forster's use of music in *A Room with a View* is far more successful than in *Howards End*. For one thing, though we may disagree about his implied estimate of the composers he uses, we have to acknowledge that he employs them with considerable tact to solve what is, after all, a difficult technical problem: how to get Lucy to reveal the truth about herself which she will not consciously admit. For another, the central truths are borne, not by Beethoven, but Wagner. Finally, and perhaps most important, *A Room with a View* is on a much more modest scale than *Howards End*, so that Wagner's music-drama has a mythic completeness sufficient at least for the meaning of the novel to find itself in. Forster's novel offers, as it were, a version of Wagner's myth, and on the whole it does so without seriously distorting character or situation.

There is no doubt that at the end of the nineteenth century the Wagnerian myths — the dramatic material out of which his music-dramas were in part fashioned — could be and often were taken as formidably inconclusive embodiments of even the most complex situations, whether psychological, social or political. And as we have already seen, Forster makes the *Niebelung's Ring* yield up the truth about Europe in 1939. Of course, this sort of application may seem impermissibly loose; and anyway how can an essay which begins with a disavowal of religious belief go on to talk of 'blessed dispensations'? Still, in fairness to Forster it ought to be said that such an objection would almost certainly strike him as unreal. For we have to remember that Forster grew up during the last years of the nineteenth century, when the answerable truths of Wagner's myths could be more or less taken for granted.

What the *Niebelung's Ring* did for the world of 1939, *Parsifal* did for the world of 1908. It made sense of at least certain features of the contemporary world, and *A Room with a View* takes its own meaning from the truths which Forster assumes are embodied in Wagner's music-drama. I want to show how it does this, but first I need to indicate the fact of Wagner's compulsive appeal at the time of Forster's youth and early manhood, and to suggest how the *Parsifal* myth might be apposite to his concerns.

II

In the essay which I have already mentioned, *Not Listening to Music*, Forster admitted that he was once 'especially fond of Wagner'. No doubt his stay in Germany — he was there at the beginning of this century — gave him the chance to experience Wagner-worship at first hand; and this may have had something to do with the considerable affection he came to feel for the country itself. But whatever additional point might have been given to his awareness of Wagner by that stay, the years in Germany could not have created it. For the fact that Forster was born in 1879 means that he grew up at the very time during which Wagner's reputation became, quite simply, gigantic. As a result, any literate person then coming to maturity would inevitably be caught up in some reaction to the man and his art; you could not ignore him or his popularity.

There is no great need to labour this point, it is well enough known already. But there may be some use in suggesting that claims to ignorance quickly reveal themselves as poses; it strengthens the feeling of Wagner's ubiquitous reputation. As late as 1902, for example, Shaw was playing this particular game.[5] In that year *The Perfect Wagnerite* went into its second edition, and Shaw added a preface in which he said that:

The preparation of a Second Edition of this booklet is quite the most unexpected literary task that has ever been set me. When it first appeared I was ungrateful enough to remonstrate with its publisher for printing, as I thought, more copies than the most sanguine Wagnerite could ever hope to sell. But the result proved that exactly one person buys a copy on every day in the year, including Sundays; and so, in the process of the suns, a reprint has become necessary.[6]

Amusingly enough, Shaw has to accept here that the image of himself as sponsor of failed causes will not extend to Wagner; not even *he* can make the master unpopular. And you have only to turn to Beardsley's *Venus and Tannhauser* to see that Shaw's discovery was several years overdue. It is true that at first sight Beardsley's use of the myth may serve merely to suggest that Wagner enjoyed a vogue with *fin de siècle* artists, and was therefore unpopular — a word which, for them, had the useful ambiguity of meaning either little known or widely disliked. But a closer look confirms that Beardsley is, in fact, reacting in predictable sort to Wagner's popularity. The fey impropriety of his *Venus and Tannhauser* is merely a way of spitting on the altar.

It may also be useful to delimit, fairly roughly, the period of Wagner's unquestioned supremacy, in order to show how closely it coincided with Forster's own early years. Thus it can be said that the reputation had not by any means won its way before 1880. In 1878, for example, the year before Forster was born, Edmund Gurney published an article in the July number of *The Nineteenth Century*, in which he says:

In his theory and much of his practice Wagner has missed this fact, that true aesthetic correspondence is due to the subtle and harmonious blending of emotional appeals *severally expressive and beautiful in their kind*; so that not only in professing to unite the 'symphony' with the drama does he ignore the structural differences between high organic development in music and in poetry, but in detail after detail, and probably owing to an unconscious want of melodic fertility, he has cut off the very chance of a vital union. The mere garment of one art thrown over another will do little if their two essences are not interfused. Wagner, in exact opposition to Beethoven, confessedly sits down to evolve music out of long strings of external conceptions, with the result that his music, however brilliantly coloured, tends to sink into arbitrary symbolism.[7]

I quote that, not so much for the details of Gurney's objections, as to draw attention to his tone. The points are made with a show of decent argument, and there is nothing in his unforced assumption that Wagner's work is legitimate material for criticism to indicate that Gurney regards himself as a voice crying in the wilderness. But the fact is that such a tone could hardly have survived the next ten years. Samuel Butler, for example, recorded his opposition to Wagner in these terms:

I went to the Bach choir concert and heard Mozart's *Requiem*. I did not rise warmly to it. Then I heard an extract from *Parsifal* which I disliked very much. If Bach wriggles, Wagner writhes. Yet next morning in the *Times* I saw this able, heartless failure, compact of gnosis as much as any one pleases but without one spark of either true pathos or true humour, called 'the crowning achievement of dramatic music.'[8]

The difference in tone from Gurney is not simply to be accounted for by the fact that Butler is confiding his thoughts to a notebook. It is rather that he is made very angry by the assumption of *The Times* reviewer that, in finding *Parsifal* 'the crowning achievement of dramatic music', he was offering a critical commonplace — which he was.

Now that entry could not have been made before 1882, since *Parsifal* was first performed that year, and in its feeling of familiarity with the work it is likely to belong at earliest to the middle years of the 1880s; and it could, of course, belong to any time up to 1902. Which makes the point about Wagner's reputation neatly enough. From the middle 1880s it grew with enormous rapidity to colossal proportions, and in this it was no doubt aided by the considerable efforts of the English branch of the Wagner Society which, in its quarterly magazine — called, inevitably, *The Meister* — was busy making available in English all Wagner's works. And a quick glance at Shaw's three-volume *Music in London — 1890-94*, confirms the degree to which Wagner dominated the concert hall.

Yet in spite of the vast appeal of his music, it would be wrong to assume that interest in Wagner began and ended there. By the end of the century, he held a position second to none less as a composer than as *the* type of the great artist. Nor is this very surprising. In an age which had increasingly found it necessary to reinforce or replace religious truths by the truths of art, artists were increasingly turned into sages. Real love for Wagner entailed a pilgrimage to Bayreuth.

Forster grew up with this fervent admiration for Wagner all around him. He would have known of the importance of Bayreuth and with it of *Parsifal*, and also of the near-religious awe in which the master was held. And these three features of Wagner's reputation are intimately linked, as Butler's fury has suggested, and as I now want to make clear.

III

In March 1891, Shaw wrote in his music column a reply to a letter which he had seen in one of the daily papers.[9]

For the life of me I cannot see why the recent suggestion that the score of Parsifal may find a place on Signor Mancinelli's desk at Covent Garden should be scouted as 'profane'. I leave out of the question the old-fashioned objection, founded on the theory that all playhouses and singing-halls are abodes of sin. But when a gentleman writes to the papers to declare that 'a performance of Parsifal, apart from the really religious surroundings of the Bayreuth Theatre, would almost amount to profanity', and, again, that 'in the artificial glare of an English opera-house it would be a blasphemous mockery', I must take the liberty of describing to him the 'really religious surroundings', since he admits that he has never seen them for himself. In front of the Bayreuth Theatre, then, on the right, there is a restaurant and a sweet-stuff stall. At the back, a little way up the hill, there is a café. Between the café and the theatre there is a shed in which 'artificial glare' is manufactured for the inside of the theatre; and the sound of that great steam-engine throbs all over the Fichtelgebirge on still nights.[10]

The terms of the letter from which Shaw quotes clearly indicate how *Parsifal* and Bayreuth were typically regarded at this time. The work was a sacred drama and performance of it required consecrated ground. And for all the aseptic commonsense that he shows in answering the letter, not even Shaw disputes the fact of *Parsifal's* truly 'religious' nature. So, in discussing Mendelssohn's *Elijah*, he remarks:

> it is not really religious music at all. The best of it is seraphic music, like the best of Gounod's; but you have only to think of Parsifal, of the Ninth Symphony, of ... the inspired moments of Handel and Bach, to see the great gulf that lies between the true religious sentiment and our delight in Mendelssohn's exquisite prettiness.[11]

Taken together, these two quotations show how, for the late nineteenth century at all events, *Parsifal* occupied a particular place in Wagner's *oeuvre*: it is not religious simply because of its subject-matter — for Mendelssohn's subject is, if anything, more religious; and we can assume that although the gentleman whose letter Shaw savages might feel that the ninth symphony expressed 'the truly religious sentiment', he would not scout as profane the suggestion that it should be performed elsewhere than at Vienna. In other words, no single factor explains *Parsifal's* unique appeal; several combine to give it its aura. And, however, briefly, these need enumerating.

In the first place it is not difficult to regard *Parsifal* as occupying a position very similar to that of *The Tempest*. Since both were taken to be last works each could be interpreted as the final message of the dying master. Indeed it is an aspect of the desire to turn artists into sages that, in the 1890s, this view of Shakespeare's play should have gained currency. And with rather more justification *Parsifal* can also be turned into a final testament, for Wagner himself saw it as the last work he would ever write for the theatre, and his immediate circle knew of this resolution. Besides, resolutions often become prophecies, and it was no secret that Wagner was in abysmally poor health, nor that he might die at any moment. According to his biographer, Ernest Newman, the task of Wagner's closest relatives and friends was to keep him alive until he could finish his work.

> On Cosima fell the major burden of these last distressful years. Richard could afford to indulge himself in fits of peevishness and the dark discouragements arising from his heavy work and broken health. But for Cosima there was no relief possible even of this sorry kind: she had to endure infinitely in patient silence, sustained by one thought alone, that of keeping him alive for the completion of his mission.[12]

The mission referred to was, in fact, *Parsifal*, and that Newman should choose such a word instructs us how to regard the attitude of Wagner and others to his last great enterprise.

Several other factors contributed to the aura which from the outset surrounded the stage-dedication-play. Although Wagner seems to have begun the actual composition in 1878, his poor health made for slow progress, and the scheduled performance dates had repeatedly to be postponed — a fact certain to increase speculation and concern. Moreover, Newman says that Wagner was especially fearful of any production, dreading the disparity between his dream and the stage actuality; and we are told that during rehearsals he suffered torments over the inadequacies in the presentation of certain scenes. It is not overmuch to sense that embedded in this anguish was an accompanying fear — that *Parsifal*, of which so much had come to be expected, would disappoint its audience. The fear is surely present in Wagner's desire that *Parsifal* should be given at Bayreuth alone, and that it should be performed for an audience of patrons? Newman says that the composer's most agonising problem lay in preventing commercial companies handling the work, and he adds:

We can hardly doubt that had he been unable to solve this problem in any other way he would have gone to the extreme length of withholding the work even from Bayreuth, for a production there would mean that the Munich Intendanz would at once exercise its legal rights, and after that the descent of *Parsifal* to the German theatres *en masse* would have been practically certain.[13]

In this frame of mind Wagner, in September 1880, wrote to his patron, the 'mad' Ludwig of Bavaria:

how, indeed, can a drama in which the sublimest mysteries of the Christian faith are shown upon the stage be produced in theatres such as ours, before audiences such as ours, as part of an operatic repertory such as ours? I could have no ground of complaint against our Church authorities if they were to protest, as they would be fully entitled to do, against a stage presentation of the holiest mysteries complacently sandwiched between the frivolity of yesterday and the frivolity of to-morrow, before a public attracted to it solely by frivolity. It was in the full consciousness of this that I gave *Parsifal* the description of a 'stage-dedication-play'. I must have for it therefore a dedicated stage, and this can only be my theatre in Bayreuth. There alone should *Parsifal* ever be performed. Never must it be put before the public in any other theatre whatever as an amusement; and my whole means are devoted to finding out by what means I can secure this destiny for it.[14]

It would have taken a man several times more obtuse than King Ludwig to miss the point of such a letter. He annulled all previous contracts for the play; and in a private letter he told Wagner: 'I am wholly in accord with you that *Parsifal*, your solemn stage-dedication-play, shall be given only in Bayreuth, and never be desecrated by contact with any profane stage.'[15] There is no reason to suppose the King had his tongue in his cheek when he wrote that letter, and the significance of his terms hardly needs insisting on: they look forward to the letter Shaw ridiculed, and show that for its contemporary audience *Parsifal's* over-riding importance lay in its being no mere work of art. For it was the master's last production, its subject was sacred, it could be seen only by the initiated, and they had to make a pilgrimage to see it. Small wonder, then, that it should come to occupy so special a place, or that it should seem to reveal truths beyond the reach of ordinary art.

Parsifal deals with the opposition between Christian and Pagan forces. Wagner's work is a version of the grail legend, and it relies for most of its details on the thirteenth-century *Parsifal* by Wolfram von Eschenbach. It may help if I set out, very briefly, the position at the opening of the music-drama. The former grail king, Titurel, is in his grave, but is mysteriously kept alive by being always in sight of the holy grail. He and his knights have the duty to guard the grail and also the holy spear, but they are constantly under threat from Klingsor, the magician, who time and again has lured grail knights into his garden and then turned them against their master. He has been helped in this by Kundry, a beautiful and seductive woman who, because she laughed at Christ on the Cross, has been forced to wander through the world ceaselessly laughing. Klingsor has gained power over her against her will and she longs to repent; but in spite of this she always turns against the bringer of repentence. She has now lured Amfortas, Titurel's own son, into the garden. Amfortas has wanted to begin his reign by killing Klingsor, but once he got into the magic garden the sight of Kundry made him forget his mission and he dropped his spear, which was then captured by Klingsor who wounded him with it. At the beginning of *Parsifal* Amfortas lies wounded but unable to die. He can be healed only if his spear is re-captured from Klingsor and laid on the wound, and only someone who is totally innocent will be able to manage this — a holy fool. This is, of course, Parsifal, who is a total outsider — he comes from the forest — brings health to the diseased, recovers the spear and cures Amfortas, rescues Kundry from Klingsor and baptises her.

In most details of the fairly complicated plot, Wagner stays so close to von Eschenbach's version that his divergencies can fairly be regarded as minor. There is, however, one major departure from the source. In his *Parsifal* Klingsor retains control of Kundry by deliberately unsexing himself, and this detail seems to have been his own invention; it is not in von Eschenbach nor, so far as I have been able to discover, in any version of the legend prior to his own. As we shall see this detail is very important for *A Room with a View*; and indeed I want now to return to Forster, and suggest some of the reasons for his coming to see in *Parsifal* a theme that could accommodate what he wished to say in his novel.

IV

The English Institute Essays for 1959, *Edwardians and Late Victorians*, contains a very interesting essay by Richard Ellmann, called *Two Faces of Edward*. Ellmann is struck by the fact that Edwardian literature is thoroughly secular, 'yet so earnest that secularism does not describe it'. And he both illustrates and tries to account for this fact. 'Almost to a man, Edwardian writers rejected Christianity, and having done so, they felt free to *use* it, for while they did not need religion, they did need religious metaphors'.[16] And: 'The Edwardians were looking for ways to express their conviction that we can be religious about life itself, and they naturally adopted metaphors offered by the religion they knew best.'[17] And again:

The Edwardian writer granted that the world was secular, but saw no reason to add that it was irrational or meaningless. A kind of inner belief pervades their writings, that the transcendent is immanent in the earthy, that to go down far enough is to go up. They felt free to introduce startling coincidences quite flagrantly, as in *A Room with a View* and *The Ambassadors*, to hint that life is much more than it appears to be, although none of them would have offered that admission openly. While Biblical miracles aroused their incredulity, they were singularly credulous of miracles of their own.... The central miracle for the Edwardians is the sudden alteration of the self; around it much of their literature pivots.[18]

This is well said, and to a limited extent Ellmann's generalisations hold true for Forster. Yet credulity is perhaps overdoing it, if only because Lucy Honeychurch's conversion has about it a feeling of seriousness whose rightness it is as difficult to avoid acknowledging as it may be to account for it. However we may want to regard the miracle — if that is the right word — we are unlikely to see in it the work of a 'singularly credulous' man.

Still, Ellmann's awareness that the Edwardian novelist wanted to 'be religious about life itself' can certainly be applied to Forster, and so can his noting the Edwardian's use of religious metaphor. Indeed *A Room with a View* centres its concern on the two words 'Love' and 'Truth', and these take on a peremptory authority from the religious metaphors which so frequently provide their immediate context.

Superficially, the novel is a slight enough comedy. It is about a young girl's education in the ways of sexual and social snobbishness, which on the one hand she is educated to accept and on the other to reject. But this subserves a far more radical theme, expressed through a paradox whose present familiarity should not obscure the force it would have had in 1908. Briefly it is this: that the appointed guardians of middle-class values, governesses and clerics, are the dedicated representatives of a class-consciousness which, for all its apparent decency and tolerance, kills off the hope of a free individual life; and that they are opposed by individuals who are, therefore, social outcasts: of necessity because they are iconoclasts of conventional morality and religion; by choice because they will not conform to demands that thwart a full life. In other words, those who apparently protect society are killers, and those who apparently threaten it have the vitality which is 'life itself'. I realise, however, that to set the paradox down like this is to make the novel seem windily portentous. Can so apparently slight a comedy bear this heavy load? If Forster were the 'singularly credulous' man that Ellmann suggests, then not. But, for reasons that I shall try to show, it both can and does.

A Room with a View opens in Florence at the Pension

Bertolini, where Lucy Honeychurch, a young girl of conventional middle-class background, and her chaperone, Charlotte Bartlett, are sharing rooms without a view. Staying at the
same Pension are two working-class men, George Emerson
and his father. Their rooms do have views and they offer them
to the ladies. After much argument and soul-searching Miss
Bartlett ungraciously accepts their offer. There is another
guest of note staying at the Pension. That first evening, when
the Emersons are being so obtusely importunate about exchanging rooms, the ladies discover that Mr Beebe, a clergyman whom they had both previously known, is also at the
Bertolini, and that when he returns to England it will be to take
up the living in Summer Street, the Surrey town where Lucy
lives.

During her stay in Florence Lucy begins to suspect possibilities in life at which she had not previously guessed; she is
profiting, we are told, from the 'eternal league of Italy with
youth', and her progress towards the education of self-
discovery reaches its first climax when, on a general outing,
George kisses her. But she is 'saved' by Miss Bartlett, intent on
offering Lucy a different education, and whisked off to Rome.

The second half of the novel takes place in Summer Street.
Here, Lucy becomes engaged to a man she doesn't love. His
name is Cecil Vyse, and he is clever, rich, and well connected.
But Lucy's conformist plans of entertaining the grand-children
of famous men — plans which cause her a good deal of half-
recognised inner distress — are disrupted. Cecil, who in all
ways is a social snob, meets for the first time the Emersons in
the National Gallery, where they are mispronouncing Botticelli's name. He invites them to become tenants of a small and
hideous cottage in Summer Street, and they accept his offer. So
Lucy and George meet again; and again he kisses her. But
'Lucy had developed since the spring', and she has been so well
educated by Miss Bartlett that she is able to repulse George,
and will not admit to loving him.

For all that, however, this kiss does produce some direct
results. Lucy breaks off her engagement to Cecil. She then
plans to go to Greece with the Miss Alans, two old spinsters she
had met at the Pension in Florence. Miss Bartlett and Mr
Beebe approve the plan and plot together to block Mrs Honey-

church's objections. But at the last moment old Mr Emerson saves Lucy. Quite by chance she encounters him in Mr Beebe's vicarage, and he forces her to confess the truth; that she has been deceiving herself all along in pretending she does not love George. This is her conversion. And the novel ends with the two young people back at the Pension in Florence, sharing their room with a view.

Even this bare outline of the plot makes clear, I imagine, that Forster's novel is intended to be a fiction committed to a critical view of middle-class Edwardian society. And the outline should also be sufficient to show that with Forster, as Trilling notices, correct political attitudes are raised to the level of moral perceptions. It is for this reason that the values by which the Emersons live are seen as morally superior to those which constrain Lucy; their acceptance of the equality of women goes with their concern for integrity in personal relations — 'Truth' and 'love'. Incorrect political attitudes, on the other hand, are proof of moral impercipience. Inevitably, therefore, Cecil is to be judged by his attitude to the Emersons and Lucy. He judges the men by extrinsic matters of taste, clothes, and speech. And in his courtship of Lucy it is soon apparent that he cannot conceive of any relation other than 'the feudal', that he is incapable of understanding 'the comradeship after which the girl's soul yearned'. So when he tries to tell her he believes in democracy — as a smart young man would — she snaps back, 'you don't know what the word means'. Her reply convinces him only of the fact that her rebelliousness is best remedied by removing her from her family circle into one of polite London society; and of such a remedy we are informed:

A rebel she was, but not of the kind he understood — a rebel who desired not a wider dwelling room, but equality beside the man she loved.[19]

The comedy of Cecil's impercipience reaches its peak in his readiness to see Lucy as a work of art. When she finally loses her temper with him, he feels in an aggrieved way that 'she had failed to be Leonardesque ... her face was inartistic'.

So far there is nothing in Forster's treatment of Cecil which takes him beyond the range of social comedy. The judgements made against him are typical, but that is part of the mode: sins of class self-sufficiency, of snobbishness in ideas and taste, male complacency — all these are present in the type Cecil represents: he is very much the product of his society. Yet Cecil is also typical in another, more radical sense, which comes out in the following description:

He was medieval. Like a gothic statue. Tall and refined with shoulders that seemed braced by an effort of the will, and a head that was tilted higher than the usual level of vision, he resembled the fastidious saints who guard the portals of a French Cathedral. Well educated, well endowed, and not deficient physically, he remained in the grip of a certain devil which the modern world knows as self-consciousness, and whom the medieval, with dimmer vision, worshipped as asceticism.

Cecil's sterility is here being emphasised in terms that cannot easily be related to the sort of typicality he has so far been given. Neither can George's condemnation of him. 'You cannot live with Vyse', he tells Lucy:

'He's only for acquaintance. He is for society and cultivated talk. He should know no one intimately, least of all a woman . . . . He is the sort who are all right so long as they keep to things — books, pictures — but kill when they come to people'.

It is very important we note here that Forster is not discovering the cause for Cecil's sterility by enquiring into the sort of person he uniquely is. There is no effort, that is, to uncover it through psychological insight, feeling for the way an individual psyche is acted on by, and reacts to, social factors, though this would seem to be the way for the social critic. Instead Forster's terms are highly allusive. Judgement is not restricted to Cecil's social typicality; it works centrifugally — 'He was medieval' — with the result that he becomes typical in a more absolute sense.

And once one notices Forster's tendency to carry typicality beyond boundaries imposed by social considerations, it can be seen to apply to all the novel's key protagonists. For example, when Lucy sees George in Florence:

She watched the singular creature pace up and down the chapel. For a young man his face was rugged and — until the shadows fell upon it — hard. Enshadowed it sprang into tenderness. She saw him once again in Rome, on the ceiling of the Sistine chapel, carrying a burden of acorns.

George, that is, is the opposite of Cecil; his virility matches the other man's sterility. It allows for social comment, of course: the man beyond society's constricting claims attains to a fullness denied to those subdued by them: damn braces, bless relaxes. But by bringing in Michelangelo's nude youths — symbols of the body's perfection, of fruition — Forster gives George a larger significance. And for all the coyness of his reference to those nude youths on the ceiling of the Sistine Chapel it would be difficult to condemn him of empty portentousness, because by and large he so unobtrusively makes this idea of fruition grow out of the social comedy. Thus clothes are used in *A Room with a View* as extrinsic marks by which class self-consciousness is mistaken for real value. When Lucy accidentally comes on George during his swim with her brother and Mr Beebe, and in his nakedness he forces her to bow to him, she reflects: 'She had bowed — but to whom? To Gods, to heroes, to the nonsense of schoolgirls. She had bowed across the rubbish that cumbers the world.' The rubbish is the heap of men's clothes, and the last sentence there demonstrates how sure Forster's narrative grip is, how little he seems to betray the slackness of singular credulity. For it *can* be a continuation of Lucy's thought — she recognises the clothes as rubbish that cumbers the world; or it *can* be Forster telling you what she had in fact done, whether she recognised it or not. And the very indirectness of the sentence allows with admirale tact for the indirect processes of Lucy's mind, the difficulties she has in coming to perceive the truth that is borne in on her. She approaches it when, trying to defend Cecil's rudeness to her mother, she acknowledges that 'Good and bad taste were only catchwords, garments of diverse cut'.

It is the tact, then, implicit in Forster's employment of clothes and the body's nakedness, that lets him carry George's significance beyond the social terms the novel may seem to be settling for. That is why he makes much of Lucy's half-glimpse of the truth that George embodies, so that her turning away from it is presented as a particularly serious offence. *A Room with a View* is at this point much more than social comedy; it is a symbolic statement of truths which Forster obviously wishes to suggest underlie society *per se*. And so when Lucy breaks off her engagement to Cecil, yet denies to George that she loves him, Forster notes:

It did not do to think, nor, for the matter of that, to feel. She gave up trying to understand herself, and joined the vast armies of the benighted, who follow neither the heart nor the brain, and march to their destiny by catch-words. The armies are full of pleasant and pious folk. But they have yielded to the only enemy that matters — the enemy within. They have sinned against passion and truth, and vain will be their strife after virtue. As the years pass, they are censured. Their pleasantry and their piety show cracks, their wit becomes cynicism, their unselfishness hypocrisy; they feel and produce discomfort wherever they go. They have sinned against Eros and Pallas Athene, and not by any heavenly intervention, but by the ordinary course of nature, those allied deities will be avenged.

There is a strange intensity of tone about that passage, considering that it is directed against what might on the face of it seem to be fairly trivial social sins: of cynicism and hypocrisy. And what are we to make of that donnish interpolation about Eros and Pallas Athene, especially since failure to think and feel will be avenged 'by the ordinary course of nature'. Why bring the Gods in at all? But you do not have to look hard for the answer. Forster needs to compensate for the Christian overtones released by his sentence about 'passion and truth', and 'strife after virtue'. It is in such phrases that we recognise the truth of Ellmann's perception: that the Edwardians wanted to use religious metaphor to express their conviction 'that we can be religious about life itself'. The trouble about using such a phrase of *A Room with a View* is that Forster's customary tact makes it seem clumsy; and yet the truth is that he *is* prepared to be deeply serious about life itself, as the passage above shows and as does this following one, in which Miss Bartlett works to bring Mr Beebe over to confirming Lucy in her sin:

Mr Beebe considered.
'It is absolutely necessary', she continued, lowering her veil, and whispering through it with a passion, and intensity, that surprised him. 'I know — I know'. The darkness was coming on, and he felt that this odd woman really did know....
'Yes, I will help her,' said the clergyman, setting his jaw firm. 'Come, let us go back now, and settle the whole thing up.'
Miss Bartlett burst into florid gratitude. The tavern sign — a beehive trimmed evenly with bees — creaked in the wind outside as she thanked him. Mr Beebe did not quite understand the situation; but then, he did not desire to understand it, nor jump to the conclusion of 'another man' that would have attracted a grosser mind. He only knew that Miss Bartlett knew of some vague influence from which the girl desired to be delivered, and which might well be clothed in the fleshly form. Its very vagueness spurred him into

knight-erranty. His belief in celibacy, so reticent, so carefully concealed beneath his tolerance and culture, now came to the surface and expanded like some delicate flower. 'They that marry do well, but they that refrain do better'. So ran his belief, and he never heard that an engagement was broken off but with a slight feeling of pleasure. In the case of Lucy, the feeling was intensified through dislike of Cecil; and he was willing to go further — to place her out of danger until she could confirm her resolution of virginity.

That owes some of its feeling of an encroaching horror to the packed symbolism — the 'beehive trimmed evenly with bees', for example. Yet to draw attention to the symbolism too exclusively is to coarsen the very fine poise of intention the passage has, its tact; it leads into the use of those large, general terms that do not sufficiently define the quality of Forster's writing. Evil, darkness, horror; the words are too strident. Yet it is difficult to see how to avoid them and the feeling for them is there. The poise though, checks us, because by means of *that* we see how deeply Forster buries his seriousness in the social terms the passage retains. It is not that he hides his intentions under the mask of social manners, but that they fully emerge only in and through the rendering of his comedy. For example, the sentence 'Miss Bartlett burst into florid gratitude' has a witty subtlety that one might easily miss. 'Florid', of course, because that is how a spinster governess would react to the clergyman's offer; the word defines with a beautiful precision her social unease. Yet 'florid' also means highly-coloured; and as we take up *that* meaning our minds reach back to the scene where, coming on Lucy and George kissing, Miss Bartlett had stood 'brown against the view'. Mr Beebe's promise of help produces an unnatural, heightened, gaiety that is totally at odds with her former deadly sombreness.[20] The word places Miss Bartlett socially, but it also directs us towards a far more sinister significance.

A scene such as this one suggests with great force how she and Mr Beebe attain mythic status. For the values they come to represent have a feeling of absoluteness about them, and they give the governess and cleric a typicality beyond whatever they possess as types in Forster's social comedy. And this is equally true of George and Cecil and Lucy. Yet with all of them the deeper significances are so firmly grounded in their social typicality that they have to be approached through it. Forster,

that is, operates in *A Room with a View* as a social critic, yet
through such criticism wishes to get at deeper, more permanent,
truths — about 'life itself'. And these are the truths of Parsifal.

V

As I have already suggested, Forster's use of music is tactically
important in his novel. When Lucy plays the piano truths
about herself emerge that she will not openly acknowledge.
For example, in Mrs Vyse's 'well-appointed flat' she plays
Schumann. 'The melody rose, unprofitably magical; it was
resumed broken, not marching once from the cradle to the
grave. The sadness of the incomplete — the sadness that is
often Life, but should never be Art — throbbed in its dejected
phrases....' J. B. Beer has noticed how important Lucy's
piano-playing is, but without doing it full justice; and he seems
not to recognise just how carefully Forster uses the device.
Beer quotes the song Lucy plays just before her final meeting
with Mr Emerson and refers to it as 'a song which Cecil has
given her.'[21] Which is true but less important than the fact that
it is Lucy Ashton's song from *The Bride of Lammermoor*.

But Beer is further awry in his account of the most crucial
scene of the novel. This is the Sunday afternoon when George
kisses Lucy for the second time and she breaks off her engagement. Before he arrives Lucy is asked to play the piano. She
chooses the music of the magic garden from Gluck's *Armide*.
According to Beer: 'Cecil asks her to follow this with the music
of Parsifal, but she refuses, and then turns to see that George
has entered without interrupting. Again, the playing of Gluck
and the refusal of the Parsifal music are significant.'[22] But
neither at this point nor at any other does Beer say *why* this is
significant, and on his terms I do not think he can really
explain why it should be. Here is what I take to be the most
important section of the scene: it starts where Beer's quotation
stops.

Such music [*Armide's*] is not for the piano, and her audience began to get
restive, and Cecil, sharing the general discontent, called out: 'Now play us
the other garden — the one in "Parsifal"'. She closed the instrument. 'Not
very dutiful,' said her mother's voice. Fearing that she had offended Cecil,
she turned quickly round. There George was. He had crept in without
interrupting her.

'Oh, I had no idea!' she exclaimed, getting very red; and then, without a word of greeting, she reopened the piano. Cecil should have the 'Parsifal', and anything else that he liked.

'Our performer has changed her mind', said Miss Bartlett, perhaps implying, 'she will play the music to Mr Emerson'. Lucy did not know what to do, nor even what she wanted to do. She played a few bars of the Flower Maidens' song very badly, and then she stopped.[23]

In other words, although she refuses to play the music, she *does* attempt it. And the real significance is both in the refusal *and* in the bad playing. Lucy's refusal to play the music is instinctive, indeed she fears 'that she had offended Cecil'. Forster deftly implies how split are her conscious and unconscious desires. And it shows above all in her wanting to play *Parsifal* for Cecil yet being unable to do so: 'She played a few bars ... very badly, and then stopped.' For although she may not consciously recognise it, the truth of her position is made manifest in *Parsifal*; and George's presence serves to make it the more insistent. The chapter in which this scene occurs is called 'The Disaster Within'.

A Room with a View works by presenting a basic opposition of pagan and Christian as holy and devilish; being on the side of life is being religious about it. *Parsifal* works by presenting a basic opposition of pagan and Christian as devilish and holy; again though, being on the side of life is being religious about it. Forster's 'good' people have the same motive as Wagner's — to defend 'life itself'; and though there is no point by point correspondence — Forster is not writing a prose version of *Parsifal* — the novel's protagonists owe their mythic status to his unobtrusive use of the structure of oppositions in Wagner's work.[24]

In the first place it is clear that the Emersons are strikingly similar to Titurel and Amfortas. They cherish certain values which we have seen are to be taken as sustaining and quickening: 'Love is of the body', old Mr Emerson tells Lucy; and keeping that truth in sight keeps him alive, though his age and frailty are repeatedly stressed. In addition, we are informed that he has been educating his son to inherit his own concerns and values: 'all my teaching of George has come down to this: beware of muddle'.

Yet again, George is wounded in his attempt to defeat the

enemy. Like Amfortas he breaks into the magic garden, but is dispossessed of his weapon.

From her feet the ground sloped sharply into view, and violets ran down in rivulets and streams and cataracts, irrigating the hillside with blue, eddying round the tree stems, collecting into pools in the hollows, covering the grass with spots of azure foam. But never again were they in such profusion; this terrace was the well-head, the primal source whence beauty gushed out to water the earth.

Standing at its brink, like a swimmer who prepares, was the good man....

George had turned at the sound of her arrival. For a moment he contemplated her, as one who had fallen out of heaven. He saw radiant joy in her face, he saw the flowers beat against her dress in blue waves. The bushes above them closed. He stepped quickly forward and kissed her.

Before she could speak, almost before she could feel, a voice called, 'Lucy! Lucy! Lucy!' The silence of life was broken by Miss Bartlett who stood brown against the view.

George's love is snatched away by the almost magical appearance of Miss Bartlett, who turns it against him. The wound of love: it could be cliché but is not, again because of the way the myth is contained in the social terms. Governesses exist to protect their charges against that sort of assault, to educate them into belief in 'a cheerless, loveless world'. And there is nothing incredible about George's suffering; only it *is* a sort of death-in-life melancholia, like Amfortas's inability to die. 'He has gone under,' his father tells Lucy. 'He will live; but he will not think it worth while to live. He will never think anything worth while.' Naturally he can only be healed when his love is returned — when the spear is laid on the wound.

Lucy makes frail attempts to return George's love. And there are moments when, however, unwittingly, she is brought near an acknowledgement of the meaning of their relationship, of what she has done to him. Chief among these is the playing of the *Parsifal* music: the badness of her playing there points her complicity; and her inability to make up her mind as to which side she is on is Kundry-like in its helpless vacillation. She refuses to play for Cecil, sees George, resolves that she *will* play for Cecil, but 'did not know what to do, nor even what she wanted to do'. And though she tries to escape Miss Bartlett's clutches she is little enough able to do it. In Florence the Reverend Cuthbert Eager hints that Mr Emerson was responsible for his wife's death.

'Perhaps', said Miss Bartlett, 'it is something we had better not hear.'

'To speak plainly', said Mr Eager, 'it is. I will say no more.'

For the first time Lucy's rebellious thoughts swept out in words — for the very first time in her life.

'You have said very little.'

'It was my intention to say very little,' was his frigid reply. He gazed indignantly at the girl, who met him with equal indignation .... 'I suppose it is only their personal charms that make you defend them.'

'I'm not defending them,' said Lucy, losing her courage, and relapsing into the old chaotic methods. 'They're nothing to me.'

Miss Bartlett and Mr Beebe together compose a formidable opposition to the Emersons; and in so anti-clerical a novel it is not surprising that even Mr Eager connects Lucy's interests in the Emersons with 'their personal charms'. All three fear the claims of the body, and in this they are joined by Cecil. But Miss Bartlett and Mr Beebe are the main threat; and their collusion is not only suggested in the scene where Mr Beebe promises help, but in Miss Bartlett's dressing for church 'in the very height of fashion'. It is another aspect of the brown/florid opposition.

Like Klingsor, Miss Bartlett deploys Lucy to hurt the enemy whom she identifies from the outset; when she takes over George's room in Florence she sees his mark of interrogation pinned over the wash-stand; for him it stands for an open questioning of life, for her: 'Meaningless at first, it gradually became menacing, obnoxious, portentous with evil'. Like Klingsor, too, Mr Beebe's strength is in his sexlessness: 'his belief in celibacy ... came to the surface and expanded like some delicate flower'.

Lucy, I have said, is not capable of saving herself. She can therefore be saved only by the intervention of the holy fool. Now in *Parsifal* these two elements — the healing of Amfortas and baptising of Kundry — are separate, but Forster manages to bring them together because, in returning George his love, the fool saves Lucy; he snatches her from the clutches of Miss Bartlett and Mr Beebe. But to do this he has to get into the enemy's stronghold as Parsifal had to get into Klingsor's castle. That is why Mr Emerson has his final meeting with Lucy in Mr Beebe's vicarage, where he has unexpectedly intruded. I realise that it might seem farfetched to make the old man both Titurel *and* Parsifal figures, but that is what Forster does. For like Parsifal he is a social outsider, and the particular quality of his innocence is insisted on throughout the novel — it is a not very acceptable saintliness. In fact Mr Emerson seems to me the least satisfactory person in the novel because he is too simply a symbolic creation, and too little realised in social terms. But however that may be there is no denying his ultimate significance, as the scene in the vicarage makes clear. For he saves George by getting Lucy to admit that she loves his son, and she is 'converted' by her admission: confession is also baptism, as the terms of the scene demonstrate. '(Lucy) could not understand him: the words were indeed remote. Yet as he spoke the darkness was withdrawn, veil after veil, and she saw to the bottom of her soul.' And though Mr Beebe comes in unexpectedly, Mr Emerson does not let him regain the girl. He tells the vicar that Lucy has loved George all along.

She turned to Mr Emerson in despair. But his face revived her. It was the face of a saint who understood.

'Now all is dark. Now Beauty and Passion seem never to have existed. But remember the mountains over Florence and the view. Ah, dear, if I were George, and gave you one kiss, it would make you brave. You have to go cold into a battle that needs warmth, out into the muddle that you have made yourself; and your mother and all your friends will despise you, oh my darling, and rightly, if it is ever right to despise. George still dark, all tussle and misery without a word from him. Am I justified?' Into his own eyes tears came. 'Yes, for we fight for more than Love or Pleasure; there is Truth. Truth counts, Truth does count.'

'You kiss me', said the girl. 'You kiss me, I will try.'

He gave the sense of deities reconciled, a feeling that, in gaining the man she loved, she would gain something for the whole world. Throughout the squalor of her homeward drive . . . his salutation remained. He had robbed the body of its taint, the world's taunts of their sting; he had shown her the holiness of direct desire. She 'never exactly understood,' she would say in after years, 'how he managed to strengthen her. It was as if he made her see the whole of everything at once.'

A frequent objection against this scene is that its terms are too vague, that moral uplift has been too easily bought. But a more valid objection is that the scene is too explicitly symbolic, too artfully composed, is too much controlled by a series of echoes, of tremors of associations with earlier scenes, phrases, words. The novel's pattern is here finally realised: 'Deities reconciled' — Eros and Pallas Athene; 'dark' — the vast armies of the benighted; 'muddle' — beware of muddle; 'he had made her see the whole of everything at once' — the room with a view in Florence, given Lucy by Mr Emerson. And *those* terms have provided focal points for a structure that itself echoes and sets up tremors of associations with the Parisfal myth. Which gives point to Lucy's feeling that 'in gaining the man she loved, she would gain something for the whole world'. The generalisation takes whatever validity it has from the scene's significance. But how much validity can the scene claim? Or to put the question a different way, is Forster's symbolist method adequate for what he is trying to do? I think we can say that it is, because although the bones of his structure occasionally poke through the surface of his text, for the most part he successfully because tactfully suggests or alludes to the levels of reference or sub-text that lie beneath his social comedy. In other words, there isn't in *A Room with a View* the kind of strain that badly affects *Howards End*. As I have said earlier, *Howards End* is a much more ambitious novel, and the truth is that Forster's technical procedures, which are those of the symbolist, simply aren't equal to his ambition. Not only that. For the heart of the problem with the novel is not so much the wrenching of a plot that is required if people are to connect, but the unfortunate naivety of Forster's liberal humanism, which *requires* the pattern of connection and yet which in the very act of producing it reveals its inherent implausibility. *A Room with a View*, on the other hand, because it is on a much more modest scale, can accommodate its symbolist structure without undue difficulty.

Notes

1 *Two Cheers for Democracy* (1951) p.80.
2 *Ibid.*, pp. 136-7.
3 *Howards End*, Uniform edition (1924) pp.30-1.
4 Chapter 6 begins: 'We are not concerned with the very poor. They are unthinkable, and only to be approached by the statistician or the poet. This story deals with gentlefolk, or with those who are obliged to pretend that they are gentlefolk.' Which, whatever you think of the irony, is a way of saying that the novel is concerned with those who together *do* form a comprehensive picture of English Society.
5 Shaw's preface is dated 1901, but the edition did not come out until the following year.

6   *The Perfect Wagnerite* (1902).

7   *The Nineteenth Century*, Vol. iv, p.66, 'On Music and Musical Criticism'.

8   *The Notebooks of Samuel Butler* (1912) p.123.

9   This and the following quotation are drawn from Shaw because, as a regular music-critic and an exceptionally intelligent man, he was in a unique position to register Wagner's importance in England during the 1880s.

10 *Music in London*, 3 vols (1932) Vol. I, pp.156-7.

11 *Ibid.*, Vol.II, p.88.

12 E. Newman, *The Life of Wagner*, 4 vols (1947) Vol.4, pp.652-3.

13 *Ibid.*, pp.587-8.

14 *Ibid.*, pp.588.

15 *Ibid.*, p.589.

16 *Edwardians and Late Victorians*, ed. Ellmann. New York, Columbia Univ. Press (1960) p.102.

17 *Ibid.*, p.196.

18 *Ibid.*, pp.197-8.

19 All quotations from *A Room with a View* are taken from the Uniform edition of 1924, London, Edward Arnold.

20 Forster's use of brown as a colour associated with horror an death is traditional enough. He may well have known the passage in *Modern Painters*, Vol.III, Part IV in which Ruskin says that for the medieval artist 'grey and brown, were ... hues of distress, despair, and mortification, hence adopted always for the dress of monks; only the words "brown" bore, in their colour vocabulary, a still gloomier sense than it does with us.' Ruskin then gives some examples of Dante's use of 'brown' and says, 'Now clearly in all these cases, no *warmth* is meant to be mingled in the colour.' *Works*, ed. Cooke and Wedderburn (1903-12) Vol.5, p.300. How closely these terms apply to Miss Bartlett does not, I imagine, need underlining. Forster had certainly read a good deal of Ruskin.

21 *The Achievement of E. M. Forster* (1962) p.60.

22 *Ibid.*

23 When Forster was writing *A Room with a View* the only performance of *Parsifal* given outside Bayreuth had been a piratical one at the Metropolitan Opera House, New York, in 1903. And the music was only generally available through a piano-score which was, of course, much sought after. Again, this suggests how sure Forster's touch is for social nuances of taste.

24 And, of course, it is here that the true significance of *Armide* lies. For Gluck's opera is also about this opposition, in which a Christian knight, Rinaldo, falls in love with a pagan woman, Armide, but is eventually recalled to his Christian duties.